To Hear the Trees Speak

To Hear the Trees Speak

ADVENTURES IN LISTENING

Olivia Sprinkel

Bedford Square
Publishers

First published in the UK in 2025 by Bedford Square Publishers
London, UK

bedfordsquarepublishers.co.uk
@bedfordsq.publishers

© Olivia Sprinkel, 2025

The right of Olivia Sprinkel to be identified as the author of this work has been asserted in accordance with the Copyright, Designs and Patents Act 1988. All rights reserved. No part of this book may be reproduced, stored in or introduced into a retrieval system, or transmitted, in any form or by any means (electronic, mechanical, photocopying, recording or otherwise) without the written permission of the publishers.

Any person who does any unauthorised act in relation to this publication may be liable to criminal prosecution and civil claims for damages.
A CIP catalogue record for this book is available from the British Library.
This is a work of fiction. Names, characters, places, and incidents either are the product of the author's imagination or are used fictitiously, and any resemblance to actual persons, living or dead, businesses, companies, events or locales is entirely coincidental.

Cover and Internal illustrations by Michelle Hockey ©

ISBN
978-1-83501-156-0 (Paperback)
978-1-83501-153-9 (Hardback)
978-1-83501-154-6 (Trade Paperback)
978-1-83501-155-3 (eBook)

2 4 6 8 10 9 7 5 3 1

Typeset in Bembo Std by Palimpsest Book Production Limited,
Falkirk, Stirlingshire

Printed and bound in Great Britain by Clays Ltd, Elcograf S.p.A.

The manufacturer's authorised representative in the EU for product safety is Easy Access System Europe, Mustamäe tee 50, 10621 Tallinn, Estonia
gpsr.requests@easproject.com

To Fiona Grace and her generation

'Whoever has learned how to listen to trees no longer wants to be a tree. He wants to be nothing except what he is. That is home. That is happiness.'

Hermann Hesse[1]

Contents

Introduction: The call of the baobab	1
Seed One: Know your roots – Silver birch, Finland	11
Seed Two: Selfless service – Banyan, India	37
Seed Three: Waking up to co-arising – Bodhi tree, Sri Lanka	61
Seed Four: Trees are kin – Eucalyptus trees, Australia	87
Seed Five: Feel the unseen – Trees of the Amazon basin, Ecuador	113
Seed Six: In tune with the rhythms of the earth – Baruzeiro, Brazil	145
Seed Seven: Joy calls me home – Olive tree, France	171
Seed Eight: Be a tree protector – Oak, UK	193
Seed Nine: The forest of the imagination – Giant sequoia, USA	219
Seed Ten: The art of being in place – Beech, UK	243
Epilogue	267
Practices	268
Acknowledgements	278
Further reading	281
Notes	283

Introduction: The call of the baobab

'No genuine book has a first page. Like the rustling of a forest, it is begotten God knows where, and it grows and it rolls, arousing the dense wilds of the forest until suddenly, in the very darkest, most stunned and panicked moment, it rolls to its end and begins to speak with all the treetops at once.'

Boris Pasternak

It is on a June morning in New York City that the baobab trees speak to me. I haven't been expecting this call. But we have some history, these trees and me. I've had an image of a baobab fixed in my mind for a long time, since I was 17.

I was in Malawi for a year, teaching English. At weekends, I occasionally went on a road trip with two other teachers. It was on such a trip that we came across a baobab tree by the side of a dried-up river. An elderly woman stood on a footbridge, just standing, looking at the memory of the river. Perhaps she was remembering when water flowed.

The baobab tree is revered as the Tree of Life in many African countries. It is at the heart of villages, a source of nutritious food and precious shade. Maybe this image lodged in my mind because of the juxtaposition between this grand tree, with its swollen trunk and spreading branches, the emptiness of the riverbed, and the slight figure of the woman, contemplating what had gone and what was to come. The baobab stores water in its trunk so it can survive times of drought. This was a time when the rains had not come. Out of shot, in the picture in my mind, under the rainless, cloudless Malawian sky, are white hessian sacks of grain stamped 'USAID', piled up outside a shed ready for distribution.

On that June morning in New York City, 27 years later, I leave my apartment on the 24th floor of a building in lower Manhattan, ride down in a mirrored elevator to the Art Deco lobby and say hello to the doorman on the way out. I descend into the subway and hustle my way into a crowded carriage. As I hang on to a pole, swaying to keep my balance and jostled by the bodies of strangers, I wonder at my life lived so much of the time either high in the sky or underground. I navigate the maze of exits at 42nd Street Station, which I now do on autopilot, and walk through the forest of high-sided billboards in Times Square. *Good Morning America* is being broadcast across the country, shots from the shiny sunny studio filling a giant screen. Theatre signs compete for the attention of tourists who have not yet started to fill the streets. The Naked Cowboy is not yet performing his songs. Office workers like me are making our way to desks high up, behind glass walls. I take a deep breath, inhaling the mix of car exhaust, weary humanity and a sour undernote of last night's hot dogs and onions. Giant yellow m&ms dance on a tall billboard, looking down at me with wide grins. I look up and smile at the topsy-turvy nature of this world. I feel a little like Alice in Wonderland, surrounded by cavorting confectionery. Alongside me at street level, a few skinny trees stretch their limbs skywards, their body clocks no doubt confused by the 24-hour barrage of lights on Broadway.

Introduction: The call of the baobab

I enter the office through the clunk of the revolving doors, which keep the ice-cold of the air-conditioning in during the summer, and the ice-cold of the New York winds out during the winter. I click my way through the security turnstile and wait for the elevator and its stopping-at-all-floors-particularly-when-you-are-running-late-for-a-9am-call journey.

I am first into the alcove of an office that I share with two colleagues, with a straight shot view back down to Times Square. I open up my emails. A headline in a newsletter jumps out at me.

> 'Giant African baobab trees die suddenly after thousands of years.'[2]

I read the story beneath the headline. Researchers are attributing the sudden collapse of the baobabs to climate change. I feel a gripping in my heart and grief for these baobabs that are dying. I think of their presence at the centre of village life and the impact on the people who live with them. If these 1,000-year-old trees that have lived through many cycles of drought are dying because of climate change, then what does this tell us about the severity of the crisis that we are facing?

I think about those trees all day, as I sit through calls and put together PowerPoint presentations. My work is as a sustainability consultant. My clients are big corporations and I talk about climate change with them every day as I help them to set goals to reduce their carbon emissions or report their progress against their sustainability targets. But climate change is too often an abstract concept, lines on a graph showing rising concentrations of carbon in the atmosphere and a corresponding rise in global temperatures. I am frustrated that change is not happening fast enough, and that it sometimes feels like tinkering around the edges.

I know the urgency of the story told by the rising carbon numbers. But the baobabs are an embodiment of the effects of climate change that are happening right now. Who is listening to the message that those trees are sending us? Trees have grown on this earth for 300 million years, long, long before we arrived on the scene. They created the conditions for us to come into being by transforming the atmosphere into one that would support human life. And now we are changing that atmosphere with our carbon emissions, with consequences for all of us. What are we doing? What am I doing? What is my place in this changing world?

I go home that evening to my apartment on Pine Street, the street name a nod to the past. This area of lower Manhattan had once been a forest, and then farmland, before it had become a forest of skyscrapers. I take a fresh notebook from a shelf. I write on the first page. 'A history of the future of the world in 12 trees. Or maybe 10. Baobab, eucalyptus, oak, redwood, birch.' What could the trees have to teach us about how to live – before it is too late?

That I am having such a deep emotional response also catches me by surprise. It has been so long since I have experienced such a current of feeling. I have been in an emotional drought. My father had died suddenly eight years before, and my marriage had ended abruptly three years ago. I have closed off my heart to protect myself against another shock.

At the age of 44, I am separated and don't have children. This hadn't been how I had envisaged this stage of my life. I carry the grief of not having children, and grief for the family life that might have been. Life just didn't work out that way. I am childless by circumstance, or childless not by choice. I didn't meet the right person at the right time. Friends suggested having a child on my own but that was not something that I wanted, having grown up in a home where my father was often absent, even

Introduction: The call of the baobab

before my parents divorced. I married at the age of 39, still hoping for children. But that wasn't to be. I carry the grief, but I have not sat with it, held it. I have shied away from it. It is not a grief that is acknowledged in society, and I have not faced it. Instead, I have numbed my heart. Yet this story of the baobabs has stirred emotion deep inside me.

On my list of trees to visit, the baobabs are first. The tree of life, which is now dying.

Then there is the eucalyptus. I breathe in the word. The name itself opens my lungs. And brings back memories, from the eucalyptus trees in Malawi to when I finally met them many years later on their home territory in Australia.

The oak. The iconic tree of England. A feature of the landscape in which I had grown up.

The giant sequoia. These massive, ancient beings, natives of California, where my father was from. I had visited them in their homeland when I had gone to visit my father there when I was a teenager. And there had even been one in the garden of my childhood home in Derbyshire.

The silver birch. The tree of Finland. The backdrop to childhood summers, and long days spent by the lake, and of countless walks since then through the woods near my mother's house.

Each of the species is already being affected by climate change. Not necessarily in such a dramatic way as the baobab, but the impacts are happening.

My mind is made up. This is a now-or-never moment. I am so taken aback by the directness of the call to listen to the trees and the stories they have to tell, I feel I have no choice but to say yes. It is as if the baobabs had spoken to me. I have to make this journey to the trees. Who knows if I will get another invitation? The trees aren't going to ask me twice.

★

Three days before I heard the call of the baobabs, I'd been surrounded by tall, dense trees, old-growth hemlocks, covering the steep sides of the Catskill Mountains. I was at Menla, the cultural centre of Tibet House and the Dalai Lama. I was attending a deep ecology weekend course, the simplified meaning of this being how we are all interconnected, human and non-human beings. I had signed up wanting to understand more about the theory and have the opportunity to be in this place, among these trees and mountains, instead of in the urban forest.

On a break, in the afternoon of the second day, I was sitting by a large pond in the centre of the grounds, looking out across the water to the mountainsides and forest. A tall, elegant, young Black man drifted down the hill to the water's edge. He pulled two wooden flutes from his bag.

'Do you mind if I play?' he asked.

'No, of course not.'

He turned the flutes over in his hands, evaluating which to play.

'What wood are they made from?' I asked.

'Zebrawood and cherrywood.' It was clear which was which. One of the flutes was striped dark and light. The other was a rich golden colour, liquid as maple syrup.

He started to play on the zebrawood flute. The sound was as pure and clean as the waters of the pond, as true as the hemlock trees on the valley sides. As he played, a woodpecker started to knock in response. He began to match his playing to this sound. The vibrations echoed between man and bird. Call and response. Each calling, each responding. He stopped, picked up the other flute, played again.

'Where did you learn the songs?'

'The woods.'

After he left, I continued to sit with his answer. The vibration

Introduction: The call of the baobab

of the music was still resonating within me. I sat on the soft grass and breathed in the air filled with the forest. Hearing the interaction between man and bird was proof to me of how we are interconnected, if we choose to listen. I had been learning this weekend about the eight principles of deep ecology, which included the richness and diversity of life forms, and their inherent value in themselves. The last of the eight principles of deep ecology is that if we believe in the seven previous principles, we have 'an obligation directly or indirectly to participate in the attempt to implement the necessary changes.' I wondered what my contribution could be. And how I could learn the song of the woods.

Three days later, it seemed like I had received my answer from the baobabs.

I talk with a friend about my journey. 'We've all read stories about climate change that have broken our hearts. We don't all drop everything to go find out more about it,' she says.

I nod my head in agreement. I recognise that the seeming simplicity and straightforwardness of the story of why I wanted to set out on this journey hides layers of complexities I don't even understand myself. Maybe that is one of the reasons for the journey. To be curious about the why, to understand its roots in my past and, through this understanding, change my trajectory and create a different future for myself. This is a journey not only about the trees, climate change and our collective future, but my own future. I am aware of my position of privilege to be able to quit my job and travel for eight or nine months. I am also aware that I am able to do this because I do not have a partner or children.

I had originally thought to plan out the whole trip at the beginning. But, maybe from listening to the guidance of the trees,

I come to the conclusion that I need to leave some room for magic and mystery. I book the flights up until Australia, which will take me four trees into the journey. I will see where the trees take me from there.

Seven months after reading about the baobabs, I spend my last night in New York alone in a trendy hotel in Brooklyn. I look out of the floor-to-ceiling glass window at the empty streets, white with snow. I am exhausted from a day of final packing, putting my boxes into storage, cleaning and leaving my apartment for the last time. It is bitterly cold outside, even for January, and the wind is swirling. The next day I will fly to Finland. Just like that, I am uprooted. Or I have uprooted myself. Again.

Seed One: Know your roots

Silver birch, Finland

'If we surrendered to earth's intelligence we could rise up rooted, like trees.'

Rainer Maria Rilke

The snow falls, tentatively at first, as if not sure of itself, of its place here, whether it should still in fact be rain and disappear into the ground, rather than settle on the earth. It gathers its courage, its volume, its pace. The flakes fall and strengthen their belief in the power of the collective.

Snow conceals but also reveals. My feet are insulated in wool socks and rubber boots. But I want to tread in a way that I can feel this place. Give life to my feet through the memory of running through the garden here, childhood barefoot, stepping on the grass but, perhaps, giving the land life as well through my movement.

The old yellow barn is in front of me, the paint faded by winter storms and all-night summer suns. Once cows lived here. My mother and her sisters milked the cows and helped their mother to make butter, turning the paddle of the wooden churn. It now stands idle and dusty in a corner and the barn has become a store of old bicycles, garden forks, rakes and snow shovels, tools for each of the seasons.

The yellow house is behind me. To my left is the oak tree which my mother planted with an acorn brought from England, some years before she moved back. The tree is strong and sturdy, but the trunk is squat, its branches spreading out close to the ground, keeping low to the earth, unsure perhaps of the unfamiliarity of this climate. The snow piled on the branches makes the tree seem an elevated extension of the earth.

Next to it, by the side of the house, grows the birch tree under which my grandfather and grandmother had their wedding picture taken in the 1930s. I wish that I could hold this photo in my hands, this link to the past, but the image itself has been lost, even if the memory of it has been passed down. The birch tree would have been smaller then. Now it is stately and mature, itself a grandmother tree, with thickened white bark and the characteristic black marks on its trunk. A legend from the Ojibwe people in North America tells that these marks were caused by the tree protecting a boy who went out to get fire from being struck by lightning. In Scotland and in Eastern Europe, birch trees were often planted by the house to protect them from lightning. The birch is a guardian tree. And if the oak is of the earth, the birch's element seems to me to be air. In the summer, the leaves are translucent shimmers of green light and conduct the whispers of the wind. Now, the snow thickens the branches.

There is a short slope of a drive up to the road from the garden. If it keeps snowing, I will need to do the snow-clearing later, pushing the wide red scoop, making a path.

I feel the snow landing softly on my face. Its touch is not unwelcome. The nerve endings in my skin tingle. The trees are still, holding their branches out to receive the snow like a blessing. The wind is quiet. Sometimes the wind cuts through here, seemingly on an express mission straight from Siberia.

I listen to the silence. It is hard to believe that only 48 hours ago I was in New York. In another snowy landscape. My home there was no more. I have no address.

The trees have uprooted me. They have called me on a journey. And as the wind is made visible by the trees, I think that the deep reasons that have blown me here and will carry me onwards will also only be made visible by the trees.

I have never lived here, but it is the one place I have returned to throughout my life, this house in eastern Finland, close to the border with Russia. I must have visited here every year since I was born, at least once, and often twice. So, at a guesstimate, let's say 60 times.

I turn to my left and walk westwards. I can see the edge of the birch woods ahead. Birch trees are said to symbolise beginnings, and also the cycle of life and death. In the beginning is the end. The silver birch tree is the national tree of Finland, so I could say that my tree DNA is 50 per cent birch. I do seem to have beginnings and endings in my blood as well, given how many times I have moved house, or job, or relationships.

Yet for me they have a different meaning. They are my constant, their white bark with the gleam of a north star. They are sentinels, the keepers of that which is precious, from ancestors, to lakes, to the moss-lined hush of the forest. I had to start my journey here. This is where my relationship with trees is rooted. Yet I realise that while the trees have always been a backdrop to my life, I have taken them for granted. I have spent time with them as I have spent time with family, but not asked questions of them. I have not paid them as much attention as I might have. To begin to understand my relationship with trees, I need to understand the rings and layers that have grown over time.

The Finnish word for the birch tree is *koivu*. Birch is harsh-sounding to my ear. *Koivu* has a soft musicality to it. Its vowels shimmer like the light among the birch leaves and ripple like the water on the lake. The word itself sings, enchants. The pine and the spruce are the dominant species in the Finnish forest, but it is the silver birch (*Betula pendula*) which has emotional pull. For me, one of the most beautiful sights in the world is the trunks of the birch trees glowing white on a long Finnish summer evening, with the blue of the lake as a backdrop.

The white bark of the birch is functional as well as poetic. It does not absorb the sun on winter days, as trees with dark bark do. As a result, the trees avoid going through a cycle of rapid heating and cooling which can cause damage. Its whiteness comes mostly from a chemical called betulin. Humans have learnt that betulin has many properties advantageous to them, including being anti-cancer, anti-inflammatory and anti-bacterial.

The birch trees are the keepers of my ancestors. On Christmas Eve, in keeping with Finnish tradition, my brother, mother, aunt and uncle and I go to light candles in the churchyard where my grandparents and great-grandparents are buried. The silver birch trees grow tall and strong and straight, at the intersections of the paths and at the boundaries, watching over the people and their rituals, sheltering, protecting, comforting with the familiarity of their presence. Looking from above, yet with us at ground level.

Each Christmas we carry out the same ritual. With my gloved hand, I scoop a hole in the snow in front of the gravestone of my grandmother and grandfather. I light a long match, and my brother shields it from the wind with his cupped hand, as I move the flame to the candle wick. I place one candle in the snow, and then another, and step back and watch them radiating their light into the crystal-white surrounds and upwards towards the names carved on the stone.

I bow my head in silence and remember. The kindness of my

Seed One: Know your roots

grandfather, the black and white chessboard between us as he taught me to move the pieces. My grandmother feeding me with Karelian stew and meatloaf with an egg in the middle and fresh vegetables dug from the garden. I nodded in understanding as they spoke, but wished I had been able to speak their language.

We continue to my great-grandfather and great-grandmother's grave, and that of my grandmother's cousin, who had no children of her own. In the corner of the churchyard, there is a place to put candles to remember those who have departed but who are not buried here. The snow is aglow with flames of remembrance. There was no funeral ritual for my father, in accordance with the Christian Science religion that he belonged to. There was a silence around his dying, in that he did not tell his children that he was fatally ill. He had never been seriously sick in his life and we all assumed that he would live into his eighties or nineties as his father, mother and aunts had. Yet he was in his early seventies when he passed away. I light a candle for him and find a place for it. In the Celtic tradition, birch trees are said to hold the souls of ancestors.

Birch trees offer us this lesson – it is our roots which can provide us with resilience in a changing world. For it is the roots of the birch trees which are likely to stand them in good stead as the climate continues to warm. One study[1] has shown how rising levels of carbon dioxide allow them to grow more roots and absorb more nitrogen than aspen trees. The work of Suzanne Simard[2] has shown how birch trees share nutrients and carbon with neighbouring fir trees through the mycorrhizal networks, sometimes dubbed the 'wood wide web'. The wider our roots reach, the more likely we are to be able to access the resources which will enable us to thrive. At the same time, if we have those resources, we can then share those with others in need. Generosity is another quality the birch tree is known for.

I continue on my walk, past the horses in their field, and the farm at the top of the hill, and turn right. I am now entering the woods. Birch trees line one side of the road, pine trees the other. It is February, so the trees are still wintering. They have moved sugar to their roots, like a bear storing fat for the winter. When temperatures rise in spring, the trees will start to move this sugar, dissolved in tree sap, from the roots to the twigs, providing the energy needed for new growth. In Finland, there is a tradition to tap the sap from the trees and make birch water, which can also be fermented. It is recorded that the Governor of Lappeenranta, a nearby town, served his visitors sparkling wine made of birch sap in 1754.[3] There is now a rapidly growing market for birch water, driven by the health benefits, which include lowering blood pressure and reducing cholesterol.[4] My mother tells me that her mother used to tap the birch trees for the sap, which she then reduced to make a sweet syrup.

Tu Bishvat is the Jewish New Year of the Trees, a holiday which celebrates the sap starting to rise. I wish for rituals in my life which could connect me with the trees. But on my journey, I will have time to learn.

I have never been here in the spring to see the emergence of the new leaves, or for the all-night bonfires by the lake for midsummer celebrations on 21 June. Or for the turning of the leaves in the autumn, or to see the red caps of the fly agaric mushrooms at the foot of the trees, fed by their sugars, and in turn helping the tree roots to absorb the nutrients from the soil. I have a limited view. My mother used to say that if I would come here for a summer as an adult then I would be able to learn the language. But I would need to come here for a year to start to learn the language of the seasons – and even then I would only be a beginner.

I have felt the loss before of not speaking the Finnish language.

Now I feel the loss of not having been witness to the different seasons in this place, which my ancestors would have known and lived with and adapted to, like the trees. I feel like I live out of tune with the seasons. In my life in the city, I observed the trees coming into leaf and the turning of the colours. But I did not adjust my activity or pace according to the time of the year. And then I wondered why I felt a lack of connection to place – and to nature.

When I was nine years old, I wrote in my diary that my favourite thing to do in the summer was to go swimming in the lakes. Every July, we would come here to my grandparents' house. We would bicycle to the nearby lake. When we first came the road was unpaved, and it was as ribbed as an old-fashioned washing board, bumping us up and down as we rode on our bikes with brakes that you had to remember to back-pedal if you wanted to stop. At the top of the hill overlooking the lake, we left our bicycles, leaning them up against a tree and fastening a thin lock, not really believing that anyone would take them. If it was earlier in the summer, there might be precious ruby jewels of wild strawberries, punctuating the moss. Sun-warmed sweetness, the concentrated essence of summer. Later, the blueberry spotting would start, picking out the small berries hiding under their leaves. But we were on our way to the lake, so would not pick them right away, apart from a few, just as a taste. The path wound down between the birches and the pines, cushioned with brown pine needles. There would be the first glimpse of the lake, the deep blue glistening beneath the green of the leaves, and our pace would quicken. The path emerged round the corner from the swimming beach that we always went to, with the sand sloping softly into the water. Many of the local children learnt to swim here and they would then graduate to the swimming spot a couple of bays away, where there was a short pier and a diving tower. Their shouts and splashes as they divebombed into the water echoed around the lake.

I would peel off my clothes to my swimming costume, and venture into the water, the slope of the sand providing a gentle entry up to waist level, at which point I just had to launch myself in. Little fishes swam in the shallows and would sometimes delicately nibble my legs, testing out this invader into their waters. I revelled in this freedom of being. I splashed and swam and floated until my teeth started to chatter.

Coming out, I wrapped myself in a rough, sun-dried towel. My mother would hand me a snack of my favourite food, a *Karjalanpiirakka*, or Karelian pie, creamy rice pudding held in thin rye pastry, crimped at the edges, spread with butter and topped with slices of boiled egg, all washed down with a bottle of blackcurrant juice, made with berries from the garden.

The birch trees were the ones nearest to the water. When I floated on my back, I could see their white trunks lining the edges. They were the keepers of this space of freedom. The wind silvered their leaves and rippled the surface of the water.

In Swedish, there is a word *smultronställe*, which literally means place of the wild strawberries, but has the deeper meaning of a special place that is close to your heart, where you feel at ease and at one with the world. This was my *smultronställe*.

The two landscapes of my childhood, from the age of four, were the Derbyshire countryside and this one. My mother and I, and my brother when he arrived on the scene when I was eight, would spend weeks in the summer in Finland, and then return again at Christmas. My father would sometimes join too, before my parents separated when I was ten.

We didn't have woods like these where I lived in Derbyshire.

Seed One: Know your roots

It was farmland and pasture and gardens. I saw trees as individuals rather than as part of the collective. There were the oaks dotted around the fields and the horse chestnuts with their spiky fruits and shiny conkers to collect. At my school, there was a small area of woodland, which we called the dingle, where we could build dens.

But it was in Finland that I could truly lose myself in the trees. Where the trees created a world.

I walk on through the woods. If I continue straight on, I will reach the primary school to which my mother and then my brother went. When I was small, I would go ice-skating there, the gravel football field covered with water to transform it into a skating rink.

But I am not going to take that road today. I turn to the left on to a narrower road. I still haven't seen any cars. Sometimes I see a dog-walker passing by on the other side of the road. I pass two houses, one on my right, the next on my left. Both are nestled among the trees, both are wooden houses built in the last 20 years or so. One is painted grey, the other is red.

Approximately 75 per cent of the land area in Finland is forest. It is estimated that there are 22 billion trees, which equates to 4,500 trees for every Finn. Finnish forests are the densest in the world, with on average 72,000 trees in a square kilometre. Given this volume and density, the forests in Finland have an important role to play in storing carbon. Trees absorb carbon from the atmosphere during the process of photosynthesis and convert it to woody biomass. Carbon is also stored in the soils in forests. It's been estimated that the trees in Finnish forests store approximately 700 million metric tons of carbon, with a further 1,300 million metric tons stored in the soil. That adds up to 2,000 million metric tons of carbon locked up in the Finnish forests.[5]

The balance between the use of the forests as carbon sinks and as the source of renewable raw materials, as an alternative to fossil fuels, is one which will become increasingly important to navigate in the years to come.

The woods I'm walking through are likely to be owned by a local farmer. About 60 per cent of forest land in Finland is owned by individuals, with approximately 14 per cent of the population being forest owners. This is partly a result of the forest policy that was implemented in the 1920s, after Finland became independent from Russia in 1917.[6] Tenant farmers of large estates were able to buy the fields and forests they had been managing, and these have been passed down in families.

My family don't own woodland. But we do have a tradition of working in the wood industry. This area has one of the highest concentrations of pulp mills in Finland, partly because of the network of lakes, which means that trees can be floated to the mill. It is a common sight to see a huge raft of logs bobbing on the water, waiting to be processed. My grandfather worked in a pulp factory nearby. It was the main employer in the area and the town itself is called Pulp. The red-painted wooden houses with the broad white porches and swing benches in the gardens, among the birch trees around the lake where we go swimming, were built by the paper company for workers at the factory.

In my grandfather's time, pulp and paper accounted for half of Finnish exports. Now, this stands at about ten per cent. But Finns are at the forefront of innovating new ways to use trees that can contribute to the transition to a low carbon economy. Maybe this is because of an abundance of trees and is simply a practical response from innovative people. I like to think as well that it is due to the close proximity with the forests that inspires new uses.

Finland has set a target of being carbon neutral by 2035, which is 15 years ahead of the timetable set by the Paris Climate Agreement. An article in *Forbes* magazine cites the 'kaleidoscope of trees, technology and talent'[7] that will enable the city of Helsinki to meet this goal.

The UPM pulp mill at Lappeenranta used to be a standard pulp and paper mill. It still produces these paper products but is now also a leader in innovation. It is the world's first commercial-scale biorefinery to produce renewable wood-based diesel and naphtha. Naphtha is the hydrocarbon building block that is used to make fuels and plastics and is usually derived from fossil fuels. UPM have developed a process which allows naphtha to be made from crude tall oil, a residue from the pulp production process. It is turning residue into a product that can be used to replace fossil fuels. The bioplastic made from this naphtha can be recycled in the same way as conventional plastic and the renewable diesel can power vehicles.

When I'm given a tour of the plant by car, it is by Ville, a bearded scientist who also has a passion for photography. We don't go into the network of buildings and towers that make up the factory. We stop by the side of the lake that the plant is situated on, a classic picture of the Finnish lake, fringed by trees. 'I often pause here to take pictures,' he says. In 2015, Ville was the first person in the world to drive a car powered by this renewable diesel. He shared the moment with his three children, picking them up from school in the test car. With the shift towards the electrification of vehicles, it remains to be seen whether renewable diesel has a long-term future, but it has a role to play in the transition.

Ville acknowledges that more questions are being asked about what the impact is on biodiversity of the managed forests and whether forests should be left to grow rather than turned into products for our use. But he says that the volume of forests in Finland is still growing – Finnish forest growth has doubled in the last 50 years – and that the forests need to continue to be sustainably managed.

The pressure on the Finnish forest products industry is likely to grow in the years to come, as the importance of forests as carbon sinks comes to the fore. At the same time, this needs to be balanced with the possibilities that wood and forest products offer to reduce emissions in other areas, whether with bio-based plastics or using wood for construction, instead of concrete. And with forests at the heart of Finnish culture, Finland is starting from a position of strength compared to other countries such as the United Kingdom, which have been deforested long ago. As Ville says, it is important that people have access to the forests so they can maintain their relationship with them.

As I continue on my walk through the woods, I reach a dense stretch of trees, the road cutting through the middle. The snow has stopped falling but the clouds remain. The woods end and open up to fields. There used to be horses in the field to the left but the family who owned them has moved on.

The road re-joins the main road, and then I'm back at the farm and the junction where I had turned off before. From the top of the hill, I can see the yellow house. My mother was born in the old wooden house that stood on that land, where the ivy grew through the walls. She had been born in the depths of the Winter War that Finland was fighting against Russia on a day that was −42°C. My mother was a twin. Her father returned a few months later from the front lines to meet not one new baby, as expected, but two.

As a young child, she helped her parents build the yellow

Seed One: Know your roots

house. She left Finland for the first time at the age of 17 to be an au pair in London. She decided that she wanted a job where she didn't have to sit in an office and which would allow her to travel, so she trained to become a nurse. After she had completed her training in Finland, she worked in hospitals in London and then in the Canary Islands. It was there she met my father who was visiting on business from the United States – my father was an entrepreneur with many different business interests over the course of his lifetime, which led him to work and live abroad.

My favourite picture of my parents was taken standing on this road, the Christmas before I was born. I would arrive into the world six weeks later in London, a month early. In the picture, there is snow on the ground. My mother is looking impossibly glamorous, like a movie star from Hollywood, wearing a fur hat and smiling with all the happiness in the world. My father is smiling proudly, somehow managing to convey that he is aware he doesn't belong here but being with my mother gives him permission. I wonder at the distance travelled from this picture to how things ended, and the pictures which my mother has torn in two, an attempt to erase my father but leaving a white jagged line down the new border of the image, an unsightly scar. But then I think of the happiness that was captured in my wedding pictures, and how that joy did not last either.

My mother moved back to Finland from the UK that same summer I went to Malawi. My grandmother had died the year before. My parents had separated six years before that and my father had moved back to the United States. The three sisters did not want to sell the house. And no doubt my mother saw the appeal of security and being near family, plus putting further distance between herself and my father. But it must have been a huge decision, after having been away for nearly 30 years, to move back to her home village. To pack up the contents of our house in Derbyshire into a container, along with her trusty Volkswagen Polo, and ship it to Finland. To move my nine-year-old brother to a country where he didn't know the language. To leave me, as she still frequently says. How would all our lives have been different had she stayed? But she felt she had to go.

As I walk back through the garden, I think of the changes to the climate my mother has noticed. The increase in rain in the spring and summer has affected the harvest from the vegetable garden. The soil becomes waterlogged in the spring, making it difficult to plant the seeds at the right time to make the most of the short growing season. There is less snow in the winter. Some years there is not enough snow to make the cross-country skiing tracks which used to cut across the fields at the back of the house. From my reading, I have discovered there is in Finland an increased risk of forest fires, snow damage and harm from pests, as a result of climate change.

I stomp my feet on the step to shake off the snow from my boots and pull open the front door of the yellow house. I walk up the steps to the kitchen, the heart of the home. It has an old-fashioned wood-burning stove which my mother uses still, alongside the electric hob and oven. My mum is baking *pulla*, the sweet white bread, which can be fashioned into cinnamon rolls and fat plaits. She asks me in English how my walk was.

My mother spoke Finnish to me when I was little. But as soon as I started going to school in Derbyshire, I started speaking back to her in English. The work of Robert Macfarlane and others has highlighted the loss that occurs when we lose nature words from our language – we lose the ability to speak about what they refer to. I do not know Finnish or its 40 different words for snow and ice.

Seed One: Know your roots

The Finnish language is classified as 'Finno-Ugric', which means that Finnish, Hungarian and Estonian share a common root. The story I had understood was that the Finns had migrated from central Russia, with another branch of the same people migrating to Hungary. Yet, it appears, the roots of the Finns are deeper than I had thought. In the introduction of the *Finnish Folklore Atlas*, I find this reference:

> 'The Finno-Ugrians are European indigenous peoples who already lived on this continent during the last Ice Age, maybe before it, before the arrival of the Aryan and Slavic peoples. The Finno-Ugrians were among European aboriginals; they were peoples of post-Ice Age sea coasts and inland waterways, part of the ecohistory of northern forests and boglands. They belonged to the peoples who have left the oldest cultural traces on the continent.'[8]

The last Ice Age in Finland ended about 11,000 years ago, and humans arrived in the Saimaa area, where my mother lives, over 10,000 years ago, drawn by the waters for fishing and land for hunting. Lake Saimaa is the largest freshwater lake in Finland and the fourth largest in Europe. The birch trees were the first trees to arrive in Finland at the end of the Ice Age. Birch seed is very light, so it is easily carried by the wind. They are known as pioneer trees, as they are often the first to move into an area. It's not just in the symbolic realm that birch trees are associated with beginnings.

The birch tree has been a sacred tree in Finland since at least 1000 BC, along with the pine, spruce and rowan. People believed that damaging these trees would result in sickness or some other misfortune. From the 1200s onwards, when various religions attempted to convert the Finns, starting with the Catholics and Pope Gregory IV, there are records of attempts to destroy these sacred trees. But it is thought that in most cases the fear of the trees was so strong that the people did not follow through on orders to cut them down.

The earliest known document of the Finnic language, dating from the early 13th century, is written on birch bark. It is in Karelian, a Finnic dialect, and was found in Novgorod in Russia. The letters are Cyrillic, and the scratches on the bark look like an arrangement of twigs on fallen snow. There are different translations, but the gist is that it is an invocation against lightning.

On my mother's bookshelves, among the books on organic gardening and interiors dating back to the 1970s, and the shelves tracing the evolution of my reading history from pony books through to school texts such as *Middlemarch*, is a thick-spined, hardback copy of the *Kalevala*, the Finnish national epic, translated into English. It is a collection of *runo,* poems or fragments of sung epics, collected by a doctor Elias Lönnrot during his travels in Karelia in the 1830s. John Martin Crawford's 1887 introduction to his English translation of the *Kalevala* notes that 'Finnish is the language of a people who live pre-eminently close to nature... where nature and nature-worship form the centre of all their life' and therefore in the translation 'every word connected with the powers and elements of nature must be given its full value.' This must not have been an easy task.

I've dipped into it over the years, when looking for something to read. I now open it again and begin to lose myself in the rhythm of the words. The rhythm and metre of the *Kalevala* was reputedly the inspiration for the poem 'Hiawatha' by Longfellow. In his introduction to the *Kalevala,* Horatio Clare writes of its music and says, 'The lead part is sung by the earth itself; the backing singers are a chorus of bards stretching back to the origins of song.'[9]

'Kalevala' means land of heroes, and the book is the story of a number of heroes, including Wainamoinen. It is more than a story, it captures the mythology of the Finns, developed over generations. Sandy Dunlop has written that 'myth is an early psychology and operating system of a culture.'[10] Finnish mythology is rooted in nature, one in which the non-human beings are alive. I feel the double loss, not only of the language, but of the stories of the land, the roots of my ancestors.

The birch tree is one of the characters that is given voice in the *Kalevala*. As he walks through the forest, Wainamoinen hears the birch tree weeping and lamenting.

> 'I must give my bark to others,
> Lose my leaves and silken tassels.
> Often come the Suomi* children,
> Peel my bark and drink my life-blood.'

The birch is bringing attention to the relationship that people have with it, one which is based on taking from the tree, with uses of its bark including making berry baskets and cups and its branches being used to make brooms. Wainamoinen tries to console the birch tree:

> 'Weep no longer, sacred birch tree,
> Mourn no more, my friend and brother.'

However, Wainamoinen's solution is not to stop making use of the birch tree, but to give it a higher use. He creates a harp from the wood of the birch tree, and it plays the most beautiful music, enchanting both humans and non-humans:

> 'Ferns and flowers laugh in pleasure
> And the shrubs attune their voices
> To the music of the harp strings.'[11]

* Suomi is the Finnish word for Finland.

He is transforming it into music that enchants.

In Wainamoinen's adventures, the theme of enchantment is a golden thread. He seeks out 'Old Wipunen, wise magician', who is buried deep in the earth, and has trees growing from different parts of his body, including the birch tree from his temple, and the aspen from his shoulder. Wainamoinen implores Wipunen to share his wisdom with him, saying that he will never leave him until he learns his incantations:

> *'Never must these words be hidden,*
> *Earth must never lose this wisdom,*
> *Though the wisdom-singers perish.'*

And so Old Wipunen:

> *'Sings the origin of witchcraft,*
> *Sings of Earth and its beginning...*
> *Sings the orders of enchantment.'*

In Wainamoinen's closing words, he says:

> *'Nature was my only teacher,*
> *Woods and waters my instructors.'*

The Finns of 200 years ago were people who believed in enchantment, witchcraft and a wisdom rooted in the earth, and the power of stories and songs to carry this wisdom. I think back to the words of the flute-player at Menla, that it was the woods that taught him how to play.

I had set out to learn to listen to how the trees speak. Here, the birch tree is speaking in the Finnish national epic poem, rooted in the folklore of the Finnish people, passed down through generations.

Listening to the trees is not something to discover how to do. It is something to rediscover through the ancient stories. I remember the words of Martin Shaw, the storyteller, shared on a storytelling weekend on Dartmoor: 'We don't need new stories, we need to go back to the old ones.' In losing our folklore and ancient stories, we have lost this connection with a world in which the trees speak – and we have the ability to listen. It strikes me that the oral tradition of stories and songs was not only a teacher in terms of their content but also through the embodied nature of listening.

In Finland, and in other Western societies, Christianity has had a large part to play in suppressing these voices of other beings, which earlier peoples took as being an integral part of their world. The author Terence McKenna has written, 'All of the voices of nature, of the sky and the Earth, were supressed by Christianity in favour of the mystery of the Trinity.'[12] When we can't hear the trees speak, we are denying the sacred that exists in the natural world.

There is much talk about what we need to do to address the climate emergency. But in beginning my journey to listen to the trees, I am realising it is about more than that. It is, in Western societies, about rebalancing our relationship with the world – and this includes, in the words of Terence McKenna, the 'resacralisation of the world'. It is about recognising the inherent sacredness of nature and letting ourselves be re-enchanted by its mysteries.

The word 'enchantment' contains *chanter*, which means 'to sing' in French, and is derived from the Latin *cantare*, meaning 'to sing'. Song can enchant us – if we listen.

The greatest gift that my ex-husband ever gave me was a handwritten note, on creamy, rough-textured paper. He left it on my desk, folded in half. I opened it to find the words, written in brown ink with a calligraphy pen: 'Your job is to listen to the singing of the birds.' He had drawn the orange outline of a flying bird in the top right-hand corner.

I felt as if he had seen who I was, what I was here for. He had seen in me what I had been searching for all my life – a clear statement of my purpose.

This statement didn't come completely out of the blue. He had seen how I had begun to record birdsong on my phone when we went for walks in the countryside. He saw the delight that the birds in our small back garden brought me – the goldfinches that squabbled over the niger seed in the feeder, the bluetits darting in and out from the bird table, the song of the blackbird drawing my attention away from my desk. But he had crystallised it as something which was important and which had meaning.

After our marriage fell apart, I would keep coming back to these words, holding on to them as a marker of who I was. I thought about them when I visited Western Australia later that year. There was a constant accompaniment of the sounds of the natural world – birdsong, frogs, crickets, the ocean – wherever I went. On my last night there, I declared to myself that I wanted to live in a place where I could go to sleep to the sound of the crickets. On my last day, I sat in a field near a river and just bathed myself in the birdsong.

Katy Payne is an acoustic biologist, who is renowned for her work on the songs of whales and elephants. She has said 'I see my responsibility, if I have one, as being to listen.'[13] And I heard Gordon Hempton, one of the world's leading recorders of the natural world, say in a podcast, 'The thing I enjoy most about listening is that when I truly listen I disappear.'[14] When I first heard these words, I would never have thought I would find myself in the middle of Amazonia, listening to trees with him four years later.

Seed One: Know your roots

In New York, I had heard the call of the trees to listen to them. Some might call this enchantment.

It's sauna evening. Every Finnish house and apartment building has a sauna. My mother's house has two – a summer sauna in the outbuilding and a winter sauna in the basement. Only the winter one, heated with a wood stove, is in use now, all year round.

My mother goes downstairs to start the fire. A half-hour or so later, and it is ready. Birch bark is a good firestarter – the betulin which gives the bark its white colour is highly flammable. I go first, as I can't tolerate so much heat. If it was summer, then I might have a bundle of birch twigs and leaves known as *vasta* to take into the sauna, with which to beat your skin. The oils from the birch leaves and the action of them on the skin help to improve circulation. It also fills the sauna with the damp scent of the forest. In the Celtic tradition, birch twigs are known for chasing away stagnant energy, and a witch's broom is traditionally made of birch to ritually cleanse a space.

I sit on the bench in the sauna, occasionally dipping a ladle into the bucket and throwing water on the hot coals, waiting for the wave of steam to follow. A sauna is often a communal experience. In the summer, we go to the public sauna by the lake. The women sit and occasionally make small talk, or just ask if they can throw more water over the coals and look out of the window of the sauna to the blue waters of the lake. At home, in the winter, my mother will dash outside to roll in the snow. The release of the feel-good hormone that comes from rolling in the snow or swimming in cold waters as part of the sauna ritual helps to keep spirits afloat during the long winters when light is scarce. In all seasons, the sauna is truly an experience of the elements and the senses.

A few days later, I take a final walk through the woods. I stop and ask the trees for a blessing for the journey. I place my hand on the trunk of a birch tree. I feel its smoothness and its ridges. I absorb its winter quietness as it rests and gets ready for spring. I think of how it is known as the tree of new beginnings, and the soul of ancestors. As I look to my journey ahead, I ask my ancestors for blessing too.

My mother and I travel to Helsinki on the train the following day. It's been a long time since we've done this journey through the woods together, a journey that each time feels like both a re-entry into and a separation from a world – the world of my mother's home, and where I come from too.

We spend time with my brother and sister-in-law, waiting for the arrival of their first baby, due the day before my birthday. That day comes and goes. The baby prefers to keep tucked away out of the world for an extra while. So we take long walks at the edge of the frozen February sea, cook up nutritious meals, and swim in the heated sea pool in Helsinki harbour.

One evening, we gather in the apartment of my brother and his wife, with my mother and Gloria, my cousin's wife, who is visiting from the United States.

Gloria is a concert violinist and composer. She takes her violin out of its case.

'Why don't you choose a poem, Olivia?' she says. 'You can read it, and I'll play and we'll welcome the baby to the world.'

I think for a moment. 'How about "Wild Geese", the Mary Oliver poem?'

The haunting strings that Gloria plays are like the call of the wild geese, filling the small space of the apartment:

> 'over and over announcing your place/in the family of things.'

Seed One: Know your roots

To know your place in the world, to be of a place – I wish this for the baby. And for myself.

She is also being born into a world that is rapidly changing. In 2100, the baby, if she lives that long, will be 81 years old. The predictions are for a 3°C rise in temperatures by then, well above the 1.5°C that is seen to be a 'safe' limit.

The day before I'm leaving, she still has not arrived and is more than a week overdue now. I say goodbye to my brother and his wife before they head to the hospital for observation. Part of me wishes that I was staying, and I wonder if I could have postponed my flight by a few days. But then that would have thrown all the reservations and schedule out. I would have to meet the baby when I get back.

That evening, I am still struggling to fit everything into my bag.

'It has to go, I can't take it with me.'

I hand the carved wooden Finnish drinking cup, made from birch wood to my mother. My brother had given it to me, no doubt imagining that I could enjoy drinks around the campfire with it on my travels. But it just wasn't going to fit. This 60-litre rucksack had to carry all that I needed for the next nine months, from the heat of India to an Australian winter in the Blue Mountains, and that was just the beginning.

So it went on, filling a bag to leave with my mother.

'You can always buy things if you need them,' she says.

'I just won't be able to fit them in my bag,' I snap back.

Eventually, I manage to close the zip. I silently curse all those travel bloggers who boast about travelling the world with a 40-litre bag.

The next morning, I hug my mother goodbye in the apartment we are staying in. When I went to Malawi, she had come to

Helsinki Airport to hug me goodbye. That was 28 years ago. We haven't lived in the same country since then. My mother often says to me about my decision to go to Africa when I was 17, 'Now I know how my mother felt when I left home at the same age to go to England and be an au pair.' She was worried for me setting out on my own, but she no doubt recognised something of herself in me. She had always said to me that she just wanted me to be happy. We had never spoken about me not having children, but she was so thrilled when she knew a grandchild was on the way.

Given my family history, perhaps it was not surprising that I had wanted to travel since I could read and write. I have a book from when I was six years old, called *A Book About Me*. On the front cover is a green insect with long antennae, wearing a top hat and carrying a giant pencil. In response to the prompt 'My first magic wish', I wrote that 'I wish I had a bird to ride.' I wrote that the bird could take me to 'Aprica Finland or Paris Spain Japan Ameripa' (*sic*), and that 'I might even like to visit India.' I had been fortunate enough to visit all the places on my list, except for Japan and India.

Now, here I am, 39 years after writing that I wanted to go to India, setting out on the journey. The plane taxis through the snow-covered fields of the airport, fringed with forest.

As the plane takes off, I gaze down at the trees. I think of the story *The Birch and the Star*, a well-known story in Finland. It was written in 1915 by Sakari Topelius and is set in Finland during a period of Russian occupation, from 1713 – 21. Many children were separated from their parents at this time. Two children, a brother and sister, are taken in by a Russian family. After ten years, they decide they must go and search for home and run away at night. 'We have a sign on our home,' the boy says. The sign is a birch tree in the farmyard and a star shining

Seed One: Know your roots

through it. The children walk for more than a year and ask everyone they meet for directions to the birch and the star. They are also guided by two birds. Eventually, the two birds settle in a birch tree on a summer evening, while the first star shines through its branches. The children knock on the door and are re-united with their parents. The lesson of the story: the birch guides you home. But I have a journey to go on first.

Seed Two: Selfless service

Banyan, India

'Trees are sanctuaries. Whoever knows how to speak to them, whoever knows how to listen to them, can learn the truth. They do not preach learning and precepts, they preach, undeterred by particulars, the ancient law of life.'

Hermann Hesse[1]

As I wait in the long, long line for immigration and customs at Chennai, bleary-eyed and disoriented in the early morning I had landed into, I try to check whether there is any news from Finland. But there is no Wi-Fi. I would have to wait longer.

I am grateful that I have organised a taxi to take me to Puducherry, my first destination, a three-hour ride away, instead of having to navigate the journey by bus. In the back of the taxi, I close my eyes from time to time, partly from tiredness and partly so I won't see the rush of the oncoming cars, as the taxi weaves in and out of the traffic. Even though it is the middle of the night, the roads are full of vehicles of all shapes and sizes. At 4 o'clock in the morning, the driver stops to buy a coffee from a small stall by the side of the road. I get out to stretch my legs, walking a few laps of the dusty lay-by, a gap in the crowd of low buildings. A cow casually wanders past. I am in India.

*

Later that morning, I connect to Wi-Fi at the guesthouse, and a message from my brother pings through on WhatsApp. Fiona Grace has arrived safely into the world. I let out a prayer of thanks and relief. In the picture on my phone screen, she is pink-faced, eyes shut, wearing a pink and white knitted cap, a little hand scrunched up into a ball. She was born as I was in the air.

Fiona Grace. If I had had a daughter, I would have called her Lila Grace. I hadn't told this to my brother or anyone else. *Lila* is a Sanskrit word which means 'Divine play'. It is the folding and unfolding of the cosmos. It is the delight and enjoyment of this moment. And *grace* is rooted in gratitude. The verb is derived from the Old French, *graciier*, which means 'to give thanks to, praise to'.

I am staying in an old colonial house, with the rooms arranged around a courtyard. Puducherry is a former French colonial town by the sea, once known as Pondicherry. The houses are whitewashed or painted shades of pink and yellow. There is a broad promenade along the seafront, which fills up in the evening with families and couples out for a stroll, watching the red sun sinking into the sea while maybe eating an ice cream.

Puducherry is home to the Sri Aurobindo Ashram. Sri Aurobindo was one of India's leading spiritual figures and the founder of a practice known as Integral Yoga. His spiritual partner was a French woman, who became known as The Mother. The community of Auroville, a few kilometres from Puducherry, was her vision. She envisaged that this experimental 'universal township' would contribute significantly to the 'progress of humanity towards its splendid future by bringing together people of goodwill and aspiration for a better world.' Auroville was founded in 1968, with representatives from 124 nations present, who had each brought soil that was mixed together and placed in a white marble urn.

Seed Two: Selfless service

The reforestation project where I am going to volunteer is part of the Auroville community. I discover via an Instagram caption that it is known as a 'City for the Future'. This seems promising, given my intention to learn from the trees how we can better live into the future.

After three nights of recuperation and learning the lay of the land of the town, I head to Sadhana Forest. With some negotiation I manage to get a tuk-tuk for a price near to that which I had been told I should pay. We squeeze my rucksack in, and we are off, heading through the busy streets of Puducherry and then on to the main road, jostling among other tuk-tuks, dusty cars and open-backed trucks. The driver assures me he knows where he is going. It turns out that he knows the general direction but not the actual turning from the main road. After some driving up and down a slip road, looking at possibilities, eventually someone points us to the right road and we turn off down a bumpy unpaved track, winding through an increasing thickness of trees. Then we are there, among wooden buildings with thatched roofs. Two security guards are lying down in 3 o'clock shade.

I am greeted by a young woman with short-cropped brown hair.

'Welcome! Have you just arrived?'

It's a good assumption, given my backpack and two smaller bags that I'm carrying.

'There's a tour going on at the moment, if you would like to join?'

I leave my bags, and she takes me to the tour. Maria from Mumbai is the leader. I learn that she came for three days in October, and she is still here four months later.

I am plunged straight into an introduction to the compost toilets – and to Sadhana's no waste philosophy. They are not the usual compost toilets with one hole but there are two separate holes to use: one for the yellow liquid and one for the brown solids. This is for the benefit of the trees. Pee is collected and mixed with charcoal, as it is rich in nitrogen and a good source of this essential nutrient for the trees. Poo is collected so that it can be used as fertiliser. It is mixed with sawdust and left for a year in barrels, during which time it breaks down and becomes 'humanure' and is then ready for use on the trees. The only water used is for cleaning yourself. There's no toilet paper either. This is common in India and many other parts of Asia. And, of course, toilet paper is made from trees. Approximately 1,440 rolls of toilet paper can be made from one 40-foot pine tree – or 14 years' supply for one person, based on an average of 100 rolls per year.

After the tour, I talk briefly with Aviram, who founded Sadhana Forest with his wife Yorit. They came here from Israel 15 years ago. He is tall and balding, with a warm presence. He had just hosted a group at lunchtime of people with cancer. One woman had started to cry.

'I can feel the love in every piece of wood here,' she had said.

In the evening, there is a 'non-talent talent show' and people gather together in the main hall. Someone sings the song 'Crazy', another person reads a story of a puppet who doesn't realise that he is controlled by a puppet maker. Another of the volunteers tells his story of cycling across the desert in Iran.

On my way to the bamboo hut dormitory, I see a full moon framed through the trees. A black cat stops to be stroked. I write in my journal that there is so much I don't know about the trees.

I wake to the sound of a wooden flute drifting through the darkness, played by a music-maker walking through the grounds of the forest, breathing life into a song of Hanuman, the monkey god. I want to go back to sleep again. There are rustlings from

Seed Two: Selfless service

the people around me, spots of light as headlamps are turned on, the crinkly sound of the plastic curtain of the makeshift changing room near me. The sounds of the music fade and come back again, as the music-maker returns for a second time to stir the deeper sleeping souls. I press the light button on my wristwatch. 5.41. I need to get up. I grab a dirty T-shirt and trousers from the day before. There is no point in putting on clean clothes now, just clean underwear. I crawl out from under the mosquito net to the changing area. Dressed, I try to walk gently on the creaky floor and make my way down the steep bamboo and rope steps. Time to face the toilets.

Luckily, I only have to pee this morning. At the drinking water taps, I shake charcoal powder on to my toothbrush. Only biodegradable toiletries are allowed at the forest.

I was drawn here by the opportunity to volunteer and also the concept of *sadhana* in relationship to trees. *Sadhana* is a Sanskrit word, and at the forest it is defined as 'Discipline undertaken in pursuit of a goal or spiritual practice.' The song of Hanuman was fitting: the monkey god symbolises inner self-control, faith and service to a cause. Here, the question being asked was 'What does it mean to live life in a way that has service to the trees, and to each other, as a central focus?' This discipline includes two *sevas*, or periods of 'selfless service', each morning between 6–8.15 a.m. and 10 a.m.–12.15 p.m. The early morning starts mean that in the hotter periods of the year at least part of the seva is conducted in the cooler morning air before the sun starts to heat up.

It is now 6 o'clock. The volunteers gather in the morning circle, in a clearing between the trees. Hellos and good mornings are exchanged in English, French, Hebrew and German. People come here from all over India and beyond to volunteer. The human voices are accompanied by the sound of the birds, giving their all for the dawn chorus. The air is resplendent with song, including the distinctive repetitive brain-penetrating three-note call of the aptly named brain fever bird. One of the group leads us in a few stretches to warm us up for the morning's work, with neck rolls, shoulder stretches, a circling of the hips, a stretch of the hamstrings. And then the final stretch: 'Open your arms wide and hug the person next to you.' The hugs continue around the circle. 'Have a great day.' 'Have a joyful day.'

It is time to find out our task for the morning. Some people are already signed up to the *cowshala* to look after the cows, rescued from the dairy industry or from road traffic accidents, and who now enjoy a happy life including daily brushing and abundant *cowpost* from the vegan kitchens (no onions, garlic or anything else that grows underground, including potato peelings, is allowed in the cowpost). Three other people help to prepare the breakfast of the porridge of the day, typically oats, rice or ragi, a type of pink millet, topped with peanuts, fresh coconut, jaggery, which is a syrup made from sugar cane, and copious amounts of fresh fruit, whether pineapple, papaya or watermelon.

The rest of us are going to head to the forest. I had emailed to ask before I arrived about what type of trees were planted at Sadhana. The reply said they planted over 160 different native trees. So I am on the lookout for what tree might be my focus.

Today is a special seva. We are going to be helping Aviram with the treatment of a tree that needs some extra attention. We file to the toolshed to gather tools, including shovels and mumptys, blades on short wooden handles which are used to break up the hard soil. We also collect the materials needed for the tree treatment: bags of dried leaves, buckets of charcoal soaked in pee and the year-old humanure.

We make our way along the brown cracked-earth path through the trees, carrying tools and pushing wheelbarrows towards the mud pool. The pool was not originally here but, about ten years ago, the volunteers pushed soil up to create a dam. Water began to percolate up to form a pool, and this in turn led to vegetation starting to grow. It also provided a welcome place for the volunteers to cool down, wash off sweat and wallow in the mud. As a result of the work to build trenches and earth dams to store rainwater, the underground water level had risen six metres in the four years after Sadhana Forest was founded. This means that the local villagers have water to be able to grow food, helping to slow the exodus to the cities.

When Aviram and Yorit first arrived, there were hardly any trees. 'The barren soil was so white and reflective that it hurt the eyes,' says Aviram. The land around here had been once richly forested. The indigenous forest of the area is classified as Tropical Dry Evergreen Forest (TDEF). The clearing of the forests intensified in colonial times from the 1800s onwards. In 2002, it was estimated that only four per cent of the natural range of the forest on this southern coastline remained, making it one of the rarest, if not the rarest, type of forest on the subcontinent.[2]

The tree that we are headed for, a banyan tree, was planted six or seven years ago by the side of the mud pool. It is about ten feet tall, slim-trunked, its bark smooth and brown-green, with branches clustered on the side facing the mud pool. We gather around and Aviram explains why it needs our help.

'When you are looking at trees, symmetry is an important indicator of health. In normal conditions, the tree should be symmetrical. But you can see looking at this tree that the water of the mud pool is on the right-hand side, and the roots are going in that direction to get water.'

I hadn't thought about symmetry in terms of the health of a

tree before. The trees can speak to us through their shape. Aviram continued:

'And we can tell that the roots are not growing on the left-hand side because there is a lack of branches on that side. The canopy is a mirror image of the roots. So we are going to do a treatment which will try to fix this.'

Aviram explains about the treatment, which is to enrich the soil with nutrients on the left-hand side to encourage the tree to send its roots that way, away from the mud pool.

'Trees are very sensitive to environmental conditions, they are checking their environment all the time. So even in four weeks' time, we should see some new branches beginning to sprout on the left-hand side as the roots begin to grow in that direction.'

Aviram doesn't use the word 'intelligence', but this is a quality that the biologist Stefano Mancuso has attributed to plants. In his studies, he found that much of the intelligence of a plant lies in its roots and root tips. Here, he has discovered 'the typical sequence of phases that mark intelligence: perception of environmental stimuli, decision making about the direction of movement, purposeful movement.'[3] The banyan tree would pick up on the change in conditions resulting from the treatment and respond accordingly.

Some of the group digs a trench on the left-hand side of the tree, carefully avoiding the few roots that are there. Others of us shape the earth that is dug out into a bund, or a curved mound of earth, on the other side of the tree, which would help to hold water when the monsoon rains came. As I stamp the soil with my sandalled feet, I think about the nature of symmetry. It applies to society as well. A lack of symmetry is the reflection of an unbalanced society, if all the resources are channelled in one direction and others are lacking. Communities such as Sadhana Forest seek to redress this balance through how they live: by not taking up unnecessary resources, eating a plant-based diet, being careful with water consumption, and ensuring that as little as possible goes to waste (even what we usually classify as our human waste).

We layer the trench next to the tree with the pee-soaked charcoal and the humanure, add water and then top it with the leaf mulch. We hope that this will be good encouragement for the tree to spread its roots in this direction and restore symmetry and balance.

On the way back, Aviram stops in front of another young banyan tree.

'This is the tree that Yorit and I want to be buried under,' he says.

They had planted it 15 years ago, when they arrived. It is more than double the size of the tree by the mud pool, both in its height and in the volume of its branches, which are symmetrical and provide good shade, as well as a resting place for singing birds.

'The mother of this tree is a banyan tree which is at the heart of Auroville,' Aviram says. I'm sensing that it is the banyan tree that has called me here. A tree which is at the heart of the City for the Future. I need to visit the mother banyan tree and find out more. It turns out this tree is the reason why Auroville is situated where it is.

The banyan is a member of the fig tree family, which has over 800 species. The Latin name for the banyan is *Ficus benghalensis*. 'Banyan' is derived from the name of the traders – or *bania* – who used to sit under the tree. One of its names in Sanskrit is *Kalpavrishka*, which means the tree that provides fulfilment of wishes. It has a long presence in Hindu mythology and culture, with texts dating back over 2,500 years describing a cosmic 'world tree', a banyan growing upside down with its roots in the heavens. Its trunk and branches extend to the earth to bring blessings to humanity.[4]

The banyan is the ultimate rooted tree. It doesn't have just one set of roots at its main trunk, but multiple sets stemming from the aerial roots that it sends down from its branches. In this rooting, it not only belongs to a community, but it creates community for the species it supports, including humans. John Milton in 'Paradise Lost' described the aerial roots of the banyan, using the mother-daughter analogy:

> 'Branching so broad and long, that in the ground
> The bended twigs take root, and daughters grow
> About the mother tree, a pillared shade
> High over-arched, and echoing walks between.'[5]

The mother banyan tree grows next to the Matrimandir, or temple for the divine mother, the spiritual heart of Auroville. I have managed to secure a pass to visit. Entry is restricted according to the wishes of the Mother. Matrimandir is the soul of Auroville and, as the guide says, you don't just reveal your soul to anyone, it takes time. Applications to visit need to be made in person at least three days in advance. These restrictions help to preserve the soul of the place and, on a practical level, keep out the daytrippers.

There are about 65 of us in our group, a mix of ages and nationalities, some of us no doubt looking for insights into our own soul. A French woman on the shuttle bus said she had been three times to Matrimandir.

'I come here to remind myself of the principle of unity.'

The first of the four principles of the community is: 'Auroville will be a site of material and spiritual researches for a living embodiment of an actual human unity.'

The bus drops us by the entrance. We hand in our bags, cameras and phones at a small kiosk. We are to enter the space unencumbered. The golden dome of the Matrimandir gleams in front of us, surrounded by unnaturally green lawns, alien-looking against the dry brown of the surrounding landscape. I wonder how much water it takes to keep them this colour.

Walking towards the Matrimandir, I stop under the mother banyan tree that Aviram had spoken of. The tree has a grand central trunk, the width of two front doors, and then many aerial roots, dropping down from the branches. This support enables the tree to continue to grow horizontally. The area it covers is perhaps the size of a four-bedroom bungalow. The largest banyan tree in the world, near the city of Kolkata in India, covers an area of approximately four acres, equivalent to four football pitches, and has over 3,000 aerial roots. It is a forest in itself and is estimated to be over 250 years old. The main trunk had to be removed in 1925 because of a fungal attack, but its network of secondary trunks continues to ensure the ongoing viability of the tree. It is no wonder that the banyan tree is a symbol of immortality in India.

The Auroville banyan tree is around 100 years old. I count 25 aerial root trunks. The guide had told us that when they were planning Auroville, the architect came to the Mother with a map to obtain her guidance on where to locate the community. The Mother had not been to the area, but she put her finger on the map. The architect went to find the spot – and it was the place where the banyan tree stood, a lone tree in a barren landscape. This was to be the heart of Auroville.

I touch my hand to one of the many trunks. I think that, not only is the banyan the geographical heart of Auroville, but it is also a model for the community. The main trunk is the heart and then there are the secondary trunks around it, forming other supports and hubs, but all interconnected. Auroville, whether by coincidence or design, is organised in this model, the map showing the town radiating out in concentric rings from the centre at the Matrimandir.

Aviram had told us how the Mother had dreamt that the mother tree was being hurt. She spoke to the engineer who was responsible for the construction of the Matrimandir and asked him to investigate. He found that the workers were hammering nails into the trunk of the tree, to act as pegs to hang their tools. The Mother had felt the pain of the tree. The engineer asked the workers to stop.

We continue walking towards the entrance of the shining sphere, its circular gold scales shimmering in the morning heat. I can't help but think of glitzy bathroom tiles and then wonder if this is a sacrilegious thought. We leave our shoes outside on the ramp leading down to the entrance and walk past the doors to two of the petals or meditation rooms, each named after one of the aspects of consciousness that the community at Auroville is seeking to develop. These two petals are *égalité* (equality) and *gnérosité* (generosity). I think back to our efforts to restore the symmetry of the banyan tree at Sadhana, to bring more equality, and to share generosity with the tree.

Inside, we take white socks from neatly folded piles to protect the floor from our feet. A ramp curls up around the inside wall, the walls covered in white triangular panels. Because I stopped under the banyan tree, I am the last one to start filing up the ramp, so I can see the whole line of people ahead of me. I feel as if I am in a spaceship, part of the crew slowly ascending to the control room, walking silently on soft white carpet. The Matrimandir was built in the 70s and it seems very much a child of its time, a *Star-Trek*-influenced vision of a space in which we could ascend to a higher consciousness.

This feeling is accentuated when we arrive at the top of the dome. It is a circular room, all white: white walls, white pillars, white cushions in two concentric circles, the outer ring with cushions against the wall to lean on. In the middle is a crystal globe, receiving a single beam of light, streaming straight down from an opening at the top of the dome. Complicated mechanics ensure the straightness of the beam of light. A mirror, controlled by a computer program, moves across the sun's path each day, following the sun like the head of a sunflower. The mirror projects the sunlight into a lens, which then in turn projects the light beam on to the crystal. There is even a photo sensor in the path of the light beam and, if it is not striking the crystal right in the centre, the computer can adjust the ray to the correct position.

I sit cross-legged on one of the outer cushions. The guide tells us not to perform any special meditations. 'Just be quiet.' That is the instruction. Feel whatever you feel, or don't feel. This is our opportunity for our soul to reveal itself. I shut my eyes and then open them again. I feel as if I should focus on the beam of light. I try to concentrate on my breath. I think of the tree outside, the contrast between the organic vitality of the tree and this white ordered space. I think of how the tree takes beams of light like this and turns the light into nutrients through photosynthesis.

After ten or fifteen minutes, there is a flashing light, our signal that our time here has ended. I do not know if I have had the experience that I was supposed to have. I have not had any revelation. All in good time, I remind myself. The soul takes time to reveal itself. Maybe the cells of my body would photosynthesise this light beam and the insight would come later. We file out down the spiral. Now there was more time to spend with the tree. People stand with one or two hands on a trunk, or wrap their arms around it, or lean back against its support, or rest a cheek on the bark. I have not seen so many people engaging with one tree before. Perhaps for them the tree is a symbol of divine consciousness on earth that could be touched, a complement to the abstract image represented by the Matrimandir. The tree as the living embodiment of unity.

Back at Sadhana, I take the opportunity of some free afternoons to spend time with the daughter banyan tree. I had set out on my journey to listen to the trees, and I was now wondering if this required a special technique. I decide that the best way to listen to the trees was just to listen to the trees. As the guide had said in the Matrimandir: 'Just be quiet.' Feel whatever you feel, or don't feel.

I walk to the daughter banyan tree. I carry my camera with me, and want to take a picture, but it doesn't feel right. Instead, I sit down under the tree, appreciating the protection it offers from the intensity of the sun. The only sounds are the birds, chattering to each other even in the afternoon heat. I find myself writing in my notebook, as if the tree was talking to me, and I am listening:

Don't look at me. It's not about me.

Look at the life that is all around me. The yellow butterfly on the blue flower. The lizard on the red stem of the rosella plant, with its red flowers and edible petals. The herb with the pungent leaves, its smell released, mint-like, as you sat down on my leaves. The birds. Oh, my birds. It makes my heart happy to hear their chatter, their different calls and whistles and songs, their tweeting and chirruping. The calls of longing, the songs of joy. The hum of the bees.

I am grateful that you pay attention to me. But please also pay attention to those around me. I'm here for them.

I stand and look up at the interlacing canopy of leaves. The tree had said of itself, 'It's not about me.' I think of seva, of selfless service. Selfless means without the self. But then maybe I can be more rather than less in selfless service. Whatever *I* is. Whoever I is. Who even am I?

I want to show the beauty of the world and help to preserve it. I want to be in service to that. I might not like using the toilets here, and I feel hot and sweaty and dirty most of the time, apart from at night, when I am cold. But does that matter, if it is all part of selfless service, if I take the inconvenience to myself out of the equation? Where there was just one butterfly before, I now see two black and white butterflies dancing with each other, and two yellow ones, circling together.

When I had careers advice at school, it was framed as how I could fit into a particular category of job, based on the aptitude and preferences test that I took. Possible careers that were put forward for me included 'international marketing' (because I had expressed an interest in and aptitude for languages) and public relations. As it happened, my career path did take me down related roads to these, leading to a focus on sustainability, albeit with much questioning of myself along the way, of whether this was what I really wanted to be doing. And focusing my questioning on what career path to follow had led me to neglect reflecting on the importance of other roles, including as a possible partner and mother.

In my deep ecology weekend at Menla, I had been introduced to the concept of 'the ecological self'. Arne Naess, the Norwegian philosopher and originator of deep ecology, had written about how the enlargement of the ego-self to the eco-self leads to environmentally responsible behaviours, because, since we are part of the wider ecosystem, these behaviours are in our own self-interest. Selfless service looked at through this perspective was about seeing ourselves as an integral part of the world, not separate from it, and acting from this place.

I thought of the difference it would make if young people – and all people – were encouraged to think about how they could use their skills and passions to be of service to the world – and how this might lead us to make other choices.

Later that day, I open a book of the teachings of the Mother. The Mother sets out the importance of selfless service, the importance for Aurovillians 'to do something every day, some activity, some work, anything, something which is not for oneself, and above all something which is an expression of goodwill for all – you are a group, aren't you? – Simply to show that you do not live solely for yourselves as if you were at the centre of the universe and the whole universe had to revolve around you.'

It is as if the banyan tree is speaking again.

'Each one should become aware that, spontaneously, one puts oneself at the centre of the universe and wants everything to come to oneself, just like that, in one way or another. But one should make an effort to recognise the existence of the whole, that's all. It's to widen one's consciousness, just to become a little less tiny.'[6]

The banyan tree grows in a way that means it loses the sense of a central self. The main trunk can be removed, but because of how it has widened and lost its focus on the centre, it can continue to grow.

I return the next day. I lie down against the earth, on warm dried brown banyan leaves. I look up through the green leaves of the tree at the sun. Above it, a taller eucalyptus tree is moving backwards and forwards, bending in the wind. The top leaves of the banyan just gently shake.

This tree, of this land, is solid and sturdy. It gives me the feeling of a mother tree.

Seed Two: Selfless service

A little white cat appears on the path nearby, calling, as if for his mother, mewling. When he sees me, he runs right over. He wants to sit on my lap, and sit on my bag, and be close to me, and be stroked and comforted. He is purring, even as he continues his crying. I don't know what else he could be saying, apart from calling for his mother. He is looking to me for reassurance, curling around me, looking at me. 'You're beautiful. You're going to be fine,' I reassure him.

And then, perhaps satisfied, he is off on his way again.

Did he just want to be listened to? Is this what the tree wants? What the earth wants? What we all want?

On the third day, I am tired. I rest my hand, and then my cheek, against the cool trunk of the banyan tree.

Just be with me, I thought I heard her say.

It's as simple as that. Just be.

How do we strip the rest away to get to that point? Beyond all the noise.

How can I just be with the ants, with the singing birds? How can I just be with what is?

The lessons of the tree are rooted. But rooted in aspiration. Reaching towards the light, while reaching into the earth for water.

Why plant trees? Brandon, the deputy director at Sadhana, shares his view on this one morning as we are waiting to start tree planting. It is about restoring the ecosystem and biodiversity and stopping further desertification. And it is also about joy.

'I'm happiest when digging,' he said, his American accent ringing through. 'And it's about being part of something that is being nurtured and seeing that your daily actions are contributing to something. We are not just here for us.'

I am taken back to the banyan tree, and the words of the

Mother. For him, Auroville is not just a human unity project – one of the principles that had been referred to at the Matrimandir. It is a unity project. It is about taking the bubble of what you identify with and extending it. 'What is the whole that we identify with? Is it unity with our community, with humans, with all living beings?'

Integral to the planning of the development of Auroville was the Green Belt. Even now, it is the responsibility of people who live in this area to plant trees. The names of the different forests sing out on the map – Fertile Forest, Pitchikandulam Forest, Revelation.

The early Auroville pioneers began by planting drought-resistant trees from Australia to prepare the ground. Green acacia and silver-leaf acacia were planted, along with eucalyptus. The acacias, known as work trees, acted as pioneers themselves, breaking up the soil with their roots, fixing nitrogen and providing shade for other plants to grow.

Once the acacias had helped to prepare the ground, the new Aurovillians could turn their attention to planting native trees. Given the absence of the original forest, they had to decide what trees to plant and where to get the seeds. This is when they turned to the sacred groves, the protected spaces around the temples which held what was remaining of the TDEF. The British had been wise enough not to incur the wrath of the gods, or the local people, by cutting down these trees, and therefore the rich diversity of trees of the TDEF had been preserved in the groves.

Many of the early cuttings and seeds that started the repopulation of the forest came from these sacred groves. These included the sacred trees commonly found around temples, including the banyan, peepul, neem, bael and ashok trees, considered to be the home of the gods.[7]

Seed Two: Selfless service

A research study highlighted the relationship between the trees of the sacred groves and gods. One of the study participants, speaking about Aiyanar, a deity worshipped in Tamil Nadu, the state which Auroville is in, said, 'As birds have a nest, for him there is a forest... As humans have homes, Aiyanar is present only if the forest is there. We have created the forest because we want the god to be here.'[8]

Planting a tree at Sadhana Forest is not just a question of digging a hole in the ground, adding some compost, putting the tree in the hole, filling the hole back in, and watering it. The process is much more involved and takes teams of people working together. To start with, the tree is not actually planted in a hole. A trench and mound system is used. Planting the tree in a mound means that you are planting it in good soil. The trench helps to protect it during the monsoon, so that the roots do not become flooded, as well as providing a water source the roots can draw from. We work in pairs on digging the trench, which is back-breaking because the ground is so dry and hard. Today, I alternate with my partner in using the different tools – we swap between swinging the heavy mumpty to break up the ground, and then digging the loosened earth out with a spade and forming a mound with this soil. We place a plastic tube in the middle and fill it with compost – the tube will be removed and re-used once the tree is established. We plant a young tree into its temporary protective shell. Meanwhile, another team rakes and gathers leaves from under the eucalyptus trees. These leaves are piled into a thick layer of mulch on the mound, to keep moisture in, stop water from evaporating and provide much-needed micronutrients to the tree. The leaves of the older trees become food for the new ones. Finally, we water the tree and sprinkle a blessing for it to grow well.

The continued watering of the trees is an important task at Sadhana, and one we do on days when we are not tree planting. The young trees need regular watering during the first years of their life, if they are to take root. Aviram takes pride in the high survival rate of the trees, which is on average 80–90 per cent, well above the average for tree-planting schemes.

Saalumarada Thimmakka is perhaps India's most famous planter of banyan trees, known as the 'mother of trees'. She started planting them when, after 25 years of marriage, she and her husband hadn't been able to conceive a child. After working on a farm during the day, she planted banyan trees at the side of a road in her village, carrying water for several kilometres to tend to them. Her trees became her children. She has planted over 300 trees, which now line the road for four kilometres between her village and the next. 'I am very happy seeing all my children. We have looked after the trees with love and I am happy and proud,' she has said.[9]

Natesan Balachandran (known as Bala) is a Doctor of Botany, based at the French Institute in Puducherry. I meet with him in his book-lined office in old French colonial buildings. He speaks about the programmes to collect seeds for the TDEF. He tells of how the rainfall pattern is changing and how the plants are reacting. The neem tree is now blooming almost a month earlier than usual. Others are blooming two months ahead of schedule. But his voice comes alive with passion when he starts to speak about education.

'There's a big problem that we don't have the young scientists coming through, they don't want to work in this field. They don't want to study plants, they don't learn to identify them. People are not giving importance to plants. They are giving much more importance to the study and conservation of animals, but not to plants. And these are the base of living things, people forget this.'

Bala tells me how the traditional knowledge of the medicinal value of plants is passed from generation to generation of women. This knowledge was now being lost. But it seemed that not only was the traditional knowledge not being shared, neither was scientific knowledge.

He continues, 'It needs to start in school, starting with herb gardens, learning about cultivation. One or two schools in the area have started this now, have pots on a terrace. But it is not enough. And then at graduate or postgraduate level there needs to be much more field-oriented techniques and training. Instead of teaching in classrooms, the students need to learn from the wild and the forest. They need to learn how to do seed surveys, conserve plants. And there needs to be the funding to do the research. The government is giving money to genetic engineering and gene mapping, but not to basic research.'

I am struck by his words. How can we hope to conserve trees and plants into the future if we do not have scientists who understand them? Sadhana is trying to spark this interest, running programmes for the local schools and colleges, so that the students can come to plant trees and learn about them. I help one morning with a group of college students, passing on my newly acquired knowledge of how to plant trees. 'We didn't know this forest was here,' they say.

Rabindrath Tagore, the Indian poet and artist, wrote, 'The highest education is that which does not merely give us information but makes our life in harmony with all existence.' He founded a school in West Bengal, based on the idea of tapovans, or forest monasteries of ancient India. Pupils were taught outside under the trees. In his poem, 'Brahman', Tagore describes how the pupils in the tapovan sat in a circle under an old banyan, hearing the birds, the bees and sound of water, and sang songs of the Samaveda. The Samaveda is an ancient Vedic Sanskrit text and it has verses specially composed for singing in the forest. Here is a vision of life lived in harmony with all existence. A lesson that comes from sitting under the banyan tree and singing to it.

In Auroville, I visit an exhibition of baobab bark prints from Namibia. The artist had taken bark rubbings of a 3,000-year-old baobab tree and discovered the figures of people and lions within the bark. The catalogue notes state that some people think that trees absorb the stories of the people around them. Maybe trees, including the banyan tree, are like a lightning rod to the earth, conducting energy back into the ground, collectively rooting society. What would the Matrimandir be without the banyan tree? Would the spaceship just take off without its roots? I find myself wondering what we would be without trees. We, whose early ancestors descended from the trees, over three million years ago. We, who have existed only a fraction of time compared to the trees, who have been on this planet for over 300 million years.

I have had a glimpse at Auroville of a particular path to a city for the future. The work of planting trees to establish and continue community provides hope that the restoration of land which man has previously made desert is possible. The community is working to an ideal. The banyan tree at the heart of Auroville is a model of community. Yet, it seems that, even here, there is still a continuous struggle, a tension between the vision and the path they are following. The lack of water is an increasing concern due to worsening drought and changes in rainfall, even though the planting of trees has increased the water table level. The question of whether a community will continue to be viable here into

Seed Two: Selfless service

the future hangs in the air. And it is a question not just for Auroville, but for the much bigger surrounding communities.

I think of my niece, Fiona. Andri Snær Magnasson has spoken about how the current generation growing up now has an inbuilt purpose. They will not go to university and then wonder what to do with their lives, struggle to find a purpose, as many of his generation and mine, now in our forties and fifties, did. If they are making chairs, he says, they will not just be designing another chair – they will have to be making the most sustainable chair possible.

The Mother wrote, 'It is in work done as an offering to the Divine that the consciousness develops best.'

The banyan tree said, 'It is not about me.'

'How can I be of service?' How would my life be different if I asked myself this every day? What would the cites for the future look like if this was the question that young people were brought up with?

Being rooted is about what you can give to a place and people, and what you in turn can then receive. I imagine that being a mother can help you to put down roots, as your child becomes a focus of attention. Perhaps I need to think differently about how I can be a mother, like Saalumarada Thimmakka. Motherhood is one of the greatest acts of selfless service, and also a source of joy.

I have been planting young trees in the City for the Future. But it is time for the next stage of my journey. I have met the birch and banyan. Now, with a head full of thoughts about community, service and planting for the future, I prepare to move on once again. I am travelling to Sri Lanka to visit a notable tree planted over 2,000 years ago: the Jaya Sri Maha Bodhi at Anuradhapura.

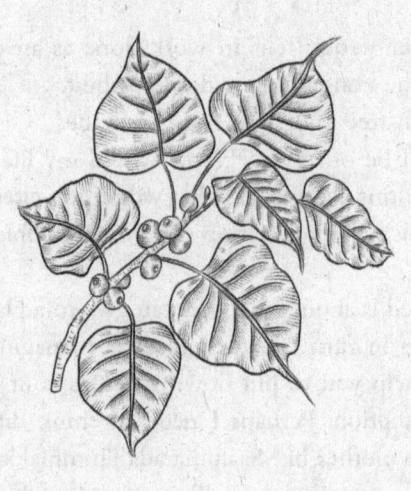

Seed Three: Waking up to co-arising

Bodhi tree, Sri Lanka

'Do I actually acknowledge that, with sensing the world, comes a degree of responsibility? Do I, in the way I see the world, also co-produce it or produce it or share the narrative or perhaps even have the role of authorship?'

Olafur Eliasson, *But doesn't the body matter?*

I stand at carousel number four at Colombo Airport, waiting for my bag to arrive, after a short hop of a flight from Chennai. I watch the bags rotating past me on the luggage belt. There is a large Philips mixer/grinder box with a fragile sticker. Is there actually a mixer/grinder inside or is it holding some other contents? I wonder if bundles of colourful fabric are for a business or gifts brought back by a generous family member. Oversized suitcases and small bags circle by. To me, each one represents hopes and dreams. Hopes for a successful business. Dreams of a relaxing vacation. Hopes of spending time with family without arguments. Dreams of moving to another country. My grey-green rucksack appears, wedged between two suitcases. What hopes and dreams am I carrying in my bag from country to country? How are they changing?

Princess Sangamitta travelled to Sri Lanka from India over 2,000 years ago. In her baggage, she had a branch of the bodhi tree under which the Buddha had sat to gain enlightenment. She was the daughter of the Indian emperor, Asoka. Asoka had converted from Hinduism to Buddhism, and Sangamitta became a Buddhist nun. King Tissa of Sri Lanka, a friend of Asoka, had converted to Buddhism, after Asoka's son, Mahinda, travelled to the island to meet with him. King Tissa then invited Sangamitta to Sri Lanka to help establish Buddhism among women there. Asoka was initially reluctant to let Sangamitta go, but she persuaded him. The princess arrived at Jambukola, a port in the north of Sri Lanka, after a long journey which included sailing down the Ganges and an ocean crossing. It is recorded that King Tissa welcomed her in person, wading into the ocean when he saw the ship approaching on the horizon. The procession from the port to the capital, a distance of 60 miles, took five days, and people in the procession included her brother, 11 nuns, the king and the royal entourage. What were the hopes and dreams Princess Sangamitta carried with her, along with the branch of the bodhi tree? She remained in Sri Lanka for the rest of her life, successfully establishing a Buddhist order for women.

Hopes and dreams and listening to these would become a theme for my time in Sri Lanka.

In my dream it was night, and the dark waters of a river were dotted with paper lanterns, floating downstream, glowing with light. I stood on the banks of the river, looking in wonder at this spectacle and this ceremony.

Three nights before the dream, my father had died at his home in France. The dream was still vivid in the morning daylight. I looked up online what its meaning might be. I found out that there is a Buddhist and Taoist festival in which paper lanterns are floated on rivers. The Buddhist festival is called Ullambana. It is a day to honour the departed spirits of ancestors. In Japan, the festival is called Toro Nagashi, which translates as 'streaming lanterns'. The purpose is to send off ancestors' spirits and guide them back to their world.

I had never heard of this tradition before. How had it come to me that in my dreams I was saying goodbye to my father's spirit, performing a ceremony of farewell which was denied to me in real life?

It had been a shock to receive the news of my father's death, via a phone call from my stepmother when I was at work. There was to be no funeral, and with my brother and half-brothers and half-sisters living in the United States, I couldn't get together with them. However, a few days later, my aunt, my father's sister who lived in San Francisco, was visiting London. We went for a walk in Hyde Park and I told her about my dream. She stopped and looked at me.

'At the end of World War II, so when your father was seven years old, there was a ceremony at the family pear orchard in Sacramento. The purpose was to celebrate the safe return of our father, and his brother and sister, from serving in the war in Europe. In the ceremony, we lit paper lanterns and sent them floating down the river.'

It was the first time that I had heard this story. It added another dimension of wonder to the image of the floating lanterns that had appeared in my dream. It was a powerful reminder for me of how we are all connected to a consciousness that is bigger than us. And that we can listen out for those images, whether they come in dreams or from nature, which can guide us on our way.

I wanted to follow up on the significance of the dream. I emailed my father's cousin, the one family member I knew who was a practising Buddhist, to tell him about it and ask for any suggestions about how I could find out more about Buddhism. I had fond memories of visiting his home in Colorado with my father many years ago, when I was teenager. The wooden house was set by the side of a clear blue mountain stream and surrounded by a shimmering of aspen trees. He was a mountain climber and skier and former National Geographic photographer, and I remember thinking that his was the kind of life of adventure and creativity that I wanted to lead. In his reply, he encouraged me to look up the books of some Buddhist teachers and pointed me to some websites.

In the months that followed, I read a few of the books and took a meditation course at a local Buddhist centre, seeking relief from my grief. Once, I called the ambulance, thinking I was having a heart attack, unaware that I was in the midst of a panic attack. I had started to experience pains in the body which, in retrospect, I can only explain as the accumulation of unprocessed grief, a freezing of this ice-cold river into crystal shards that stabbed my legs and arms. As I sat on the meditation cushion, I did experience a quietening of the swirling of my mind, even if the pains were still there.

In my exploration of Buddhism, I learnt how the Buddha had gained enlightenment after sitting under a bodhi tree for 49 days. It is said that the Buddha had been wandering for five years, seeking the answer to the question 'Why were people suffering?' He sat down under the bodhi tree and decided not to leave until he had found the answer to the question.

It was not by chance that the Buddha sat under a bodhi tree. Hindus already revered the tree as sacred. Lord Krishna declares in the Bhagavad-Gita, 'Of all the trees, I am the peepal tree,' with *peepal* being another name for the bodhi tree. In India, *sadhus,* or holy men, choose to sit under them for meditation. Its Latin name is *Ficus religiosa,* in recognition of its importance in both Hinduism and Buddhism.

Bodhi is usually translated as 'enlightenment' in English. The root of the word, *budh,* means 'to awake', so the literal translation is 'awakened'. In Buddhism, bodhi is the understanding possessed by a Buddha regarding the true nature of things. The tree was named after its role in the Buddha's enlightenment.

When I started researching my journey to the trees and read about the Jaya Sri Maha Bodhi tree in the ancient town of Anuradhapura, Sri Lanka, I knew I had to visit. It was planted in 236 BC and is the oldest tree recorded to have been planted by humans. If Buddha had gained an answer to his question 'Why were people suffering?' from sitting under the tree, then maybe I could gain some answers of my own about how to live – and how to live in this time of rapid changes to the climate. This particular tree was an offshoot of the one that the Buddha had sat under, brought to Sri Lanka by Princess Sangamitta. The original tree was no longer living, so this was as close as it was possible to get.

Anuradhapura is 103 miles as the crow flies from Colombo, somewhat further by train. At the airport, I navigate my way past the scammers who assure me that the bus isn't running and that I will need to take a taxi. I find the bus which is going to the station. I am completely covered with sweat by the time I take my seat on the train. I have reserved a seat in a second-class carriage and I am grateful it turns out to be next to an open window. Fans fixed to the roof of the carriage turn listlessly; the window offers much more relief once the train starts to rattle and creek its way slowly forward. A boy sits next to me. He's maybe 12 or 13 years old, his mother and father are sitting in front. I wonder about his hopes and dreams. It is a Sunday afternoon – perhaps they have been visiting family in Colombo for the weekend.

The train makes its way past the backs of houses, where people are sitting outside watching us go by, and continues through small stations and railway crossings, where tuk-tuks and motorbikes and cars wait for the train to pass. We cross through lush meadows fringed with palm trees and dotted with water buffalo with attendant white egrets on their backs. As my sweat begins to cool, I am reminded of the shared humanity that comes from travelling together, so different from if I had taken a private, air-conditioned, individual taxi, just looking to get to my destination as fast and as conveniently for myself as possible.

I have booked a room in a homestay and the owner meets me at the train station in Anuradhapura. As he drives, he tells me about the complex water irrigation system that was set up over 2,000 years ago to serve the town and is still working. At his home, he sets out a fresh coconut pierced with a straw and a plate laid with pieces of cake. I am grateful for the combination of freshness and sweetness. I sit on the little patio outside my room and breathe in the warm evening air.

In the morning, I set out to make my acquaintance with the Jaya Sri Maha Bodhi. My host tells me that I can cycle to the tree and lends me a bicycle. I experience the familiar feeling of freedom of setting out to explore by bike. I ride a couple of kilometres along the main road to the town, and then experience the familiar feeling of getting lost. I stop and ask, and go in the direction that I am pointed in, until I realise that this is not the right way. After consulting my offline Google map, I take a one-way track in the opposite direction, my blue dot on the map now moving towards the bodhi tree.

I lock up the bike in the car park and head to the temple. Temple-goers must tread barefoot and I leave my sandals at the kiosk that looks after shoes. I silently thank my host for advising me to bring a pair of socks to protect my feet from the burning heat of the stone. I make my way with the steady flow of white-clad Sri Lankans and foreigners, most not dressed in white, through the gates. There are a couple of large bodhi trees, identifiable by

Seed Three: Waking up to co-arising

their distinctive heart-shaped leaves, in the immediate grounds. But neither of these is the Jaya Sri Maha Bodhi. My gaze is directed up the white-painted temple steps to where, behind walls, I can see a tangle of branches of a couple of trees, stretching skywards, also adorned with green leaves. There look to be two taller trees and a smaller one. One of these is the oldest, most sacred tree.

I walk up the steps towards a large altar, piled high with white and purple lotus flowers and bowls of rice left as offerings. A young white couple approaches and the woman adds a lotus flower to the gathered mass. Her partner takes a picture of her with the flowers. I catch myself judging them for treating this as another photo opportunity, but then check myself. Here I am, taking pictures too.

It is the army's responsibility to protect the tree and a guard stands near the altar. He is talking to another couple. As they move off, I approach him. I ask him about the significance of the flower offerings.

'When we offer flowers to the Buddha, it reminds us that what happens to the flowers happens to us. We die and we are reborn. We imagine our life. We remember that death is not the end of our life. And that the next life is depending on what we are doing now.'

'And which is the oldest tree?' I ask him, wanting to make sure I am looking at the right tree behind the wall.

'The oldest one is the smallest one,' he says. 'People think that the oldest tree should be the biggest one. But if you think about people, the oldest people aren't the biggest people, they get smaller with age. It is the same with this tree.'

He explains about the other trees. 'The other trees have sprung up around it to protect it from the monsoon winds, sheltering it.' These trees are the oldest tree's bodyguards.

I have read that there is a public holiday tomorrow because of the full moon and that this is marked at the temple. It is known as a *poya* or *pooja* day.

'What's happening for the full moon pooja tomorrow?' I ask.

'There are additional ceremonies here at the temple. We observe the five precepts of Buddhism every day, but on the full moon there are three additional precepts: we only sit on the floor, we don't eat after midday and we don't listen to any music or TV.'

'If you come again tomorrow,' he adds, 'I will bring some books for you to look at and some old pictures.'

I thank him and say that I will see him tomorrow.

Since it is possible only to see the thin branches of the Jaya Sri Maha Bodhi, reaching up from behind its wall of protection, I go back down the stairs to the temple courtyard. There I sit on the dusty ground under one of the spreading bodhi trees, the outline of the distinctive leaves with their long, pointed tip already familiar to me. The leaves have a long petiole or stalk, which means they flutter and shimmer in the faintest of breezes. A family of seven approaches the tree where I am; they could be grandfather, grandmother, father, mother and three children. The grandfather starts to pray. He prays with his whole being, his words gaining speed and volume. The father holds on to the trunk, a faraway look in his eyes. The mother ties a white ribbon to a branch. I wonder who they are praying for. The little girl, maybe five or six years old, turns to look at me shyly a few times.

I feel out of place. I am a tourist. But it is more than that. I am confronted with the inadequacy of my response, the lack of a basis to genuinely make an offering and connect with the world in this way. I feel the contrast between myself and the way that the grandfather is praying. His prayers and his body are one.

I am not a Buddhist. I haven't been brought up in this culture. Perhaps it is unfair to myself to compare my response. But in this moment, I feel the absence of not having an equivalent practice. I went to a Church of England secondary school, where incense was swung as the priest walked down the vaulted aisle and we engaged in what I called 'stand up, sit down for Jesus'. Before that I went to a Christian Science Sunday school, in a brown brick building in a town 20 miles from where we lived. It was something I had to do once a week and, as far as I was concerned, just served to take me away from my explorations in the countryside surrounding my home.

As I listen to the family's prayers, I realise I do not have the habit of communicating with that which is bigger than me, whether a tree, or nature, or a god. And I do not have the rituals that can become as familiar as habits. I do not have this connection between my body and my prayers. I don't even have prayers.

There would have been practical reasons for the Buddha sitting under the bodhi tree as he sought the answer to his question of why people suffer. The tree provided valuable shade. But I like to think that it gave the Buddha more than respite from the intensity of the sun. In the days and nights he sat under it, he would have heard the music of the wind blowing through the leaves, seen the interplay of light and shade through the branches. Perhaps he traced the heart-shaped outline of the leaves over and over. Maybe he was focused on his breath and took in the oxygen that had been breathed out by the leaves of the tree. Maybe he was grateful for the support of the tree against his back. He would have observed the insects crawling on the ground and heard the song of the birds who landed in the tree and made it their home. He would have felt the interconnectedness of his body and his nature with the wider nature that supported him.

After 49 days and nights, he got up from under the tree, ready to share the answer to the question: 'Why do people suffer?' His core realisation was that suffering is caused by our illusion of separation. Joanna Macy, the Buddhist activist and scholar, wrote, 'What the Buddha woke up to under the bodhi tree was *paticca samuppada*: the dependent co-arising of all phenomena, in which you cannot isolate a separate, continuous self.'[1]

From sitting under the tree, he had lived experience of the beautiful interconnectedness and interdependence of all life, a web of relationships. He saw the patterns at play and the interplay between them. What was important was 'the way things work, how events happen and relate to each other."[2] From his insight into dependent co-arising, the Four Noble Truths emerged, which are at the core of the Buddha's teaching. The first is, simply, that life always involves suffering. The second truth is that the cause of suffering is our belief that we are a separate, solid, independent 'I'. The third is that we can end our suffering, that we are the solution. And the fourth truth is the path that the Buddha offers for the way out of suffering, known as the Eightfold Path: right understanding, right intention, right speech, right action, right livelihood, right effort, right mindfulness and right concentration.

As I sit under the bodhi tree, I reflect on the second truth, that the cause of our suffering is our separation, believing we are separate from nature, from each other. I can see through my own limited window of experience and understanding how sitting under the tree observing the shifting patterns of the leaves and of the clouds and of the mind would have led the Buddha to understand that suffering comes from not acknowledging our interconnectedness. Climate change is a result of our separation from nature, acting in ways which prioritise human interest over the effects on the wider world of which we are but one part.

This founding story of Buddhism is so different from that in the Christian tradition. In the Bible, it is the tasting of the fruit of the tree of knowledge that causes Adam and Eve to be expelled

Seed Three: Waking up to co-arising

from the Garden of Eden. A separation from nature occurs as a result of this act. In Buddhism, by sitting under the tree, by being with the tree, the Buddha gains the insight of our interconnectedness that leads to his awakening.

Under another bodhi tree in the courtyard, a group of women are sitting on the ground, chanting, their voices rising and falling softly together, the tree absorbing the reverent vibrations. Here is co-arising, as they sing the world that they want into being through their offerings and prayers.

A couple of years after my father's death, I took a weekend workshop with Jill Purce. Jill is one of the leading chanting teachers in the UK and has also extensively studied Tibetan Buddhism. In a downstairs room of her home in London, surrounded by artifacts from her years of travels, we practised the sounds of Mongolian overtone chanting, learning to make unfamiliar sounds and let the sounds resonate together. I didn't experience a healing of the unexplained pains in my body, but I did gain temporary relief in the act of making sound together.

The feel-good factor of chanting is borne out by the science. Studies have shown that chanting can increase feelings of positive mood, relaxation and focused attention, while decreasing stress and anxiety – the vibration of chanting helps to bring our nervous system into a state of rest.

I couldn't understand the meaning of the words that the women were chanting under the bodhi tree. But I could feel the connection to that which is bigger than us. It was also a reminder of a lineage of women gathering together that was started here in Sri Lanka by the arrival of Princess Sangamitta, bringing the branch of the bodhi tree and establishing an order of Buddhist nuns.

Later, I look up what the chants might have been. Chants are traditionally sung in Pali, a dialect related to Sanskrit and thought to have been spoken by the Buddha. The opening of one of the main chants expresses praise and honour to the Buddha:

Namo tassa bhagavato arahato sammā-sam-buddhassa
Namo tassa bhagavato arahato sammā-sam-buddhassa
Namo tassa bhagavato arahato sammā-sam-buddhassa

> *Homage to the Blessed One, the Worthy One, the supremely Enlightened One!*
> *Homage to the Blessed One, the Worthy One, the supremely Enlightened One!*
> *Homage to the Blessed One, the Worthy One, the supremely Enlightened One!*

Jill has spoken and written about how 'Enchantment literally means to be made magical through chant.' She said in an interview: 'I think that's what chant is really about – it's praising wondrous nature, this magical place, this divine being, whatever it is. Praising it with gratitude.'[3]

Cycling back to the homestay, I pass a long, brightly coloured mural painted on the wall of a school. The mural is divided into scenes. In the first scene, a girl with ribboned braids in her hair, wearing a white shirt and skirt and red-and-white striped school tie, and a boy with white shirt and blue shorts, are planting a coconut, its leaves sprouting up above the ground. In the next scene, a woman is watering the coconut plant with a hose. The coconut now has palm-like leaves. In the following picture, the tree is fully grown and is bearing coconuts. A woman stands under it with a black and white cow, carrying a bucket in her hand, maybe with milk from the cow. There is also a banana tree, pineapple plants and flowers – a garden farm has sprung up around the one coconut that was planted.

Seed Three: Waking up to co-arising

There is a State Minister for Coconuts in Sri Lanka. In 2020 the Minister, in a statement filmed while he was climbing a coconut tree, urged the planting of coconuts on every available plot of land, to make up for the shortfall of 700 million coconuts in the country. So there may be more of these murals coming to walls around Sri Lanka.

In the last picture on the mural, there is a gathering of men and women in front of a river, with baskets of fish. It is not clear if this is linked to the coconut story or if the artist is celebrating abundance in all its forms. Yet the interconnectedness of the actions and outcomes is clear. I think of the Japanese saying, 'If you want to catch a fish, plant a tree.'

A Japanese scientist has proved the truth behind this adage. Katsuhiko Matsunaga showed that, as leaves from trees break down, the fulvic acid that they release binds with iron in the soil, and when this oxygenated iron runs into the oceans, it enables phytoplankton to perform photosynthesis and provide food for the fish.[4]

Sri Lanka has 1,340 km of coastline. The risks from climate change that Sri Lanka are facing include loss of ocean biodiversity and damage to coastal infrastructure. At the same time the remaining forests in Sri Lanka are being cut down at a rapid rate, and just one third of natural forest remains. This loss of forest contributes to erosion and landslide risk, and eventually to the loss of fish in the sea. Research has also shown that the resilience of rainforests is being affected by climate change. In one forest, there was a decline of 17 per cent in biomass of the trees over a 40-year period, with the Ceylon ironwood the most affected. Periods of drought as a result of climate change, together with fungal pathogens, are thought to be the cause of the death of the trees. Although I have not come across research on bodhi trees being directly affected by climate change, they are not separate, they are an interconnected part of this ecosystem.

At the local restaurant in the evening, I see the family I had watched making an offering under the tree. They recognise me and smile and say hello. I ask them why they have been at the temple. 'The mother is sick,' the woman replies.

I didn't ask what illness the mother was suffering from. But *Ficus religiosa* is known for its healing powers beyond those accessed through prayer and chanting. It has a long history of being used in Ayurvedic medicine to treat a wide variety of conditions, from diabetes through to liver diseases. Many parts of the tree are used, including its bark, fruit, leaves and seeds. In one Ayurvedic treatment, which is used for eczema and other skin conditions, the bark of the *Ficus religiosa* is combined with the bark of four other *Ficus* trees, including the banyan, *Ficus bengalensis*.[5] Dried figs ground up into water are used to treat asthma and the juice of the bark is used as a mouthwash to cure toothache.[6]

The next day is a poya day and there is an even greater flow of people through the gates of the temple. I feel the bare earth beneath my feet, trodden by so many people over thousands of years. I walk around to the back of the temple and up the stairs to see if I can find the guard from yesterday who had said that he would bring some books, but he is not there. I go back down to ground level and find a space to sit on the dusty ground, near to the whitewashed wall behind which is the Jaya Sri Maha Bodhi.

I watch a young girl walking in a circle near the base of the wall, sprinkling water from a clay pot. The tradition is that on full moon day at Anuradhapura, you take water from the *Tisa Vaeva*, the ancient tank, and pour the water at the foot of the tree. The

Seed Three: Waking up to co-arising

Tisa Vaeva is where the original bough of the bodhi tree from India was kept before it was planted. Watering the bodhi tree is a ritual that is practised at all temples. By watering the tree, you are giving life to someone who is in need. If someone becomes fatally ill, the practice is to visit the bodhi tree for seven days in a row to water it and pray for recovery. Women wanting a child will also water the tree and pray for fertility. I wonder if it would work for me. But I don't try. I again have the sense that these are not my rituals.

A group process past to make an offering within the temple as part of the full moon celebrations. The Buddha received enlightenment under a full moon. I wonder if this is why each full moon is a public holiday here, so that people can reflect on how they live their lives.

On the other side of the temple is a place where you can stand and offer your prayers up to the tree. Again, I feel like an outsider, like this is not my tree to offer prayers to. I had thought that in coming here I would listen to the wisdom of the tree. But this wasn't a tree that I could have direct contact with, like the birch tree in my mother's garden or the mother banyan tree at Auroville, or the daughter banyan tree at Sadhana Forest. This was a tree that had become a living symbol to be venerated, rather than a tree to be in direct relationship with. The history of the tree preceded it and surrounded it.

The people here use rituals to connect with the tree, in the hope that it will listen to their prayers. But their rituals are not my rituals. I feel pressure, from myself, to be interacting with the tree in a specific way. But I feel removed.

I stop by the base of the temple where people are standing and sending their prayers up to the tree. I offer my thanks heavenwards. I ask for guidance as I continue my journey onwards.

★

After my evening meal, I go for a walk by the lake. I stop to watch the birds and take pictures. An older man stops to talk. He says he likes to watch the birds. I walk back to the end of the path by the lake. The full moon is rising over the water. Each time I watch the moon rise, I am surprised anew to see it. It seems magical, this great sphere – the size of it, the speed of its climb. I feel a sense of wellbeing and peace rising as well.

Earlier in the day I had felt the lack of rituals I could use to connect with the world. The full moon was a clear marker of ritual here in Sri Lanka, as a public holiday and an occasion for collective ritual. Imagine if in the US or UK every month there was a public holiday to mark the full moon and take the time to reconnect with the principles to live by.

But I don't need to wait for this. We don't have to wait for a grand societal gesture. Change starts with each of us. There is nothing to stop me using the occasion of the full moon to pause, reflect and give thanks. To meditate on what the full moon reminds us of: the cycles of nature, the cycles of life, the turning of the wheel. It reminds us that circumstances will change. Of the impermanence of life, as the Buddha taught. He also taught about the importance of our actions, right action, the cause and effect. Rituals are a way of guiding our actions, to focus on what is important. And rituals don't need to be grand gestures. The way we drink our morning tea can become a ritual – it is the attention that we bring to it that sets it apart from routine. In the philosophy of co-arising, where all actions are interconnected, our actions determine who we are.

I look to the moon and send the same prayer skywards as I did to the bodhi tree. 'Guide me as to how my journey will unfold – as you have done already.'

I hear the moon say to me, 'You ask me to guide you as to how your journey will unfold. You can listen to the guidance of my cycles.'

The answer is in the question.

The next day, before I leave Anuradhapura, I explore some of the other temples. It is a UNESCO World Heritage site and one of the ancient sites of Buddhism. My first stop is Jetavanaramaya temple. It is a *stupa*, or a dome-shaped temple, in the form of a bell. It is the largest stupa in the world, reaching over 70 metres high. It is said that all the bodhi trees on the island are related to the Jaya Sri Maha Bodhi. Here, another bodhi tree grows. I sit under it. I listen to the birdsong. The roosters are still crowing, although the sun is high. I repeat the mantra I had read in Thich Nhat Hanh's book, *How to Walk*, on the flight to Colombo:

In out
Deep slow
Calm ease
Smile release
Present moment
Wonderful moment

I need to let go of expectations. Be open to receive. The present moment is enough.

I take a minibus to Kandy, my rucksack wedged in beside me. Kandy is a hill town surrounded by mountains and forests. Its most famous attraction is the Temple of the Tooth, where a tooth of the Buddha is on view. I make my way there, getting drenched by a sudden thunderstorm. But again, I feel sense of separation, rather than connection. The purpose of the temple is to venerate a piece of the Buddha, which seems counter to my understanding that Buddha was not meant to be worshipped as a god.

The next morning, before I go to the meditation centre which is to be my next stop, I visit the Botanical Gardens in Kandy. I only have two hours. The gardens are a mix of clipped lawns, stands of trees exotic to me and flowerbeds overflowing with colour.

I revel in the lushness of the trees. I look up to see huge fruit bats, known as flying foxes, flying between the trees and hanging upside down from branches. Up to 25,000 of these bats live here. The information sign tells me that they have a huge wingspan of 1.2–1.5 metres, with a body length of 23 centimetres. Just to see the air full of so much life makes me happy. I recognise a cannonball tree, with its large fruits hanging down, from one that I had seen in gardens in India. Starting to recognise trees makes me feel as if I am getting my bearings in these lands. There is an extraordinary slim-trunked tree, with her roots spreading out around her like the folds of a gown on the earth, and two branches raised to the sky like arms thrown up high in celebration or dance. I take a picture and light streams into the corner of the image, illuminating this goddess. Elsewhere, yellow heart-shaped leaves are threaded on a vine around a tree. I am filled with a sense of wholeheartedness, heart-fullness.

As I walk through the trees, I think, this is my temple, this is where I am happy, not in the buildings designated as such. I realise that the trees can be sacred to me, wherever they are. And that is my tradition.

There is a tradition of forest monasteries in Sri Lanka, as there is in Thailand. Forest monasteries sprang up to allow space for contemplation away from the urban centres. I looked into whether I could spend time at one in Sri Lanka, but there are restrictions on lay people attending and women are not allowed at some of

Seed Three: Waking up to co-arising

them. I was glad to find a Buddhist retreat centre in the hills above Kandy, which offers eight-day silent retreats. Buddha sat under a bodhi tree for 49 days and gained enlightenment. I wasn't going to sit under a tree for that length of time but I did want to have the experience of sitting in silence to see what I could learn. I also liked that this retreat was not just about sitting but included walking and working meditation. Meditation in action.

The bus to the retreat centre is the Delkota bus from the Good Sheds Bus Stand. I take a tuk-tuk to the bus stop. It has a red interior and a quote printed on the inside back wall.

> *Study nature,*
> *love nature,*
> *stay close to*
> *nature. It will*
> *never fail*
> *you.*

It seems like a sign that I am heading in the right direction. The driver drops me off by the bus. As I get on, I see one other Westerner. I figure he is likely to be going to the retreat, but I choose another seat a few rows in front. The bus fills up, and we leave.

We move slowly through the traffic of Kandy. The bus becomes standing room only, the aisles crowded. We pass through the university, with manicured lawns and cricket pitches. We start to wend up through the hills. Palm trees, pine trees, jackfruit trees. Views out over steep valley sides and over to the mountains. My heart is happy to be here. I feel the extraordinary privilege of being able to do this, to have this freedom. That I don't have children brings me sadness. But I tell myself there is no point imagining what that other life with children would have been.

I would not have been able to go on this journey, in this way, if I had had children.

The bus driver calls out that I need to get off soon. I manoeuvre my way out of my seat and stand in the aisle, wedged between people, and then the bus stops. Awkwardly, I gather my rucksack from the space next to the driver and climb down the steps. The other Westerner does get off; he is going to the retreat.

We look around for a tuk-tuk to take us the final part of the journey.

'I'm sure one will appear shortly,' I say, 'They usually do.'

And a couple of minutes later, one does. On the way up the dirt track, continuing up the mountain, the driver points out the tea plants. The women picking the tea, with big bags on their back to put the tea in, turn to smile as we pass. As we get higher, he points out the coffee plants growing above the tea, and also the green pepper and cloves. We really are in spice country. My fellow traveller is from Germany. He has black curly hair pulled back in a short ponytail, and I think that maybe he is in his thirties. He has been on a number of meditation retreats before, in Germany and in Australia. He is a veteran; I have only been on yoga retreats.

> Arriving.
> There is chanting rising up from the valley.
> The song of birds.
> A rumble of thunder.
> On the gate, 'Silence please, retreat in progress'.

In the seven days that follow, I have the opportunity to learn to listen to myself. I realise how I cannot learn to listen to the trees unless I am able to observe the chatter in my own mind and where that is coming from.

The silence of the retreat is interrupted halfway through when a wildfire threatens the meditation centre. Stories of recent wildfires in California are on my mind, and I feel the fear of being trapped by a fire, although the leader of the retreat centre is calm and confident that we will be safe. We see the orange flames advancing and smell the smoke in the air, and most of us choose to leave for the night, packing our bags and walking out of the centre to take refuge in a village further down the hill. We make our way back in the morning, past charred trees still smouldering. The blackened trees and ground, with embers glowing, seem to me like our worst fears made visible. Each of those destroyed trees is an embodiment of what is so often abstract: the reality of how humans are damaging nature and, by extension, ourselves, through our actions. It was as if the fire was spelling out a warning in brushstrokes of charcoal. It seemed poignant that the silence of our retreat had been interrupted by the fire, as we spoke to each other with increasing urgency to try and figure out a course of action. And there was the sadness of seeing the impact of the fire on the trees and the land. But the fire had not entered the centre.

At the time, it was not clear if the cause of the fire was natural, for example through a lightning strike, or if it was started by humans. Later, reading about forest fires in Sri Lanka, it appears likely that it was started by humans, with possible causes including carelessness, setting light to dead grass to obtain fresh grass for cattle and burning of degraded forests for cultivation, with the fire then spreading.[7]

As extreme events become more common, the importance of having a strong foundation to respond from becomes even more important. As individuals we need to have the mental resilience to be able to deal mindfully with whatever comes our way, and to be present to support others. The fire showed me that I still had more work to do to be able to stay steady. There is not enough awareness around climate-change adaptation and mitigation in the physical environment. But there is even less awareness around psychological preparedness. And mindfulness has a key role to play in this. In each moment, we can choose our response and create from there, instead of merely reacting. And reduce our suffering as we do so.

The last morning, we have a question-and-answer session. A participant asks a question about meditating in nature. One of the group offers a quote from Shunryu Suzuki, a Zen teacher:

'I don't know anything about consciousness. I just try to teach my students to learn how to listen to the singing of the birds.'

After the session finishes, I speak to the man who had shared these words. We can now break our silence because we are leaving.

'Thank you,' I say. 'Those words you offered from Suzuki, about teaching students to hear the singing of birds. That meant a lot to me. My ex once told me that my job was to listen to the singing of the birds. I wonder if he knew this quote?'

Suzuki was saying that the best way we could connect with consciousness, however that is defined, is to truly listen to the singing of the birds. To hear this quote now felt like a gift.

I say, 'I feel as if a circle has been closed. Or perhaps it is not a closing, but a spiralling, onwards and outwards.' It is another sign that I was on the right path.

Words gain new meaning and depth as they interact with other words and experiences, at a different point in our journeys. The teaching of co-arising also gives us insights into consciousness. Joanna Macy explains it as: 'Knower and known, mind and world, arise interdependently.'[8] In Buddhist philosophy, consciousness needs an object – but it is a two-way relationship. Our consciousness hears the singing of the birds and is in turn informed by this listening. We can choose what we listen to, and this will in turn inform who we are.

It is time for my journey to continue. The following day, I take the slow train back to Colombo. I sit in the calm sunshine at the train station, waiting for the train, which is delayed by 30 minutes. I am perfectly happy and content. I am not annoyed about the delay, as I might have been before. I listen to the piped muzak and the cawing of the crows. I listen to the singing of the birds.

Something in me has slowed down, I write in my notebook. I reflect on the possibility of a different relationship with time.

Trees operate on a different timeframe from us.

Surely that is one of the reasons that we are in awe of them. We recognise that they exist in a timeframe outside of our own. Imagine. To live for over 2,000 years. To have stood your ground for all that time. Our lives are fleeting by comparison.

From the train window, I look out at the green hills, the steep-sided valleys, a blur of trees as the train picks up speed. I watch my thoughts.

Listening doesn't always mean having to come up with a story or a message that emerges from the experience. If you are listening to a friend who is upset, or sad, sometimes it is enough to sit with them in silence.

The focus of attention in listening is not you, but who you are listening to. The only thing for you to do is make yourself open to the listening.

It is in the act of listening that the relationship between two beings is transformed. The other being knows that you are listening to them. And sometimes there is nothing to say.

I hadn't intended for my trip to listen to the trees to be a spiritual journey. But maybe the trees had other plans. One definition of spiritual is: 'Deepening that understanding [of the way things are], and repeatedly cutting through the illusion of the self.'[9] Maybe it is impossible to spend time with the trees and not contemplate what is beyond us.

In many religious traditions, trees represent the link between the material and the spiritual realms. Trees are present in the story of the life of the Buddha, not only at the time of his enlightenment but at his birth and death, as he entered this world and as he left it. His mother gave birth to him under a sal tree, a sacred tree in the Hindu tradition, and he passed away under two sal trees. Trees are a bridge between the seen and the unseen. Like listening.

In Kandy, outside the Temple of the Tooth, I had seen a sign.

What is Buddhism
As stated by the world famous scientist
ALBERT EINSTEIN

> The religion in the future will be a cosmic religion. It should transcend a personal God and avoid dogma and theology. Covering both the natural and spiritual, it should be based on a religious sense arising from the experience of all things, natural and spiritual, as a meaningful unity.
> Buddhism answers this description.

I googled the quote to check its veracity. It seemed that this was one of those quotes that does the rounds of the internet but cannot be found in Einstein's writings. Whoever said it, the core idea remains valid.

'A religious sense arising from the experience of all things, natural and spiritual, as a meaningful unity.'

Seed Three: Waking up to co-arising

The formal rituals of Buddhism are not part of my tradition. But the trees are pointing a way for me into this unity of the natural and spiritual, and into an experience of co-arising, where I can see how all my actions feed into this web that I am part of, and I am shaped in return.

On my last night in Sri Lanka, I stay at a modern hotel near the airport. I sit on the terrace outside, eating vegetable curry and rice, drinking a beer. The only other people are a couple sitting at a table nearby and they invite me to join them for a drink. The woman is originally from Ireland but has been living in Montana for the last 15 years with her American husband. We talk about climate change, among other things. As I get up to go, she says, 'Can I ask you one final question? If you had a choice right now between going to Mars and starting a new colony there, or staying here on Earth and trying to make things better here, what would you do?'

'Stay here.' There was no hesitation in my reply. The answer to me is obvious. There is no life on Mars, that we know of. The conditions are not favourable. And we have such a bounty of beautiful life on this planet, although it is rapidly diminishing because of us. Why would I want to leave?

'Really?' she replies. 'I would go to Mars, no question. We need a new beginning, we need to start afresh.'

Hopes and dreams. The baggage going around the carousel. The flags waving in the wind from the bodhi tree. We all bring our different hopes and dreams. The different destinations we have in mind.

The grass is greener on Mars.

Yet the invitation is always there to look at and feel the ground beneath our feet. And to carry a branch of loving kindness in our baggage as an offering to those we meet.

Seed Four: Trees are kin

Eucalyptus trees, Australia

> 'Surely we've cut ourselves off for long enough now – time, now, to open our minds outward, returning to the biosphere that wide intelligence we'd thought was ours alone.'
>
> David Abram[1]

Bilpin, a village 65 miles from Sydney, population 665, is my next stop after Sri Lanka. The houses are strung out along the main road that connects Sydney with the Blue Mountains. The mountains are named after the blue haze of the eucalyptus that grow on their slopes. The road is known as Bell's Line of Road. Archibald Bell was the 19-year-old Englishman who was shown the route across this land by two Darug men named Emery and Cody. Colonists who had previously attempted to cross had failed. It turned out the secret to traversing this terrain was not to travel through the ups and downs of the gullies of the landscape but to stick to the ridge line.

The greater Blue Mountains Area was declared a World Heritage Site in 2000, in large part due to the diversity of its eucalypt forests. More than 90 species of eucalyptus are found here. When I drew up my list of trees to visit, eucalyptus was one of the first to be added. It was another tree, along with the baobab, that was rooted in my memory from my time in Malawi. At the edge of the school, near where women used to gather in a circle to sing and dance, was a grove of tall blue gum trees. I loved wandering through these trees, inhaling their scent and hearing the crunch of their long, thin leaves under my feet.

The trees arrived there because of the British Empire. From 1790 onwards, eucalyptus, or gum trees, were exported from Australia to India. It is likely that these trees were *Eucalyptus globulus*, or Tasmanian blue gum, which became a workhorse tree for empire. The colonists prized the trees' ability to grow quickly in dry conditions, providing timber they needed for building. The eucalyptus trees arrived in Malawi in the 1880s. They are mentioned in a progress report from the Blantyre Mission in April 1889: 'The Mission's tea bushes are doing extremely well; the gums have seeded and we have now plants from them.' The 1896 editions of the *Central African Planter* newspaper carried advertisements by the African Lakes Corporation Limited for plants of various species, including the eucalyptus. Another edition of the same newspaper carried an advertisement for a grand piano, on sale for £40. I wondered which wood this piano was made from, and where, and what songs were played on it. Songs of empire.

Although the eucalyptus trees were not native, they grew large in my memories of Malawi. Subsequently, whenever I came across them on my travels they took me back to this time when I had struck out to discover who I was.

Later, I realised that my relationship with the eucalyptus went back further than Malawi, to San Francisco and my early childhood there. Presidio Heights, next to Golden Gate Bridge, was our local park. My early walks were among the eucalyptus trees, the thin leaves longer than my toddler feet. The first eucalyptus trees were planted in California in 1853, about the time that my forefathers and foremothers first arrived in California. Maybe my affinity with the eucalyptus, these transplanted trees, stretched back to before my childhood, their minty clean scent permeating my DNA.

So perhaps it shouldn't have been a surprise that when on my first visit to Australia, four years before this trip, I had felt like I had come home, that the land was speaking to me. There was no logical explanation for this feeling. I didn't have any family connections to Australia. Yet this strong heart feeling was undoubtedly there. I tried to figure out why. My hunch was that it was connected to the eucalyptus tree.

The famous Proustian memory moment involves a madeleine. Maybe my equivalent was the eucalyptus. Scent molecules go directly to the primary olfactory cortex and can attach to memories without us consciously processing them.

Yet, maybe this wasn't the whole story. In a conversation one day, I described this feeling of homecoming in Australia and my eucalyptus theory.

'I had exactly the same reaction when I stepped off the plane in Australia,' the woman said. 'And I didn't grow up with eucalyptus trees. I grew up in the Midwest of the USA, and we didn't have them there.'

It seemed like my theory was not cut and dried. There was more to discover. Why does Australia provoke such a strong reaction, not only in me but also in others? And what can this teach me about belonging?

A dream. Not my dream.

'I actually have recurring dreams where I'm on a landscape and there's these enormous eucalyptus trees that are bigger than anything I've ever seen in my waking life, and I remember looking at them and thinking, "That's amazing, they must be so old, these trees have stood here on this

landscape for so long, the things that they've been witness to – the changes in the landscape from the changes in vegetation to the changes in people and the cultures that walk upon it." It really makes you think about what impacts us modern, white Australians are having on this land.'

The dreamer is a participant in a research study,'[2] examining the role of the gum tree in an Australian collective cultural identity. Eucalyptus is the most common forest type in Australia, accounting for nearly 80 per cent of the native forest area.[3] They loom large in both the physical and cultural landscape of Australia.

I am staying at an artist's residency for a month, run by Rae and Yuri. Rae is a sculptor, and the curved forms of her colourful sculptures dot the property. She has bushy brown curly hair and a smile in her eyes, but there is also a touch of the steel that she uses in her sculptures. Yuri is an expert on the local area and has written numerous walking guidebooks. He looks the part of a guide to the bush, with a grey beard, a stride that connects to the land, and a straight-talking approach.

On our first day, Yuri takes us on an orientation walk through the bush. The vegetation is a mix of shrubs interspersed with the trees, mainly eucalypts. He tells us that there are nearly 800 different varieties of eucalypts, and I wonder if it will be an impossible choice to just focus on one. We walk into deep gullies and scrabble up huge rocks, giving us a view out over the green vastness of the Wollemi National Park wilderness. The park's name comes from an Aboriginal word meaning 'look around you, keep your eyes open and watch out'. It is the traditional land of Wiradjuri, Darug, Wanaruah and Darkinjung peoples, with evidence of their presence on this land dating to over 12,000 years ago. Yuri leads us into a cave.

As our eyes adjust to the darkness, we see the ochre outlines of hands on the cave wall. Aboriginal people long ago held their hands to the wall and blew ochre paint through a tube, so that the colour recorded the shape of their hands. It is as if these hands from the past are reaching out to us, a reminder of the people who lived here in close connection with their kin: the trees, the rocks, the animals, the living earth. I breathe in the air of the cave, hoping to imbibe some of that connection into my bones. We can't touch the paintings but, in my mind, I place my hand within an outline of a hand on the stone. I whisper to myself a wish that I can make art that honours this connection, this land, these peoples. And then we step outside into the sunlight once again.

Bilpin is renowned for its apples and is called 'The Land of the Mountain Apple'. There used to be more orchards, but two cider makers with popular picnic gardens remain. Other fruit trees in the area include persimmons, which we go to pick one Sunday. There is a post office, a hardware and agricultural supplies store, and a small shop which sells basics such as milk and chocolate. The nearest food store is a 20-minute drive away.

The residency is on the right-hand side of the road as you drive from Sydney. This was to prove significant when huge wildfires raged in 2020, a year after I was there. The road acted as a fire break, protecting the land and property on the other side. The residency is reached by a dirt track, about a kilometre from the main road. This track is the boundary line to the Wollemi National Park. The windows of my room face out across the road into the trees of the park.

There are six of us in total at the residency. Abbie is a poet from Malta, with long chestnut wavy hair, a fellow Aquarian, my age. Laura is the youngest, in their late twenties, also an Aquarian, and has come from New Mexico. They are an artist who works in a variety of mediums, from embroidery to drawing to performance art, but always with a focus on the ecological. The other three artists are Australian, all in their fifties – Jan is a sculptor and painter, his Dutch origin hinted at by his height and thick blond hair; Wendy is a ceramist and landscape painter, with a motherly and teacherly air; and Alison is a painter, often working on natural materials such as tree bark, her love of pattern and colour expressed in her clothes as well as on her canvases. We are all united by our love and respect for the natural world and working to convey this through our words and images.

I spend time trying to familiarise myself with the different types of eucalypts. One of my favourites is the scribbly gum (*Eucalyptus haemostoma*). It is named after the zigzag patterns embroidered into the yellowish bark by moth larvae as they tunnel between the old and new bark on the tree each year. I look at the patterns and imagine what stories might be written in these scribbles. Another is the mountain blue gum (*Eucalyptus deanei*). The trees grow tall and straight, up to 65 metres high, with greyish bark, and topped with a crown of branches. They are a favourite of koalas, who have recently been spotted in the area again. One day we go for a walk among them hoping to spot the grey bears in the trees, but they remain elusive.

I am learning that the bark of the eucalyptus trees is a distinguishing factor for identification, and they fall into broad bark-themed groups including stringybarks, ironbarks, peppermints and smooth-barked gums. The peppermints can be recognised by their bark which is thick and fibrous and interlaced, but most notably by the minty smell of their crushed leaves. They are often used for the production of eucalyptus oils as they have a high content of oils in their leaves.

In the novel *Eucalyptus* by Murray Bail, a protective father

Seed Four: Trees are kin

seeks to stop his daughter getting married by demanding that the successful suitor identifies correctly all the eucalyptus trees on his property. I am beginning to understand why this might be such a task. There is not only the bark to take into account, but the shape of the leaves, and the flowers. The common identifying characteristic of all eucalypts is that they have capsule fruiting bodies or gum nuts, which develop after the tree flowers.[4] One of the trees that I am most drawn to by its smooth reddish bark and graceful spreading shape is a eucalypt, but not a member of the *Eucalyptus* genus. It is an angophora, of which there are nine species. Classifying the eucalypts is a complex business, which has led to many changes over the years.

A week into my stay in Bilpin, I come across a quote online from Patrick White, a writer local to the area, that eucalyptus is a state of mind, not a tree. I latch on to these lines like a meditation mantra. This is the insight that I need, my justification to focus (using the term loosely) on eucalyptus as a family, rather than on an individual species. I write lines exploring the eucalyptus state of mind.

A state of mind which is a state of light and shadow and 894 variations in between.

A state of mind which is blue and red and scribbly and pepperminty and lemony.

A state of mind rooted in rock of volcano flow and spinning out to the Southern Cross.

A state of mind which charcoals, hollows, still grows.

A state of mind which is a lung-opened, inhale, exhale, expansion

State of heart.

Yet despite the lines I write about the eucalyptus trees, ending with the words 'state of heart', I am still considering the eucalyptus as a state of mind, approaching them with the thinking mind, rather than through the senses and feelings of the body.

I connect via Skype with Monica Gagliano. She is a research scientist, specialising in evolutionary ecology, currently based at Southern Cross University, where she directs the Biological Intelligence Lab. She lives in the rainforests of Queensland. She has written a book called *Thus Spoke the Plant* about her pioneering work in understanding plant communication. I ask her if the phrase 'eucalyptus state of mind' resonates with her. In her accent tinged with the song of her native Italy, she says, 'Not really. I don't think of them as a state of mind, but rather as a condition of the heart.'

She describes how she loves the pink smoothness of the skin of the salmon eucalyptus, and the contrast between the tall, strong trunk of the lemon eucalyptus and its delicate, lemony fragrance. It is clear she appreciates the trees through all her senses.

'But do you think that Patrick was trying to say the same thing, but in a different way?'

'There's a big difference,' she says. 'If we want to communicate with the plants, it needs to come from a feeling place. The thinking place will block anything.'

I repeat the words to myself.

'The thinking place will block anything.'

I had come to the conclusion myself that eucalypts needed to be approached from a state of heart. But my thinking mind was still getting in the way. As Monica pointed out, it was this thinking mind that was stopping me from listening more closely to the trees.

I am surprised to find myself talking to a scientist about this. If there was one profession that is typically associated with operating from a state of mind, it is the scientific profession. But Monica has been fighting for acknowledgement of the importance of bringing a state of heart into scientific work throughout the course of her career.

Monica has been one of the pioneers in proving plant intelligence. From her research, she was able to prove that the mimosa plant can learn and has a memory.[5] After being dropped repeatedly, the plants learnt that this was not actually a threat and therefore they didn't need to spend precious energy in closing their leaves. And they remembered this behaviour three days and even a month after the experiment.

Monica speaks to me of how cultural background defines what is allowed in science. She is clear that listening to her own state of heart and listening to the plants has enabled her to make scientific breakthroughs.

'There is a case for science to understand itself better,' she says. 'There is the idea that the subjective process is not included in science. Yet, without the subjective looking in, and imagining, there would be nothing possible.'

Monica has spent time with *cuyanderos* in the Amazon. She doesn't want to use the commonly used word in English, shamans.

'It's a colonising way of describing them.'

She feels it is putting a label on people that they would not use themselves. She speaks of how the *cuyanderos* have a very open relationship with nature and are trained to listen from very early on. Practices which help them to learn to listen may involve isolation, fasting, ingesting or smoking particular plants, and waiting for the relationship with the plants to arise. These conversations with the plants often turn into gifts for the *cuyanderos* to share, including *icaros,* which are healing songs from the plants.

Monica has been given an *icaro*: 'The entire song came; it was just complete. Someone was singing it to me, it was easy for me to learn it and repeat it.' She speaks about how you can build the relationship with the plants, if it is meant for you.

'The plants will call you – and you will know.' I wonder if I will ever hear such a song, in this way.

Monica shares with me some of her favourite plants. These include the wattle tree, also known as a mimosa tree, with its fluffy yellow balls of flowers, which speak to her of old knowledge; the grevilleas, with their exuberant blooms from peaches and cream, through to hot orange, which are 'joy coming out of the heart' and the banksias, with their brightly coloured cone-shaped flowers, which are like a café, all the butterflies and birds coming to one place to feed.

There is a clarity in the way Monica speaks that I think comes from her connection with the trees and the plant world, tapping into an intelligence that is bigger than human intelligence.

'How do you relate to Australian plants, having grown up in Italy?'

'It was a homecoming. I was looking for home, I had been disconnected from nature in Italy. The first time that I realised how disconnected I'd been was when I arrived in Australia. Here there is space to connect with nature, here there is "big nature".'

Here was another person who shared the sense of homecoming I had experienced the first time I came to Australia. Australia offered the opportunity to connect with this "big nature", something that is impossible in so many European landscapes and our bodies recognised this coming home.

I ask Monica for advice about listening to plants.

'Like all relationships, some plants are very loud and generous with wanting to share. Others are very quiet. And others are clear, saying, "Don't come close to me." It's about respecting that.

Sharing gratitude with the plants. And continuing to fine-tune your skills. It will take time to build that trust with the plants.'

It is like any relationship. I think back to the words of the guide at the Matrimandir. The Matrimandir is not going to reveal her soul to anyone – and neither are the plants. It all takes time.

But, as Monica says, 'In our current cultural situation, we seem to have no time for anything. We have no time for food – we do fast food. We do fast-food relationships. If people want to learn to listen, it takes time.'

Yet how do we 'make time' to do this?

'If it is true that by controlling time, you control everything, then reclaiming time "in here" is possibly the most powerful and revolutionary act of empowerment.'

At the Sri Lanka retreat, our teacher shared a quote from Thich Nhat Hanh, the Buddhist monk and teacher. 'The only time we have is ours.'

Time is not something outside of ourselves, a resource which is scarce.[6] We are time.

Trees are time. They are perfectly 'in time', aware of and changing with the seasons.

A dream.

In the midst of the blue gums, I am sitting with a sage. He poses a puzzle. There are two cups. A cup of cold water. A cup of hot water with rosewater in it. How do you cool the hot water without diluting the rosewater essence, using just the two cups?

'I know,' I say, after a moment. 'Pour out the cold water, then tip the hot water from one cup to another, as if making Moroccan mint tea, or cooling South Indian coffee by pouring from cup to bowl and back again.'

I didn't know if this was the right answer or not. I didn't get a response from the sage.

In the morning, I woke from the dream and thought, I could have just left the water to cool in the air.

What was the hurry?

Why was there a problem to solve?

The blue gums were speaking to me in my dreams. And maybe, through the clarity of the dream, I was learning to listen. I then just had to put the advice into action – not hurry, not need an answer.

We turn off the road, cross the railway track, and the dirt road degrades into dips and gullies. Rae parks the car and we walk the last 100 metres or so. Chris greets us in a clearing under the scribbly gums.

'Welcome.' Chris smiles broadly, shakes our hands. He is a friend of Rae's and he has agreed to talk to us about Aboriginal culture. He is an Aboriginal man, who has been on his own journey of reconnecting to his culture, after the acknowledgement of being Aboriginal and knowledge of the culture was suppressed in his grandparents' and even his parents' generation.

'Do you mind if we begin with a smoking ceremony?' he says. For a moment, I imagine that this is going to involve smoking pipes, but this is not the case.

'It's about helping us arrive, in this place,' Chris says. 'It helps to calm the mind. And people bring baggage with them when they come to a place, so this helps to clear the spirit.'

I help to gather twigs and pieces of bark for the little fire that Chris is building, to one side of the main fire, which is heating the blue kettle. Once the fire is going, Chris places a large bundle of eucalyptus leaves on it, and the smoke begins to creep through the branches. One by one, we kneel down by the fire and waft

Seed Four: Trees are kin

the smoke with our hands towards us. I squat, trying to be present to the moment. Smoke whooshes from the fire right into my face, like a trapped spirit being released. I step away.

'I guess I have a lot of stuff that needs clearing,' I say.

There must be something about sitting around a fire that quickly directs the conversation to the heart of the matter. Chris mentions that he is no longer afraid of death because of his spiritual beliefs.

'Do you mind me asking about what your spiritual beliefs are?' Abbie says.

'No, of course not, let's get right into it,' Chris says. 'This world, this is not it. We haven't left heaven, we've just had a thought that we were separate. It is a dream of separation. We are all one soul.'

He explains further. 'These beliefs align with the old peoples or Aboriginal way of understanding that our main home is the spirit world from where we come and where we go back to, and we are just here for a time until we head home again, working our way back to the main camp - which we have never really left, and are still connected to, and which encompasses us. The stars represent the spirit-world campfires of the ancestors in traditional culture.'

He pauses as we take this in.

'The gift is being okay with as is. This is also similar to Buddhist beliefs.'

'You said that you were an environmental and social justice activist. How do you square being okay with as is with being an activist?' I ask.

He looks into the flames for a moment.

'If I consider the world as a dream, I still want the dream to go well. But I'm not attached to the outcome. The world is passing, I'm not here to hold it together.'

After another moment, he adds, 'The important thing is to be fearless in the world, that's what I've tried to teach my children. And to be kinder and gentler.'

Chris continues, as he adds a stick to the fire:

'We were born into a country where there was no slavery, no servants even. Some people say that all cultures had slavery of sorts, but this is not true for Aboriginal culture. One of the English men to arrive early on wrote that the Aboriginal people are "not willing to be masters and not willing to be servants". They were very non-hierarchical. We don't have a king or a chief. The English tried to make certain men into leaders, put a chain around their neck. But the other members of the tribe didn't recognise this. The English complained that this made it difficult for them to do business or negotiate with Aborigines, as there was not one recognised leader, as there was in other parts of the world.'

Before we leave, Chris gives a couple of us the opportunity to try making hand art of the kind that we had seen on the cave wall on the first day. He gives me a hollowed-out wooden tube, filled with orange-red paint, made with ochre gathered on this land. I put the tube between my lips, and one of the group puts their hand on the trunk of a tree. I blow as if down a peashooter. The paint sputters, failing to reach the tree, let alone create an outline of a hand. I obviously don't have the technique or strength of lungs to blow the paint out at the required velocity to make an impression. Chris sees my disappointment and kindly says, 'It's totally in the spirit of okayness with what is. It maybe makes our ancestor spirits smile.' I smile and think back to the outlines imprinted in the cave.

Back at my desk that afternoon, reviewing my notes, looking out at the thick cover of eucalyptus trees, all of a sudden it made sense: the difficulty that I was having with identifying one particular tree, and of wanting to engage with the eucalyptus trees collectively. This was the original character of the land, as expressed by the people. I needed to go out and listen to the *forest*, not to the trees, and see what that told me. Maybe that great puff of smoke was what had been needed to clear my ears for a different way of listening.

I took my first steps at the age of nine months in San Francisco, in a Victorian house, made from redwoods, painted blue. I imagine pushing my chubby self up off the floor, white-blond curls bobbing. Maybe holding on to a nearby chair. Then letting go of the support and taking one step and then another, and a couple more, before my legs give way and I tumble down. My mother fussing over me and congratulating me. And getting ready to try again.

We have to learn to use our bodies as children. But then when did I stop being in my body? It is not something that our culture values. I was never taught to value my body as a source of wisdom.

Eucalypts are ideally suited as teachers in the world of feeling and using the senses. They appeal to the visual sense, with their grace, beauty and the myriad colours and textures and patterns of their bark. They play with all of our senses perhaps more than some other trees do. We hear the wind music that is made by their leaves, as well as the percussion underfoot once they have fallen and returned to earth. There is the appeal to touch, whether running your hands over the patterns on the trunk of a scribbly gum, feeling the edges of a strip of bark curling away from a tree, or stroking the velvet blackness of a charcoaled fallen trunk or limb. The trees invite a deep inhalation of their scent, so palpable and distinctive, to further open the lungs and our sense of smell. And beyond these physical senses, there is an appeal to what we call a 'sixth sense', an intuitive feeling or a state of heart.

Each walk that I take in the bush, I try to shift from a thinking mind to a feeling heart. I am discovering that a feeling heart starts with using the sense of touch and feel, as well as the other senses.

An intuitive awareness or ability to feel in this way is one that is largely buried in Western culture. Stephen Buhner in *Plant Intelligence and the Imaginal Realm* has written about how we can open these doors of perceptions again, if we so choose. One of the primary ways that we can do this is to simply approach the natural world with an open heart and the question, 'How does it feel?' and listen for the answer. Asking the question, he writes, will 'significantly increase both the visual and feeling inputs that are normally gated for you by your unconscious'.

I try this one morning, in the rainforest gully surrounding the residency. I stand beneath the trees and just decide to stay where I am. Beneath my feet I begin to feel an electric current of life passing to and fro. I shut my eyes. I concentrate on what I can feel. Listening is about sensing with my body, not hearing with my ears, or even seeing with my eyes. What can I feel? And what I can feel are these connections, pulsing backwards and forwards. I stretch out my hands and can feel these pulses in the air around me as well. It makes sense. The most effective way to listen like a tree, is to act like a tree, rooted to the ground, and connected to the air as well.

There is a Celtic word, *mothaitheacht*, which Diane Beresford Kroger describes as the feeling of a tree's presence, which is 'a feeling in the upper chest of some kind of energy or sound passing through to you'. Knowing that this is something that the Celts used to have a word for makes it seem more real. This is not just something I am imagining, but in fact there is a long tradition of listening to the trees in this way.[7]

I am on a journey of discovery to understand how to listen

in all its forms – with the thinking mind, with the body, and now also through the intuitive knowing of the heart. And understanding that the body is the doorway to the heart.

Walking back to the house, I slow right down. I photograph the lichen on a tree stump from numerous angles, bend down and take pictures of the twisting tree trunks framed through the grass trees, examine different seed pods in detail. The lichen, the grass trees, the seed pods – these are all vital parts of the forest, as much as the trees.

Two dreams:

I am sitting with my mother, my brother and his pregnant wife. The city is under attack, the invaders are coming, we know that it is going to be a nuclear attack, nuclear apocalypse. Then I am running to the top of a tower. I am all alone when the explosion happens. There is a great light, and I am falling and falling and knowing that I am going to die. I want to say 'I love you, Mum' and all those other things that I haven't said. I know that my sister-in-law is going to lose her baby too. I wake up, surprised that I am alive, that it was a dream.

Two nights later, another dream of the end of the world. Again, I am sitting with my mother, my brother and his pregnant wife, and a friend of mine from work, who has a one-year-old daughter. We are sitting in a house very like my ex-husband's house in London, which he was living in when I first met him. We are under attack again. I had been for a walk down by the river, seen all the preparations being made for the attack. I came back to the house, shutting the door quickly before the giant bugs came in. Then I saw one of these huge, oversized bugs in the house. We are sitting down at the table to eat a meal. Waiting for the attack to begin, and the world to end.

★

I turn the dreams over for meaning. The most likely explanation I came to was that I had been reading about societal collapse, catastrophe and possible extinction, and that apocalyptic events were on my mind.

A week later, it is Easter Sunday, the day of resurrection and rebirth. Alison drives Laura and me in her little Jeep down from the mountains to a confluence of two rivers. The banks of the rivers are lined with casuarina trees, the same species I had seen in the surrounds of Sadhana Forest, where they were being grown for their wood. Laura wades in the shallow waters, hunting for mussels, which are the focus of the project that they are working on, examining how molluscs are impacted by pollution of river waters. Alison and I sit on the riverbank, chatting. She shares a dream, and I then tell her my dreams of the end of the world. Alison goes to paddle. I remain sitting and an interpretation for the dreams come to me. Are they more personal, relating to the end of a possible world for me? My period was due at the beginning of April, when I arrived in Australia. It is now 20 days later, and there is no sign of it. It has been regular every month, but now – nothing. But was this the beginning of the end? Maybe. It would have been highly unlikely for me to have children at the age of 45. But this possibility was now becoming even more remote.

On the drive back, Alison tells us about giving birth to her two daughters. I am quiet. I feel grief that I would never have this experience. I knew that people were now choosing not to have children because of climate change, and not wanting to bring a child into the world to face such a future. But that wasn't why I didn't have children.

Had I cut myself off from a particular relationship with the world out of fear? Had the trees called me on this journey to learn how to be in a different relationship with the world? And to feel more deeply into this relationship? I began to wonder how much of the climate crisis was due to a lack of our capacity as a society to feel. Had we become numb or numbed ourselves in different ways, which led to where we were now?

Another morning, another walk, exploring the eucalypt forest and rainforest, descending 300 metres down to a creek. It takes us two and a half hours to walk the three and a half kilometres down, and an hour and a quarter to walk the same way back up – the reverse of what might be expected. But we spend our time on the way down stopping to look at not only the trees, but the tiny spongy forests of moss, the extravagances of lichen, the varying shapes and sizes of fungi, the clear waters of the rock pool and the cascades of the waterfall. I look from different angles, photographing, exploring this ecosystem. I am here in the now. I am not thinking about anything else apart from how beautiful the light is on the trees or the wondrousness of that golden honeycombed rock, or I am noticing the dimpled pattern on the angophora tree, or inhaling the damp smell of the ferns by the creek. In the moment, I do not reflect on that quality of being in the now, because I am so engrossed in the beauty all around me.

It is the quality of the light that enchants me again and again, the interaction between the light and the trees and, underneath, the translucent grasses. Roger McDonald, in *The Tree in Changing Light*, writes of how the botanical function of the tree is as a light collector. The tree needs to capture light in its leaves to photosynthesise food. 'Leaves were solar collectors. They generated sugars that flowed through the inner bark and changed into the woody material of the branches, trunk, and roots.'

I hadn't thought of it in these terms before. How was this light flowing into me, changing me, remaking me, making me?

As we walk up the hill on the way back, I say, 'If it is healthy to spend time in forests, then we must be really healthy.'

Research on the effects of spending time mindfully in forests, known as forest bathing, shows that it can lower blood pressure, boost the immune system, reduce stress and aid sleep. I wonder what our future would look like if we could all spend more time walking and sitting among trees. And thinking back to the Buddhist principle of co-arising, how this action would change who we are, individually and collectively.

The language that we use when we talk about – and, perhaps more importantly, to – the land, trees and animals determines how we see them. 'Can my country hear English?' asked Dinah Norman a-Marrngawi of John J Bradley, a scholar who has been working for a long time on studying her language and culture, Yanyuwa.[8] She answered her own question: 'I do not think it does, it can only hear Yanyuwa.' I am left to reflect, how I can hear the trees speak, how can they hear me, if I do not know the language of the place?

If we do speak in English, Robin Wall Kimmerer, a scientist, professor, and enrolled member of the Citizen Potawatomi Nation, has suggested using a new pronoun for our fellow living beings, which would not objectify them in the way 'it' does in English. In the Anishinaabe language, the word for living beings of the Earth is 'Bemaadiziiaaki'. From this, Kimmerer suggests the pronoun 'ki', as in when speaking of the Sugar Maple, we say, 'Oh that beautiful tree, ki is giving us sap again this spring.' And the plural for earth beings would be 'kin'. 'On a crisp October morning, we can look up at the geese and say, "Look, kin are flying south for winter. Come back soon."'[9]

Our kith and kin are those people that, hopefully, we love and that love us. 'Kith' does not, in its original meaning, refer to people but to the land that we come from, to which we belong. To one's home outside the house. In the English language, we once had this connection to the land.

Seed Four: Trees are kin

Bob Randall, an elder of the Yankunytjatjara people of Central Australia, has written of how, 'Right throughout my life, old men would point to a forest of trees or a grove of trees or just one tree and refer to it as people: "See that mob over there." This way of talking could be referring to kangaroos, trees, hills or humans. Any of us could be "that mob" or "us mob" could include the totality of that.'[10] Here is a view of the world that is inclusive of all beings.

It is hard to see how we will be able to repair our relationship with the world, unless we are able to see, acknowledge and talk with our fellow beings in a way that recognises our connection, rather than reinforces our separateness. I would argue that global warming has been caused because of our disconnection from the world around us and the impacts of our actions, and we therefore need this change in mindset – and perhaps more importantly our 'heartset' – in order to create systems to live in which are built on a renewed and reset relationship with the world of which we are one part.

Toko-pa Turner is a Canadian writer and expert on dreams. In her book *Belonging: Remembering Ourselves Home*, she writes of how by paying attention to our dreams, and those aspects of us that are alienated that appear in the darkness of our dreams, we can 'begin remembering ourselves home'.[11]

She writes: 'Dreaming is nature naturing through us' and as we begin to learn to listen to our dreams, 'This sensitivity is what makes us more porous and multilingual, bringing us into conversation with the many languages of the world.'

This recognition of the many languages of the world strikes a chord with me – and how we can be in conversation with them, whether through the language of dreams or the language of trees, if we choose to listen.

Olivia Sprinkel

Chris had spoken about the world being a dream. In Western society, we have created a separation between our inner and outer landscapes, and between our waking and dreaming lives. What if we could break down the barriers between them? Toko-pa Turner suggests the practice of saying at points throughout the day, 'This is a dream', to help us change our perception of what is real and what is not real.

Dreams have been pushed to the margins in Western society. Yet they are keepers of wisdom, like the trees. They speak to us in a symbolic language. Paying attention to our dreams is another way in which we can connect and listen to that which is beyond us. I am convinced that by doing so, we can better connect with nature and what the trees have to teach us.

What does listening to trees mean? Towards the end of my stay in Bilpin, I realise that I am defining it too narrowly.

One morning, I decide to meditate outside. The previous owner of the property was a Buddhist and she set up a stone bench on a rock clearing by the house. I sit down, the bench damp from the night before. Sitting there, I think about ways to greet the day. Most of the time I do not have this immediate connection with the earth at the beginning of the day; I start my day inside and then continue it inside. This means that the tenor of the day is completely different. Outside, I can ask the plants, 'How did the raindrops feel upon your leaves?' To ask the earth, the trees, the plants, the rocks, how they are, as you would do a friend, and then listen to their answer.

And there may be no answer, because maybe they are not in the mood for talking. Maybe it is an answer that you cannot hear. Or the answer is the feel of the breeze upon your skin, or the freshness of the rain-soaked air. Maybe it is the yellow robin, there in front of you, looking at you with curiosity and care.

Maybe it is the way your gaze is drawn to the swirling patterns of the bark on the peppermint gum that is leaning down the hill. Or the lyrebird you catch out of the corner of your eye, that is running to wherever it is running to. Or the mushroom cap, peaked as the Himalayas, if the Himalayas were two millimetres high.

Now the robin returns to land on this tree and looks at me again. I, in turn, look anew at the surface of the bark, the rock, my skin. They are meeting places of knowledge, trading posts of information in our shared world. My body is permeable. Through my body, I can listen to the world, feel the world, know the world. And feeling and knowing are not divided in different hemispheres of the brain. They are united in one place: my body, the body of the world.

The evening before the group is leaving, we smell smoke in the air. We walk out along the road, towards sunset rock. The sun is setting, and the sky is an eerie orange. We know that this is a controlled burn, not a wildfire raging out of control. We stand in silence, watching the sun go down as the fire continues to burn, as the sky flames, as we begin to feel the smoke in our lungs. The controlled burn is taking out some of the accumulated undergrowth and cutting down the risk of future fires getting out of control. Even so, it feels like a portent.

Nine months later the fires will return. And this time they will be out of control. In the 2019 – 20 wildfires, which last for three months, it is estimated that approximately 80 per cent of this million-hectare area of the Blue Mountains was burnt. I think of the goanna, the giant lizard, we saw running up a tree. Even if the animal escaped with its life, where was it going to live now its habitat was destroyed? It is estimated that over 140 million reptiles, birds and mammals were impacted by the fires. Think of that one goanna multiplied by 140 million. The scale is incomprehensible and heartbreaking. These animals and the trees and all the other plants are kin.

The residency in which I stayed was spared the flames. But in a video posted online I recognise the white picket fence of a café where we had stopped one afternoon for ice cream; now it was burnt to the ground. Other houses in Bilpin were destroyed. The word 'apocalypse' was frequently used to describe the fires.

Many species of eucalyptus depend on fire to reseed. Heat releases seeds from capsules, which land on ground that has been cleared of other vegetation and therefore competition. Some have lignotubers at their base, a swelling which contains buds and which allows new growth to sprout after a fire. Some have buds in their outer sapwood, which are protected by the tree's fire-resistant bark, and which will sprout after a fire. But the frequency and intensity at which the fires are now occurring has disrupted what was once a natural cycle and the trees and surrounding ecosystem increasingly do not have the opportunity to regenerate before the next major fire.[12]

Before I leave, I want to say thank you to this land and the trees for all they have taught me about feeling with my body and with my heart. I look down at the ground beneath my feet. I am captivated by the colours and textures. The sandy grey of the earth, carrying the rainbowed rocks, with shades of mustard yellow, dusky pink, husky purples, glittering greys and a soul of ochre. Layered above are fine stands of green grass and a blessing of eucalyptus leaves. I take pictures, framing the ground in different ways. I set the intention to continue to explore connecting with the ground in this way. I have a sense that this will help to guide me home, as I go forward into the next stage of my journey. I asked at the beginning of my stay where the invitation to listen to the land had come from. The answer was in the question. It had come from the land itself, and from the trees which grew from it – the invitation had come from kin.

Seed Five: Feel the unseen

Trees of the Amazon basin, Ecuador

> *'I have been standing all my life in the*
> *direct path of a battery of signals*
> *the most accurately transmitted most*
> *untranslatable language in the universe.'*
> Adrienne Rich, from 'Planetarium'

'Relax.'

This is the first rule of listening, according to Gordon Hempton, one of the world's leading acoustic ecologists. His voice is soft, as one might expect from someone who practises listening for a living. But it has authority, it is a voice you want to listen to. He is in his 60s, balding with close-cropped grey hair, the skin on his face weather-reddened from many long hours spent outside in all conditions. We are sitting in the grassed backyard of a small hotel in a village outside Quito, the capital of Ecuador, soaking in the sunshine after our middle-of-the-night arrival, our flights from different departure points having been delayed by bad weather. Fortified by a breakfast of freshly squeezed pulpy pink fruit juice, strong coffee and scrambled eggs, Gordon begins to ease us into a journey of listening.

'Relaxing is your most important preparation for really being able to listen. The smallest bones and muscles in the body are in the ear. If you are tense this can affect what you perceive.' As we finish our coffee, he shares two other secrets to effective listening.

'Listen to the whole place, rather than isolating individual sounds. And focus on how the sound feels.'

I think back to my time in Australia and how I had been learning to listen with the heart, and the feeling sense, rather than with the mind.

'Here you go, Dr Sprinkel.' Gordon hands over a stethoscope. 'This is for you to listen to the pulse of the trees.'

Although he has over 30 years' experience recording the sounds of nature around the world, listening to trees is new to Gordon. In his research for this trip, he has discovered that stethoscopes can detect sound and movement within trees. It will be a useful tool to help figure out fruitful places for further investigation and recording of the songs of trees.

I first heard Gordon Hempton talking about listening some years ago on a podcast and his words had stuck with me. I had emailed to ask if I could visit him in the Pacific Northwest, where he is based, and listen to the cedar trees with him. He had replied to say he would love to but during the dates I had suggested he would be leading a small group in the Amazon basin in Ecuador. Did I want to join him there? Of course, I had to say yes. I had wanted to include the trees of the Amazon because of their vital role in the world's ecosystem, known sometimes as 'the lungs of the world' and because of the deforestation taking place there, but hadn't yet figured out how and when I could visit. The perfect opportunity had presented itself.

My mother had been a volunteer in a school in Quito, the capital of Ecuador, 15 years ago and, when I had visited her, we had travelled to the rainforest. I had been enchanted by this

Seed Five: Feel the unseen

rainforest ecosystem with its lush denseness and bewildering diversity of trees and vegetation. I knew it would be difficult to pick one tree to focus on. I was going to be open to the guidance of the trees.

After breakfast, I start practising my listening. Gordon sets me up with a recorder and headphones – a red Sony recorder, about the size of an iPhone, complete with a fluffy grey wind protector to sit over the top, and specialist headphones. Sitting in the hotel's backyard garden, I soon discover how listening through the headphones to birdsong and the everyday sounds of comings and goings brings to my attention sounds I would otherwise have missed – it is like listening in 3D or Dolby Surround Sound. Individual sounds pop out, creating a more vibrant landscape, revealing the tapestry of the chatter of birds, the conversation of human voices and the barking of dogs. My listening is slowly expanding, with the help of recording equipment and an expert guide.

Gordon is one teacher of listening for this journey. The other is Randy, who will provide lessons in listening from an indigenous perspective. 'Indigenous' means belonging to a place and, as I am to find out, listening is a central practice of belonging. The Cofan people are native to the Amazon basin in the east of Ecuador, and have lived in the forest for thousands of years. Randy is a white man and a Cofan chief. Like Gordon, he is also in his sixties, white-haired, slim-built. He wears a black knee-length tunic over jeans, and a red kerchief around his neck, typical Cofan dress.

The son of American missionaries, Randy was born and raised in a Cofan village. He studied in the US and bridges indigenous and Western scientific knowledge. He is a shaman (although he doesn't like to use that term, as he believes it has been discredited) with an MSc. I am uncomfortable about the role that his parents might have had in seeking to replace traditional Cofan culture with Christianity. But, as Randy tells it, they also fought hard to preserve the culture from other outside influences. Randy's wife is Cofan, and it is clear that his heart is here. He has dedicated his whole life to fighting for the rights of the Cofan nation to look after the forest and protect the land they belong to from oil companies and palm-oil plantations. So, although his parents are not native to this place, he belongs here.

For the two-day drive to the Amazon basin, eight of us pile into a minibus. Randy is travelling on ahead. Josh, Randy's son, is our guide. He is studying in Seattle, and I imagine his confident good looks, his shoulder-length jet-black hair and broad smile winning the hearts of his fellow students. Aida is the only other woman in the group and will be my room- and tent-mate. She is a singer living in Minnesota and originally from Iran. She knows Gordon and came to the Amazon with him last year. Sam is a quiet, easy-going Californian who has just graduated from journalism school and is writing a story on Gordon. Tim has been travelling around the world, to reset his life after his wife died. Christian is also on the trip to take some time out to re-evaluate in mid-life, in the midst of a successful business career. Jacob is a photographer who will be documenting our journey.

We head out past stands of eucalyptus trees. Ecuador is another country where the eucalypts have been planted and made the country their own. *Eucalyptus globulus*, or blue gum, was first introduced, as in Malawi, in the late 1800s, but it is from the 1970s onwards that the rate of planting for timber has rapidly increased, causing the deforestation of native species and impacting biodiversity.

We climb up towards the continental divide in our minibus.

Seed Five: Feel the unseen

Cloud shadows pass over the steep sides of the mountains. We cross from sunlight into cloud and then rain as we climb higher. We pass 'bear crossing' signs. Apparently, two bears were seen once. They have never been seen again. They would have been either the Andean or spectacled bears found in the Quito region. Both types are notoriously shy and their numbers are low, which explains the infrequency of sightings.

Gordon shares more with us about the science of sound.

'Elevation and temperature both affect sound. If you increase elevation, you increase the quality of sound and there is less echo. Sound travels more slowly in colder environments. So, as we descend towards the Amazon basin, and it gets warmer, sound is going to be travelling faster.'

I had never thought before about the effect of elevation on sound. It now made sense why people would yodel on the top of the mountains, revelling in the clarity. There was a scientific reason why the hills were alive with the sound of music.

We stop for the night in Reventador, a clutch of buildings along the main road. The town is named after the volcano which rises up above it, the top covered in rain clouds when we arrive. The rain starts falling shortly afterwards, and we listen with our newly tuned ears, observing the difference between the sound on the metallic and plastic parts of the roof.

At dinner, Randy explains the significance of the volcano to the Cofan people. 'There is no word in the Cofan language for "sacred" because, at its core, everything is sacred. But the Cofan have begun to use the word "sacred" to help protect key places for them, because it is language that the colonials understand. The volcano is one of those places.'

In the morning, we climb up to the roof terrace of the hostel to look at the volcano. The top is still covered in cloud.

'What makes the volcano special for Cofan people?' I ask Josh as we gaze up at its imposing slopes.

'The volcano is a place of our people,' Josh says. 'It is part of our country, a place where we go hunting and fishing. It's a seat of power for us.'

As Josh finishes speaking, the white cloud clears and is replaced by a mushroom of black ash, propelled upwards from within the volcano, getting bigger and bigger and then lighter and lighter in colour as it rises higher and higher.

We stand quietly, watching this powerful demonstration and reminder of the aliveness of the earth – and what lies hidden inside.

'Perfect timing,' Josh says, when the cloud has floated higher.

We nod our heads in agreement.

Down the road from Reventador, we stop to see if we can hear the oil flowing in one of the pipelines raised up by the side of the road. But we can't hear oil, only emptiness. We walk on the biggest pipeline, which runs next to the electricity wires. This pipeline is for heavy crude; there is also a medium-sized one for light crude and a smaller one for natural gas. Oil blocks, contracts for oil exploitation in a geographic area, cover 68 per cent of the Ecuadorian Amazon.[1]

Further down the road, we pass the hydroelectric plant, built by the Chinese and opened at the end of 2016. In payment for the dam, 80 per cent of Ecuador's oil production goes to China (as of 2019). Two years after it opened, the dam is full of cracks and the plant is only operating at approximately 50 per cent of its predicted capacity.

We are now in the country of big-leaved banana trees, Ecuador's second biggest export after oil. There are also papaya trees, and fish-farming ponds by the houses. A horse grazes outside a church on top of a hill. At the filling station, there are security guards with bulletproof vests. We are near the Colombian border where there are regulations in place to prevent people filling extra tanks and smuggling petrol over the border to Colombia or Peru.

The tar road turns to gravel. The palm oil plantations begin. Palm oil was introduced about five years ago, and the native forest was cut down to make way for this monoculture. Different sizes of palms line the roads. In a nursery, pots of palms are growing, waiting to be planted out. Oil, from the ground or from trees, is destroying the Amazon in different ways. Nearly half of all packaged products sold in the UK contain palm oil, from biscuits to soap. The choices we make every day about what products to buy can have an impact on whether the jungle will continue to grow here and provide habitat for the people, animals and birds that depend on it.

It is time to transfer to the boat and travel up the river. We climb into an open, fibreglass canoe with a motor. It is made by the Cofan and modelled on a wooden dugout canoe. It is one of the ways in which they are looking to develop sustainable businesses. The canoes have proved popular in this part of the Amazon, but they are finding it hard to get the funding needed to expand and serve other areas, even though there is a market for them. Randy says that the NGOs prefer to fund cacao plantations, despite them being unprofitable.

This canoe doesn't have any kind of cover and, soon after we start out, torrential rain sets in. My waterproof is soaked through in minutes. I put on a lifejacket to try to retain some warmth, and have another jacket draped over my legs. I huddle against Tim for some body heat. He lends me his cap to stop water dripping directly into my eyes; even so, for much of the journey, it is difficult to look up because of the driving rain. Yet in the discomfort, I feel an exhilaration of being here in the Amazon basin, on these waters. We are on the Aguarico, or Rich Waters. We try to estimate how wide the river is, maybe 150 metres across in some places. There is jungle on one side, and plantation clearings on the other.

To describe the water system in the sky, scientists use the metaphor of rivers. These sky rivers are drying up as trees are being cut down. I remember in school biology class drawing the water cycle. I carefully coloured in the trees with their brown trunks and heads of green, the blue arrows travelling up from the soil, through the trunks and leaves, continuing up into the sky. I wrote in my best handwriting the word 'transpiration'. I drew clouds, heavy with rain, and puffs of wind to move the clouds along. Finally, I completed the picture with the blue streaks of rain falling on to the land and trees below.

The Amazon makes over half its own rainfall from evaporation and transpiration from plants. Yet if deforestation continues, the water cycle will be broken and it is forecast that up to half of the Amazon rainforest could transform into grasslands or degraded ecosystems in the coming decades.[2]

This scenario is hard to imagine as I sit in a canoe, travelling up a river, being drenched by the sky river. But that's the problem. It is hard for us to imagine the consequences beyond our immediate experiences.

We pass the village built by the oil company at great expense, with all the materials brought up the river. The Cofan children go to school here after seventh grade. The residents of the village, who are a different tribe from the Cofan, have internet and mobile phone coverage. But in exchange they have given up the rights to their forest. This is not a deal that the Cofan are prepared to make.

★

Seed Five: Feel the unseen

The boat draws over to the side of river, but not next to land, as the river has flooded its banks. It is rainy season, after all. I step out and into water that goes over the top of my new knee-length rubber boots.

The volcano had given me some clues about the journey that lay ahead, the challenge to the boundaries between what is seen and unseen, between what is deemed sacred and not sacred. Here is another fluid boundary, between water and land. Maybe it is because I am soaked through to the skin, I also feel the boundary between my body and the world beginning to dissolve.

We wade through the water, and on to dry land. Wooden walkways have been built with government funding, providing a defined route into the village and to our accommodation. There are four cabins for tourists, and a bigger structure for gathering and sharing meals. All the buildings are built on stilts to raise them above flood waters and thatched with palm leaves. The edges of the forest crowd around. Four of us share a two-room cabin and a bathroom with a shower and a flush toilet, which is more luxurious than I was expecting. There is electricity from 6–9.30 pm, when the generator is switched on and heats up water for the shower. I don't think to ask why there are not solar panels for the energy – maybe they are not compatible with the amount of rain.

Dinner, for the meat eaters of the group, is paca, a large rodent hunted by villagers. I'm glad that I am vegetarian, so I have a good excuse not to taste it, enjoying rice and beans instead. After we have eaten, Randy provides an introduction to the Cofan and their history, which goes back at least 5,000 years. They traded with the Andean people, who in turn bought from and sold to the coastal inhabitants, so there was a route from the jungle to the coast. When the Spanish arrived, they had little contact with the Cofan, until the priest, Ordones, entered the area as the first missionary. He spent three years there and documented his stay in a book called *Tour of the World*, published in 1620.

Disease spread by colonialists eventually decimated the Cofan, like it did so many indigenous peoples. Smallpox, measles, cholera and typhoid reduced the Cofan population from hundreds of thousands to fragmented, isolated populations. In the 1920s, there were only around 300 Cofan people remaining. When Randy's parents came as missionaries from the US in 1955 and conducted a population survey, the combined Cofan population of Colombia and Ecuador was 480. It is now approximately 2,000.

The year 1972 was pivotal for the Cofan. The Texaco Gulf consortium finally successfully completed the oil pipeline construction. Ecuador's government offered 125 hectares of land to anyone in this region who wanted it. The Cofan village of Dureno became surrounded by these new colonisers of their land, including other indigenous groups taking advantage of the government scheme. When this land occupation began, the Cofan didn't have a concept of landownership. Instead, they believed deeply that you own what you create. For example, if you plant a tree, you own the fruit that comes from it. It took the Cofan many years to realise what was happening to the land that they belonged to. In response, they sought to establish a village further down the river and, in 1984, they built the Cofan village at Zabalo, where we are staying.

'We want this land because we want it to be forest,' Randy states, simply. 'We see ourselves as people of the forest. The land owns us.'

This is a crucial distinction between indigenous and non-indigenous peoples. Non-indigenous people typically see the land as belonging to them. The Cofan see themselves as belonging to

Seed Five: Feel the unseen

the land and it is their responsibility to be caretakers of the forest. Yet, in order to fulfil this custodian role, they need to have official rights to the land. If their rights are acknowledged in law, they can refuse access to the oil companies, and they can continue with their way of life, including hunting and fishing. In 1992, they were granted the right to 80,000 hectares of rainforest by the Ecuadorian government, although not the title deeds. This was the first time that the National Park system had been obliged to collaborate with an indigenous group and it required a new dual model of custody of the land.

Randy explains how, in 2008, Ecuador started paying for what is known as 'environmental services', looking after the forest so that it continues to absorb carbon and preserve biodiversity. If you have intact forest, you can make an application to the programme, and it helps to provide a budget for the community. And, after a continued fight, the Zabalo Cofan people were finally granted the title to 140,000 hectares of land in 2019.

The Cofan are truly people of the forest. During our stay, they showed us how they use vines to make ropes and baskets and make spears and blowgun darts from palms. The forest is their medicine chest. On my first day, I had a sore throat and I was given a green drink made from local plants. I couldn't drink it all as my stomach started to cramp halfway through, but the next day my sore throat was better. Herbs are used to cure diarrhoea. Leaves are boiled and used as topical painkillers. If we lose the forest, we lose these plants and the Cofan's knowledge of these medicines.

Of the trees that we encounter, the most easily identifiable is the kapok or ceiba (short for *Ceiba pentandra*), whose canopy stretches up beyond other trees and dominates at ground level with its huge, buttressed roots. Also easily recognisable is the palm with stilted roots, growing out from the trunk from about one metre high, which I later identify online from my pictures as *Iriartea deltoidei*. These palms can grow up to 25 metres tall and have leaves up to five metres long. I am confronted again with the difficulty of choosing one to focus on – and wonder if this is even the right thing to do, given the diversity and interconnectedness of the forest ecosystem. In the neighbouring Yasuni National Park, 307 species of trees per hectare were counted. As in Australia, I am realising once again the primacy of the forest, rather than individual species of trees. I decide that I am going to listen to the forest, rather than one particular type of tree.

Before we leave the village for our jungle camp, I ask Randy for his advice on listening to trees.

First:

'Appreciate the immensity of the forest. Feel the number of trees. Like you feel the amount of earth in a mountain.'

Second:

'Feel what is unseen in the forest, whether it is spiritual or microscopic.' He told of how, when the Cofan people were able to look through a microscope at plants from a forest, they were not at all surprised by what they could now see. They know that there is so much that we do not usually see.

'It's a great dance,' Randy says. 'We can only see part of it.'

Gordon had suggested we listen to the sound of the place, rather than to individual sounds. The task is to expand our listening outwards, beyond what is normally heard, seen and felt. If, as Randy said, it's a great dance that we can only see part of, we can only hear part of it as well.

We head out towards the Zabalo river in the long, motorised canoes. Where the black waters of the Zabalo meet the Aguarico, pink river dolphins jump out of the water. Amazonian river turtles sun themselves on logs in the river. A hoatzin – pronounced 'Watson', and also known as the stink bird – fans its tail. And everywhere are the trees, crowding to the water, sometimes fallen in. There are trees draped with ferns, and palms armed with spikes. A pack of woolly monkeys travel through the trees, led by a big male, then a mother with a baby on her back. They throw their hands into the air, make the leap to the next tree. Brown red howler monkeys are chilling out after their morning feed. Two blue and yellow macaws fly away squawking from the top branches of a tree. Our guide tells us they mate for life. Vines loop or hang straight into the water. Blue morpho butterflies dodge along the river, iridescent in the sunlight. Fruit bats skitter alongside the boat, disturbed from their log perches. The reflections of the oversized plants are geometric and kaleidoscopic in the black water. I am going through a portal.

The monkeys in this reserve don't fear us as they do in some other parts of the forest. There is a rule that forbids hunting anything with hands. One of our guides hears a toucan's call. He replies, using his hands and a leaf to make the sound, which is more like the croak of a frog than a bird. And then there, in a tall tree at a bend in the river, another guide spots a harpy eagle. The harpy is the biggest eagle in the world. It dominates the branch. We can make out its resplendent cape of black and white feathers. A capuchin monkey is raising the alarm, making a barking call. But the eagle continues to remain still, only moving its head from side to side.

The Zabalo lands are the world's first designated Wilderness Quiet Park. Gordon has been at the forefront of a movement to recognise the importance of quiet for all species and has been instrumental in the Zabalo's designation as a Quiet Park. But even here, as we travel down river, we encounter what sounds like the noise of a generator from the oil village. Gordon says that he needs to investigate this. I reflect on how, in an ever-more-populated, noisy world, the need for quiet becomes even more intense. And how learning to listen makes you more aware of it.

Later, as we go out again in the boats to fish, an Amazon river otter pops its head up to take a look at who we are and then dips back down into the dark of the waters.

It is the first night in our jungle camp. The group's six tents are huddled under a large black tarp, propped up on wooden poles hauled from the surrounding jungle. Palm leaves form the groundsheet, providing an extra layer between us and the muddy ground. I am sharing a tent with Aida. We each have our camping mats and a sheet and a blanket. It is warmer and stickier here in this camp than back in the village. After dinner and a couple of games of gin rummy and a few tastes of whisky, brought along by Tim and Christian, we head to bed. It is raining again. And my period has started. This is the first time in four months, the first since I was in India and where I was also without regular toilet facilities. Some timing. I don't appreciate the impracticality of it. Fortunately, Aida has some pads with her, as I had left mine behind in the hotel in Quito, to save space in my bag. But maybe it is my body connecting to a cycle of bigger wisdom. I have read about how it is common for women to get their period unexpectedly when they are in the wilderness. And I am glad that my cycle will continue, having feared it might be beginning to cease.

I wake in the night from a dream.

It is a dream about hotel room keys. I had left early and forgotten to return them. I wanted to call the hotel but the line was not working.

I open my eyes. I feel that I am awake. In front of me I see

Seed Five: Feel the unseen

white shapes, knobbly and gnarly, what could be a head. The shape appears to me to be a spirit of a tree. It has eyes and is smoking a pipe. And this one spirit is joined to another, spreading out.

Scared for a moment, I don't understand what I am seeing. The spirit looks at me, and reassures me that everything is okay, I just need to relax. It continues smoking.

And then I am moving into another world, seeing into a root network. A three-dimensional world, there, right in front of my eyes, one that I feel that I can reach out and touch. I see a seed sprout, the shoot growing up in front of me, and a beetle scurries past in my view. A glimpse into this whole other world we can't usually see. The root network gradually fades.

I sit upright, with no doubt that I am awake now. I reach for my pen and notebook to record what I have just experienced, so I don't wake in the morning and find I have forgotten the details. My pen won't write, so I make notes on my phone instead. I get up to go to the toilet, pulling on my rubber boots outside the tent after checking them for ants. I squelch down the path into the jungle, turning over in my mind what I have just seen. It is 2.45 in the morning and the insects are singing at full volume. I feel that I need to record this moment, this privileged access to that which is not normally seen. Back at the tent, I rummage around for my recording equipment, hoping that I don't wake Aida. I walk a little way along the path to the river and record for a couple of minutes. I add a voice note to the recording so I can identify it later: date, time, 'the sound of awakening'.

Two and a half hours later, I hear Gordon getting up in his nearby tent. He comes to my tent to make sure that I am awake to hear the dawn chorus.

Gordon has set up his recording equipment near the river. It is a specially constructed set-up, on a tripod stand, with two directional microphones, and headphones connected through an amplifier. Three of us take it in turns to listen through the headphones for a few minutes at a time and then just to listen with our naked ears. The songs of the birds swell, become a cacophony. Listening to the sounds through headphones reveals new details, different songs, which are then easier to tune into just with the ear once we have heard them. I can hear the low rumbling growl of the howler monkeys added to the mix. Gordon tells us that they could be a mile away. I wonder why they are called howlers rather than growlers.

I try to put into practice Gordon's advice to listen to the sound of the place, rather than individual sounds. The feeling I have is similar to the one that I had when I saw the web of underground connections in my night-time encounter. Here is an auditory web. All the sounds are intertwined. I think of the sounds that have already been lost from this web. And how if the growl of the howler disappeared, there would be a key piece missing. This is one of the reasons why the work that Gordon and others are doing on sound recordings in the field is so important. It means we have this record for future reference and we can understand exactly what we might lose, and are already losing.

I hear an insect buzzing around my head. I feel my own insignificance. I am as small as this insect buzzing. I go through my life thinking that I am so important, concerned about my own little problems, but it is not about me at all. I feel this now but how can I really internalise this and act from this place?

'*Cuen se daca*,' 'Let it happen.' Gordon and Aida had this Cofan saying tattooed on their arms after their visit here last year.

Things will be unveiled in their own time. I had written in

my intentions for the trip that I hoped to call forth the spirits of the trees if they wanted to communicate with me. I had been trying to get a glimpse of this other world. Now I have had it. I know that this unseen world is there. Who knows when or how the next glimpse might be? But it's not something I can make happen. I can only let it happen.

As night becomes day, I can feel my heart beating, vibrating with the place. I feel like dancing. Swaying, pulsing to the beat. Randy had called it 'the great dance'. It is a dance I want to be part of.

I share my night-time experience with Josh. He smiles his broad smile. 'It sounds like the forest people visited you.'

I am truly privileged to have been given access to the world of the forest people. I feel as if the world I am looking at, listening to and experiencing has an extra dimension. And I am at peace – as if I am sinking into the place. I feel the ground beneath my feet. Today is the day we are going to listen to the trees. Gordon has brought along different equipment for us to work – or play – with. The first piece we use is a microphone that he has specially rigged up for this purpose. It is a hydrophone, usually used for recording underwater, a black ovoid shape, to which he has fastened a red golf tee that can be inserted into the ground or into a tree to act as a probe. We start with pushing the probe into the earth, hearing how sound travels underground. I can hear the vibrations if someone stamps their feet a few metres away.

The next experiment is to try the microphone in a tree. Gordon uses a small hand drill to make a tiny hole in the trunk, and then inserts the probe into the hole. There is a lot of background hiss so it is hard for us to tell what is the noise of the tree and what is static. But it seems like there is a sound of a gulp and gurgle that could be the movement of water. I remind myself that this is all an experiment and we cannot expect to get clear, definitive results on our first attempt.

We move to another big tree. I listen to it first with my stethoscope, to detect sound we can then explore further with the microphone. I can hear a pulsing sound through the stethoscope in the middle of the tree trunk, about three feet up. We then try listening to it with a contact microphone placed on the trunk. Here is what we had been hoping for, a clear sound of the tree pumping water up its trunk. *Yes!* We try drilling a hole in the same place and listening that way, but the results aren't so clear. The act of drilling has altered the environment and perhaps what was occurring in the tree. The contact microphone is our tool of choice going forward. This is a discovery in itself.

I continue to listen to other trees with the contact microphone, but I'm not really hearing anything. I remember when I was brushing my teeth in the morning, I found myself looking at a broad, smooth-barked tree behind my tent and had the feeling that this tree had something to do with the forest people that I had encountered in the night. I go over to a nearby tree of the same kind and place the contact microphone on the trunk, again about three feet from the ground. The sound here is so much louder than I had heard on the other trees. I then rest the microphone on the top of a triangular root buttressing the tree. And there it is, the clear, unmistakable sound of a stream of water, running up the root into the trunk of the tree. *Eureka!* I make recordings in both these locations of the tree before excitedly reporting back to Gordon.

To be able to hear and record the water travelling up the trunk is listening to a tree in a way that I had never done before. It is amazing to consider the mechanism that allows water to be transported all the way to the top of a tree, whether it is 50, 80 or 100 metres tall. Listening to the tree in this way also makes me consider what a tree hears or feels. From the microphone I can hear the vibrations of birdsong and people talking, so the tree, I think, is likely to be able to feel these vibrations too. When people talk or sing to plants and the plants respond, they are responding to these vibrations.

Standing there, microphone on the tree, listening, I am also observing the tree, witnessing the moss that is growing, the intricacies of the bark, the dangling vines, the ants and other insects scurrying to and fro, becoming aware of some of the life that a tree supports. I can also feel my own heart beating more loudly and clearly. Joseph Campbell, the author and mythologist, wrote 'The aim of life is for your heartbeat to match the beat of the universe.'[3]

For a few minutes at least, I feel that I am in sync. Gordon reflects my experience back to me.

'You've reminded me about the importance of the act of listening, and the part that feeling plays in listening.' He shares a quote from Heidegger, 'True listening is an act of worship.'

In a way, whether we heard anything or not was irrelevant. It was the act itself that was important. It was even more special because we were able to hear the pulsing of water in a tree, like the blood pumping through our veins. The rainwater being carried up the trunk of the tree, to be released back into the air, so it could return again to nourish life. On an average sunny day, the trees of the Amazon release 20 billion tons of moisture into the air.[4]

The following day provides another lesson in listening. I am floating down the river in a canoe, being carried by the current, with Sam and Toto Vente, a guide. I am taking pictures of the reflections of plants in the stillness of the river, the sun appearing from behind the clouds from time to time. We pass a palm tree sticking out of the water near the bank. I can hear the sound of falling water. It does not make sense that the tree is dripping. I look again and I see something move. I think it is a monkey, it is the only animal in my sphere of reference that comes to mind. I motion for us to turn the canoe around. We draw closer. I can see a furry, damp body clinging to the tree, and then a claw, with long nails, around two inches long. A sloth! The canoe is now right under the tree, and we can see the black and white body, slowly climbing the tree. It stretches one arm up, and then moves its legs carefully, precisely, one at a time. As it climbs higher, we get a better view, the black and white striped back with a brown mark in the middle, and then its black round head with its etched-on permasmile. It seems like nothing would ruffle this one. It doesn't make any sound, its expression doesn't change, it just keeps on climbing, deliberately, until it reaches the top of the tree.

The sloth's journey is not done yet. It starts to climb towards the tree branch that is leaning over from the other side of the river. We watch it cross over, silhouetted above the middle of the river, and make its way into the deep branches and out of sight.

Slow down. That is the sloth's undoubted lesson for us. I wouldn't have spotted it if I hadn't been in a slow, curious state of mind, wondering where the water was dripping from, pulled in by both the sight and sound of the water.

Back at camp, we share our story. Josh said it was rare to see a sloth. He had only seen one once, when they felled a tree and only afterwards realised the animal was in it.

It is our last night in the jungle camp. Tim and Christian share the remaining drops of whisky from their flasks. I take a sip and feel the bright warmth spread down my throat. The next day we will return to the village and then we will set out for two nights in another part of the jungle on our own, our 'solo'.

Seed Five: Feel the unseen

I take the opportunity to ask Gordon a question that has been on my mind.

'Will we be marking the beginning of the solo with a ceremony?'

I had undertaken a solo in the Spanish Pyrenees a few years ago. Before we had left for our solo spots, we had given thanks to the land and set an intention to open ourselves to any gifts that the land might want to share with us.

'No,' Gordon replies. 'It is better to go out on such a journey without any expectations.'

'But it's not about having expectations,' I say, aware that my voice is rising, along with a feeling of heat inside me. 'It's about the ceremony being a tool or technique which both acknowledges the land and allows us to be more open to listening to what the land has to say. I don't mean anything elaborate, just something simple.'

'But you are still creating expectations. And if you have expectations, then you are not going to be open to what you might hear. Because you are listening from the mind of your expectations, not an open mind.'

'Well, I guess we have a difference of opinion.' I become quiet. I don't feel in a position to argue with Gordon. But an act of ceremony feels important to me, like introducing ourselves before our arrival, an act of respect, rather than just turning up unannounced.

We have one night back in the village, to wash and try to dry some of our clothes. Randy prepares us for our solo. He speaks about the different layers of the forest, about using the five senses, and then going beneath the feeling layer. He describes the layers of the unseen, and how all the different worlds are thinly layered on top of each other so it is possible to move between them. I feel fortunate to have had a glimpse of this when I saw the root network that night in the jungle.

He talks of how humans are destroying the environment and the web of interconnections. An example: the oil spill kills the algae, which means the minnows don't have food, which in turn kills the birds because they don't have anything to eat either.

And he speaks of how the spirits are being driven out of the forest.

'There is one particular type of spirit, which is a human-like figure about three foot high. It makes a sound like the squirrel cuckoo. We heard it one evening in the village. The call had been heard passing houses going down the river, over the span of an hour. I saw it and it was sad because it was looking for a place to live. I said that it was welcome to stay in our forest.'

It is only later that I make the connection between the spirits – the forest people – and the people of the forest. The forest spirit is moving down the river, looking for a place to live, as it is chased out of its home. The Cofan were forced to move down the river to find a new home because of people moving on to the forest land they belonged to. And the forest itself can't move.

The next morning, after breakfast, Tim asks Randy if there are any practices that the Cofan people would do before heading out on such a solo journey. Again, the short answer is 'No.'

But, because Randy is a storyteller, we receive a longer answer as well. The short version of the longer answer is that because everything is sacred for the Cofan people, there is no need for special ceremony.

'Indigenous people are above all practical and take a very practical view of the land. For example, there is one community member whose passion is pig hunting. And he wouldn't think about having a sacred connection with the land in those terms because it is just so deeply ingrained in him.'

Randy elaborates on the concept he shared with us on the first night, of how the Cofan have learnt to use the language of the sacred to defend what really matters to them. He gives the example of the graveyard in the Cofan village of Dureno, where he is going to be burying his mother's and father's ashes in a few days' time.

'For the Cofan, the location of the graveyard is practical. It is on the outside of the village, and it is on sandy soil, so it is easy to dig. Because it is sandy soil, we also know that at some point it will be washed away back into the river, so it is not a location as such that we are deeply attached to. The government wanted to put a road into town. The people put forward all the reasons why they didn't want this to happen, and the negative impacts it would have on the town, and the government didn't listen. Eventually, the Cofan put forward the argument that the road will go through the graveyard, which is sacred. Immediately, the government backed off. The Cofan used the term "sacred" to apply to the graveyard, because this was a concept of "sacred" that the government could understand. But really we were using the term to protect what was actually sacred to us – the integrity of the village, the forest and fields. The government couldn't understand how the village, forest and fields could be sacred. But they could understand, in their terms, how a graveyard could be sacred.'

Randy leaves us with a final thought. 'Indigenous people need to create a vision of the future, rather than going back to the past. If they have custodianship of a large percentage of the world's remaining forests, mountains and deserts, what does that future look like?'

Eighty per cent of the world's land-based biodiversity is located on indigenous peoples' territories. While they customarily own more than half the world's lands, they only have legal ownership of ten per cent of it.[5] Without legal ownership, they can't protect it in the way that they know how to.

Randy and the people at Zabalo have succeeded in gaining the rights to be custodians of a portion of the forest. But, so far, they have not been successful in gaining access to electricity and the internet, which they see as key to the long-term survival of the village, and therefore their role in preserving the forest. Having internet would allow people to study from here and would also allow college graduates to be based in the village after they graduate, as they could work online, rather than having to move to the city. And electricity would enable communications, but also enable people to have refrigerators and freezers. Freezers would mean that people could go hunting and then freeze the excess meat, which makes it last longer, and introduces more variety and nutrition into the diet. At the moment, the only option for preserving meat is smoking it, which reduces the nutritional value. Hunting is an important part of maintaining people's connection with the forest, one of the ways they learn about the plants and animals.

The village downstream had to trade its right to the forest in exchange for the oil company supplying electricity and internet access. It seems clear to me that Randy has a vision of the future in which indigenous people can use the benefits of modern technology to continue to live in the places which they belong to, and protect and preserve them, while staying connected to the forest and all its many layers.

I set out on my journey into the jungle without ceremony. We walk through the forest single file – Josh, two guides, Jacob, Tim

Seed Five: Feel the unseen

and myself. It feels good to be hiking, with the weight of the pack of on my back. I talk with Jacob about his experience of Buddhism. He says people make decisions based on what they think will make them happy, but in the end it doesn't make them happy, because they can't see the full picture and they don't have all the information for making their decision. I remember what Randy said, about how there is so much that is unseen.

The rain starts to fall, and soon becomes the torrential downpour we are now familiar with. At first there is a freedom in this complete soaking and then it just becomes uncomfortable. When we reach the spot for my solo, down a hill, by a bend in a stream, John, my guide, makes a shelter for me out of palm branches. I help to drag the cut branches through the forest and pass them to him. I pull down vines from the trees and he uses these to tie the branches to the pole structure. In this very small way, I feel connected to the forest, using it to create a shelter. Given the quantity of rain, we also put up a tent inside the shelter. When John leaves, it is 4 o'clock and the rain has stopped. He has started a small fire for me and I take time to tend it, to blow into the embers, to watch the flames curl around the damp wood, as the smoke blows into my eyes. I wash my face and hands in the stream at the bottom of a steep, muddy bank. At 5 o'clock, it starts to rain again. I collect my trousers and hat which are hanging from a branch to dry and retreat inside my tent, moving my bags inside as well. I put on the new clean shirt I was saving for a special occasion. Its most important quality to me at this point is that it is dry.

Bringing the bags in my tent means that I bring the ants and flies in as well. I spend half an hour or so playing 'squash the bug'. I don't want to get bitten by these ants. Being in the tent is like being on the inside of an ant hill, as I watch the ants crawling around the outside. As it gets towards dark, I meditate for half an hour, and then spend an hour writing in my journal about the day's events. I write that I am grateful to be here, that is such a privilege to experience this forest in this way. Even here, away from other humans, I can still hear evidence of humans, from the noise of a plane flying overhead. Randy had noted before when we heard the planes that the stewards on the plane would be handing out forms for arrival in Peru, and that people would be sitting up there in cramped seats. I think of all these different layers of existence co-existing.

Towards 8 o'clock, I eat some rice and peas, and caramelised peanuts. I go to pee, putting on my waterproofs and my wet socks and boots. I let a moth into the tent who has a glaring pink eye. Then, half an hour later, I write in my journal 'And now my stomach feels dodgy, like I need to poo. This isn't…'. I don't even manage to write 'good'. I am struggling to get my trousers and boots on to get out of the tent once again. I barely make it in time. A stream of brown liquid comes out of my rear, and some of it before I manage to pull my pants down. I am in the jungle, in the mud, in the rain, in the dark, and I have shit in my pants. I am getting bitten by insects. This is not the nature connection that I was looking for.

I carefully make my way to the stream, trying not to fall down the muddy bank. I wash my pants and do my best to wash myself. Back in my tent, I try to dry off and pray that this is the last of the episode. The plan had been to stay here for two nights. But given how I am feeling, I do not want to spend another day and night here. I decide then that I am going to go back in the morning, when Josh comes to check on me. I am not going to stick this out for another day and night just to say I did it.

I do not need to get up again in the night. I do not have any dreams that I remember. When I wake, I listen to the sounds of the dawn chorus, capturing the moment on my recorder, the sound of the new day swelling all around me. I pack up my stuff and wait for Josh to come. I am glad to be going back to camp.

What had Randy said? The indigenous people's view of nature is above all practical. I did not have a transformational, spiritual experience in my night alone in the jungle. But I did have to be practical in looking after myself. Maybe my body was getting rid of something, purging me of unseen bacteria, or the unseen of a different kind. It is not always for us to see.

Back in camp, I have two dreams. A colleague, who doesn't have children, decides to adopt two boys. In the dream, I wonder if I could adopt children myself.

In the second dream, I am with an ex-boyfriend in a big, old, dilapidated house. We are having a dinner party there, and also planning to go on a canoeing trip. I meet a good-looking guy. He gives me a book. I am moved. He asks if I know the book. I say that I've read another book by the author, one about a runaway. This is about the hero's journey. The guy says to me that he can give me a baby. 'You'd do that for me?' I ask.

My period had started again and it seems that being in the rainforest is bringing my longing for a child to the forefront of my dreams again.

In her essay, *The Greening of the Self*, Joanna Macy writes of a conversation that she has with John Seed, director of the Rainforest Information Centre in Australia. She asked him how he faces the despair as he struggles to protect the remaining rainforests. He replies, 'I try to remember that it's not me, John Seed, trying to protect the rainforest. Rather, I am part of the rainforest protecting itself. I am that part of the rainforest recently emerged into human thinking.'[6]

It is the notion of my self that has been challenged many times here in the forest. How does it change things if I think that I am part of the rainforest protecting itself? I have been questioning how I can be of service. And this is still valid as a question. But maybe it becomes easier to answer if I think of myself as the part of the rainforest recently emerged into human thinking. What happens if I ask myself, 'What would the rainforest do?' That changes everything. I am not acting from and to protect a limited concept of self. I return again to the Buddhist philosophy of dependent co-arising, where we are part of an interconnected web and our actions determine who we are.

Wendell Berry wrote, 'The concept of country, homeland, dwelling place, becomes simplified as "the environment" – that is what surrounds us. Once we see our place, our part of the world, as surrounding us, we have already made a profound division between it and ourselves.'[7]

Randy and Gordon and the trees have been teaching me to break down the barriers between myself and that which I am part of. It is clear to me that a vision of the future has to include an indigenous relationship to place, in which we are not separate and separated from the land. We must listen to indigenous peoples and increase the share of the land of which they have custodianship and ownership. The governments of the world will continue to set climate and biodiversity targets which are not met. Indigenous people do not need to set targets for the land they belong to because their view of the world has always been forest-positive and nature-positive.

The Sarayaku people of the Ecuadorian Amazon have put forward the concept of 'Kawsak Sacha' or 'Living Forest'. They want the Ecuadorian government to recognise territories as a 'living, intelligent and conscious being'[8], and to recognise indigenous governance in these territories. José Gualinga Montalvo, a leader of the Kichwa People of Sarayaku, has written about how dreams are an important part of the interconnection between humans and forest, a form of communication. 'Communication in dreams is with plants, with trees. This can be with the tree itself... it can be with the forest itself, with the sacred lagoons.'[9]

I was privileged to be given a glimpse into this communication when I had my vision of the root network. It was a momentary peek into an indigenous world view, and I could have some understanding of what we lose without this intimate relationship with the world. The forest that we can see and this unseen realm depend on each other. The recognition of the concept of 'Kawsak Sacha' would, in the words of José Gualinga Montalvo, 'guarantee the intrinsic relationship we have with this non-visible world which, in our philosophy and worldview, is living territory'.

It's our final day in the jungle. There is a large ceiba tree nearby that I have seen towering over the village but have not yet visited. Now's the opportunity. It is a last chance for listening to a tree here as well.

The ceiba is about a ten-minute walk away, through some banana trees, past a flock of squawking macaws. There is no way of knowing from afar how big it really is. It is huge. Not just in terms of height, but in its presence on the ground, with giant buttressed roots. The tops of the root buttresses are themselves taller than me and jut out about the same distance. The tree has a relatively shallow underground root system, so these buttresses help to support the tree. I walk around the tree to gain a sense of its size. I walk slowly, to navigate the branches and the roots on the ground, and to stop to look up, but it takes me over three minutes. I walk around again, counting my paces: it measures 56 paces in circumference. It is probably not more than 200 years old, according to Randy. It seems incredible that such a large tree is not older. But these trees can grow up to four metres a year and can reach up to 60 metres tall. I can't begin to estimate how tall this one is as it stretches skywards. A large limb has fallen from the top. This alone is as thick as a good-sized tree. The fallen limb provides a chance to see the hand-shaped leaves, which are otherwise many storeys in the sky, at the crown of the tree.

A yellow and black butterfly sits on the fallen limb, opening and closing its wings. This is a real, not a proverbial, butterfly in the Amazon, flapping its wings. It continues to sit, feeding on something in the wood, turning around occasionally, continuing to fold its wings.

I move to stand by the centre of the ceiba. I look up. There is a whole other world up there, a forest in a tree, festooned with epiphytes and ferns, home to a world of insects and birds. Drops of water from this morning's rain slowly fall. And one day, one of those other big branches, will crash to the earth. And it too will slowly begin to decompose into the forest floor, adding nutrients to the soil that will feed a whole other ecosystem. But for now, there are just the drops of rain. The branches interrupted their initial descent to earth. Now they are continuing their journey. A drop lands on my nose as I am looking up.

I stand quietly, alone. The rest of the group has returned to the village.

The spider web. The dappled light. The bark of a dog from the village. The sweat on my skin. The trill of a bird. The buzz of a fly. The silence of the butterfly landing on my bag. The drip of water. The expanding pool of light. The exploration of an ant. The faint movement of the fern in the humid still air. The pulsing of the crickets, the rise and fall. Maybe it is a grasshopper trilling, not a bird. A mosquito whining. The spider web trapping sunlight. The epiphytes draping the fallen log. The vines tumbling from the tree. And still the butterfly flaps its wings. Who knows what the effects might be?

Seed Five: Feel the unseen

I stand in the middle of this web of connections. The forest has shown me these interconnections, from the roots beneath the ground to the web of sounds, to the impact of product choices that we make in supermarkets far away from here – and, in my night-time vision, what lies beyond what we usually see. The ceiba is known as the tree of life to other peoples in South America. But the Cofan people don't have a sacred tree. All trees, all life is sacred to them.

'Listen to the whole place.' This is how Gordon had asked to me listen. 'Listen to the immensity of the forest', Randy had said.

I feel the immensity of the web of interconnections, which goes beyond one tree. And yet, standing under this ceiba, I'm grateful this tree exists as a reminder of what a tree looks like when it is allowed to reach its full potential. It is a portal to that web of wonder and of belonging. I relax. It is what the rainforest would do. And then it would continue to grow. If we allow it to.

Seed Six: In tune with the rhythms of the earth

Baruzeiro, Brazil

> 'The tragic reality is that very few sustainable systems are designed or applied by those who hold power, and the reason for this is obvious and simple: to let people arrange their own food, energy and shelter is to lose economic and political control over them.'
> Bill Mollison, *Permaculture: A Designers' Manual*

> 'Humans could reconcile themselves with the planet, finding a way to be useful and welcomed in the system, but we don't realise that, we can't see because we have disconnected ourselves from life on the planet, thinking that we are the intelligent ones. We can't see that we are just part of an intelligent system.'
> Ernst Götsch[1]

I lie in Kura Kura treehouse, the second highest treehouse in Brazil. I open myself to the morning sounds of the place, listening with my full body. I let the body absorb the sounds, I don't try to make sense of them with the mind. If the tree is a microphone, then the body is too. If we are what we eat, then we are what we hear as well. It is all input to the body, the sound waves travelling into and vibrating in the depths of our being. I think of the sea creatures whose organs explode because of the man-made sound waves striking into their bodies.

I am far from the sea. I am in the Cerrado, a vast, two-million-kilometre square area, the size of Mexico, which stretches across 23 per cent of Brazil. I first heard about it in the context of the deforestation of this most ancient of savannahs. The diverse grassland is being turned over and the trees are being cut down for cattle farming and soybeans, along with other monocultures. The international agribusinesses behind this deforestation, and their customers, including the fast-moving consumer goods companies and fast-food restaurants, are the antithesis of the slow farming practices that have been practised here for generations. The Cerrado's health is vital for the country's more famous ecosystem. The Amazon, and another seven out of the country's 12 river basins, have their source here. It is one of the oldest biomes in the world and the biodiversity is astonishing. Five per cent of the planet's animals and plants are native to here. It is home to more than 10,000 plant species, nearly half of which are unique to the region, over 900 bird species and 300 types of mammals. Among the endangered animals living here are giant armadillos, jaguars, maned wolves and tapirs.

I lie in the treetop and feel the different songs of birds in me. 'I contain multitudes,' as Walt Whitman wrote. The coo-ing of the dove provides a base note, other birds adding trilling, chirruping and chirping. Quick notes and longer songs. One note repeated. A winding-up of song, the notes rising higher and higher. Another song which is a letting-go, a winding-down. A tight fluttering of notes. The rattle of the woodpecker. Each of those songs is a woodpecker's beak, knocking some part of me open. I stretch and awaken my body to the day. Through the treehouse structure,

Seed Six: In tune with the rhythms of the earth

I can see to the east the citrus-orange sky above the mountains.

Last night I climbed 31 narrow, wooden steps to reach my treehouse eyrie, holding on to railings made of branches, leading me upwards, three turns of the spiral. The staircase opens to a hatch in the floor of the treehouse. The tree supports the structure from the outside but also from the inside. A tutti-frutti-coloured hammock is slung between the branch of the tree reaching through the floor and the wall of the treehouse. A red, white and blue circular rag rug brightens and softens the space. A folded futon is covered with cosy pillows and blankets.

Now, I stir from the futon mattress and pull on leggings and a T-shirt. I make my way carefully down the stairs, holding on to the wood of the railings polished by many hands, touching the rough bark of the tree trunk. My day is starting with a physical connection to the wood and to the trees. My body awakens further through this contact and with the concentration of navigating the narrow stairs.

I sit on the bench on the deck near the small round swimming pool. My eyes closed, I hear the flutter of bird wings at the feeder. I open my eyes and watch the birds coming and going. The black birds, the little grey birds, the doves, the hummingbirds. I move to the circular yoga shala with its thatched roof. As the sun continues to climb higher and higher, brighter and brighter, I salute it. Reaching upwards, bending, folding, stepping back, curving up, pushing back. Five breaths. Step forward. Reach up again. Stand and feel the sun. And repeat as the sun continues to climb.

At the end of the day, as the sun is setting, I sit on the same bench where I started the day. I feel the difference in the energy from the morning. There is a quietening, a stilling in the air. A bird pipes out the day. My energy quietens too.

Later, I climb back up the steps to the treehouse. I rock in the hammock while I write in my journal and read a few pages of a book. Then I close the hatch to the world downstairs and climb under the blankets to read some more, before releasing myself to the sleep of the trees.

There is a simple beauty in being synchronised with the rhythm of the day, one that is slow and in keeping with the heartbeat of the earth. This is the lesson that I am learning in the Cerrado, to slow down to the rhythm of the earth.

I am staying near a small town called Alto Paraiso, in the state of Goias. The sign at the outskirts of the town declares 'Man in Harmony with Nature'. This is an aspiration rather than a statement of fact. 'Alto Paraiso' means 'High Paradise' and the area is renowned for being located on the world's largest quartz crystal bed, 200 kilometres long and 30 kilometres deep. When I read this, I'm intrigued. I don't have a collection of crystals but I wonder at how it affects a place to be sited on top of a 1.8-billion-year-old crystal bed and how it influences the people who live there. I find there is, unsurprisingly, a large number of crystal shops lining the dusty main street in the town, and it has attracted those who are interested in healing and mystical arts. The town also has links with outer space. There have been frequent reports of UFO sightings in the area and the gate to the town is in the shape of a giant flying saucer.

The focus of my interest is more down to earth. Part of the richness of the Cerrado, like the Amazon, is in the diversity of its 800 tree species. I was drawn here to learn about this savannah forest, so different from the Amazon, yet crucial to its survival. It is known as the 'upside-down forest'. The small trees and shrubs that can be seen above ground are only a small proportion of the total plant; some of them have as much as 75 per cent of their biomass underground. Their long, complex root systems allow them to tap into water deep down, which is necessary in a region that is dry for much of the year. This network of roots means that the Cerrado is a huge carbon sink, storing an estimated 13.7 billion tonnes of carbon dioxide, which is more than China's annual emissions. However, its destruction means that is also becoming a source of carbon emissions.

I'm faced again with trying to select one tree from many that I can learn from. In the end, it is a chance encounter with a nut-flavoured drink that sets me on the trail of the baruzeiro tree (*Dipteryx alata*), although I first come across this tree at Terra Booma.

I am walking with Carlos and Henny in what they call 'their lab'. Terra Booma is not a lab in the indoors, white-coated sense of the word and there is not a chemical in sight. But it is a place of observation and experimentation. It is a farm where, for the past three years, Carlos has been planting according to agroforestry principles, listening to the results and learning. Banana trees are planted among eucalyptus. The fluttering leaves of the young eucalyptus will fall to the ground and provide organic matter to enrich the soil. The large drooping leaves of the banana provide shade to smaller plants, like the lines of tuft-top pineapples growing at the foot of the trees. Sunflowers hold their yellow faces to the mother sun. The ground-cover plants hug the earth and help the system to be self-sustaining, locking in moisture and also enriching the soil. Butterflies flit between flowers. I feel the peacefulness and harmony growing here, the plants working together.

Carlos has deep brown eyes and bouncy dark curls, held down by a pointed straw hat. He was studying agriculture when he first came across the work of Ernst Götsch, the pioneer of syntropic agriculture, also known as successional agroforestry. 'Ernst was saying the complete opposite of what we were being taught, but his approach made so much more sense to me.' Carlos started researching more into Ernst's work, and then went to study with him.

I was familiar with permaculture, a design concept that can be applied to all areas of life, with one of the key principles being the creation of closed-loop self-sustaining systems. Syntropic agriculture can be seen as the practical application of one aspect of permaculture, focusing on food production.[2] Ernst Götsch's method starts with regenerating the soil. Much of what is classified as sustainable agriculture is based on substituting inputs which are harmful to the environment with more sustainable versions, for example chemical fertilisers are replaced with organic ones, or pesticides are replaced with natural solutions. Syntropic agriculture is not based on better replacements operating within the same system. It is a fundamentally different approach. It is described as process-based agriculture, rather than input-based.

'We follow the natural way,' says Carlos. 'We observe what happens with natural vegetation, and we mix our planting in the same way.'

Carlos describes how when Ernst first arrived at his farm in Bahia, Brazil, in the early 1980s, the land was completely degraded. It had been cleared for intensive logging and then abandoned, nothing grew, and the water sources had dried up. Its name was 'Fugidos da Terra Seca', which translates as 'Escaped into Dry Land'. Now there are 17 springs flowing and Ernst grows the finest cacao in Brazil, which fetches four times the price of conventional products.[3]

Process-based, rather than input-based. 'The biggest external input… will be knowledge,' wrote Ernst Götsch. I turn this concept over in my head, like turning over the soil of my mind, breaking up the hard clumps of earth that have formed there. In the West, our culture and society has become input-based rather than process-

Seed Six: In tune with the rhythms of the earth

based. We want the quick fix and so we add the artificial fertiliser to degraded land in the hope that our seeds will grow there. We are not prepared to put in the work and allow the time for the soil to become healthy again, to follow the process through for the restoration of the land. Syntropic agriculture is the intelligent optimisation of the process, which requires constant observation and learning, so that necessary adjustments can be made.

'There is no quick answer.' These are the opening words on the website about the work of Ernst Götsch.[4] When Carlos came to Terra Booma, the land had been used for growing beans and was depleted of nutrients. The first task was to enrich the earth, using cow and chicken manure. The team then started with planting to help break up and add further nutrients to the soil.

With nearly three years of results, Carlos and the team are now beginning to draw conclusions about what works and what doesn't. For example, in the beginning, the team said that they wanted to break away from planting in lines, mainly as a reaction to the planting methods of monocultures. They tried planting in islands, with a banana tree at the centre and other plants arranged in a circle around it. But the plants didn't grow as well in these circles. In addition, lines enable easier planting and management. The team have reverted to planting in lines, but always keeping in mind the two main principles: stratification and succession. Stratification is having plants of different heights and succession is planting to ensure that there is a good flow of harvesting and replanting.

Another observation was that some of the vegetables that did not thrive in the vegetable garden grew more successfully when planted in the forest. Onions were huge, tomatoes kept producing fruit, sesame also thrived, but not corn, although that was a success elsewhere.

'It's all about observing and listening to nature,' says Carlos. He has a quiet manner, introducing each of the plots with great care and attention. He clearly listens to each of them and seeks to understand what needs adjusting, whether it is the soil requiring organic matter, the plants needing more water, another combination of plants, or planting at different times and stages in their life, from seed or as a seedling. There are so many factors at play, along with those that can't be controlled, such as the weather.

'There's no competition in nature,' says Carlos, 'only unconditional love. If one plant dies, it is surrendering itself to the others and to the earth. It is all about co-operation.'

This is a world view that is at odds with conventional wisdom, the survival of the fittest. By enabling a diverse range of plants to grow in harmony with each other, farmers using this method are increasing the total size of the pie, not reducing it. Later, I watch a video about another farmer who has also studied with Ernst Götsch and now farms a plot of land in New Zealand. He explains how one tree, for example a banana tree, might produce five to ten per cent less than one grown in a monoculture. But when all the crops produced from the plot of land are taken into account, it will in total produce double the amount of food that a monoculture would.

I wonder why a system that makes so much is sense is not more widely applied. The answer dawns on me that it relates to the process. Creating a complex system requires more care and attention than a simple input-based approach.

I think about the lessons for this in my own life. I've had a theme of the year for over ten years. It's an intention, a way of being that I want to focus on for that year. The first was 'The Year of Saying Yes', chosen when standing on top of a sand dune in the Sahara Desert at New Year. I wanted a year of saying yes to adventures. The year that I separated from my husband, I had

Seed Six: In tune with the rhythms of the earth

chosen the theme of 'The Year of Wilding and Witching'. The theme had come to me because I had a sense that I wanted to bring more wildness, in terms of both my inner and outer landscapes. Maybe I had had an inkling of what would help sustain me during that year. An earlier theme had been 'The Year of Olivia's Kitchen'. This was not about cooking but the recognition that in order to live a thriving life I needed to create the conditions for this. It wasn't just about adding more inputs. But so often in my life, if I have wanted to fix or change things, rather than looking at the 'soil' and the process to make it healthy, I reach for more inputs. Sometimes those are quick-fix inputs such as buying something new, or it is the hope that an input such as a new job or a new relationship will make things better. Instead of searching for a new input, I would do better to focus on the process.

Our current system of consumption is based on exploiting what we see as resources that are at our disposal, for us to take, make things from, and then waste. Götsch has said, 'Human beings are part of this system. Instead of exploiters, we can be creators of resources.'[5]

This is the fundamental shift in perspective I believe that's needed in our society, from consumers and exploiters to creators.[6] Carlos and the team here had made that shift – and to being process-based rather than input-based, allowing space for stillness to observe what is happening, rather than living in the fast lane of constant movement.

The diversity of trees that are planted at Terra Booma illustrates the importance of having many trees working together. The species include food-giving trees, some familiar to me such as the banana and avocado, and some that are not, such as the baruzeiro, a nut tree native to the region. The lobeira is another tree which is native to the Cerrado, is fast-growing and doesn't need nutrient rich soil, so it is ideal for growing on degraded land such as this. The fruit can be used to make sweets and jams. It's also known as the Wolf's Plant, as the fruit is a staple of the maned wolf's diet.

'What's your view on planting non-native trees, such as eucalyptus?' I ask Carlos. The eucalyptus forest monocultures in the Cerrado are controversial because of the destruction of the biodiversity of the savannah, the large amount of water the plantations require, as well as disputes about communities being displaced from their land.

'They are a good thing for us,' he replies. 'They grow fast, they provide shade, and they provide plenty of organic matter. Maybe in 15 years' time we won't need them any more because the soil will be restored and we will have established our forest with native plants, but now we are grateful to them for what they can offer in the system we are creating. We are looking for a native replacement but haven't yet found one.'

'Have you noticed any effects from climate change?'

'The main one is that the seasons are less predictable,' he says. 'There used to be two distinct seasons, the rainy season and the dry season. Each one lasted about six months. Now in the rainy season, we sometimes have a mini summer. This means that we need to make sure that irrigation systems are in place to compensate for the lack of rain.' At Terra Booma, they are fortunate to have an artesian well to draw on for most of their water needs. At the same time, they take great care to recycle grey water back into the ecosystem and minimise the use of water.

The team at Terra Booma are not only taking a different approach to agriculture, but to the way that the farm is run. The aim is to replicate the way that natural systems work within human systems, with shared and participatory governance. There isn't one boss.

'We take decisions together every Monday morning,' Henny explains. She exudes the same warmth and care as Carlos, her long fingers reaching out to the plants as we pass by. As we walk among the abundance of different plants growing together, pineapple, papaya and okra, she says, 'We know that we need diversity, we need the tomato and the banana and the corn. If we were all corn, then everybody would die.'

Each person is responsible for leading a different moment. Someone is responsible for observing the system, someone for irrigating, someone for feeding the trees.

Henny uses the term 'sociocracy' to describe how the team work together. It's not a concept that I'm familiar with.

'Another way to describe it is social agroforestry. Complementary abilities with a common purpose.' This makes sense to me. Like the plants have their different roles in the ecosystem and support each other, so it is with the human team. There is no need for a leader with a capital L.

This doesn't mean that it is a free-for-all, far from it. 'The more focused we are on planning, the better we can be,' Henny says. 'If we don't have planning, we are leaving things to happen by chance.'

One of the principles of sociocracy is a commitment to continuous improvement, ensuring that there is a feedback loop. 'One of the biggest things we have learnt is not to be afraid of cutting – the plants will regenerate. And regular pruning actually encourages the trees to grow back more vigorously. When they are pruned, they also send out a regrowth hormone through their roots, which encourages the plants around them to grow more strongly as well.'

I can see how social agroforestry means that everyone knows

their place – in a positive way. And they know who they are. If they are a tomato, they are not trying to be corn, and vice versa. I leave Terra Booma feeling inspired by the example of how agriculture and organisations can be life-giving and life-enhancing.

The lodge I am staying at is situated well off the beaten track, down a bumpy, pot-holed dirt road, about half an hour on the back of a motorcycle taxi from Alto Paraiso. Along with the two treehouses, there are a handful of individual huts, as well as a couple of rooms in the main house. Here there is a tall tower looking out over the sunsets of the savannah and this is where the owner, Mari, lives. It turns out that the story of how she came to be the custodian of this land is in keeping with the crystal mysticism of Alto Paraiso.

Mari is a tall, willowy woman, her long blonde hair draped over her shoulders, a nod to her Finnish roots. Her father is Finnish, her mother is Brazilian, and she was born in São Paulo, in the 'super megapolis' as she describes it. She has also lived in London, where she once ran a well-known cabaret club in the heart of Soho. It was while she was living in London she started to feel a pull back towards nature, which she had first felt in her childhood. She enrolled in a degree in zoology at King's College, London, and graduated with first-class honours. She had thought she would go to work in Africa, as she had already spent time there, studying the animals and birds in the savannah.

Then, as she tells me, 'All of a sudden, I met a person who put me in touch with his girlfriend, who was studying jaguars in the Pantanal in Brazil. She offered me the opportunity to work with her, helping to collect data. The Pantanal is the biggest wetlands in South America, and is thriving with wildlife, home to lots of jaguars. This was my wonder job! I went back to Brazil, bought a Land Rover, cut a hole in the roof so I could use it

Seed Six: In tune with the rhythms of the earth

for observation, and decked it out with the equipment I needed. I was there on and off for five years, but London was still my home.

'Yet every time I stopped to meditate, I felt the connection with nature so strongly. A little seed started to grow inside me about leaving London one day. But I had four cats, and I couldn't leave them.' She pauses to take a sip of her tea.

'I was pulled towards this other special place in Brazil, called High Paradise, the biggest quartz crystal place on the planet. I started to go once a year. One day, when I was in London, a lady called. I had stayed at her place and she had done readings for me, which were very precise, about the past. Now she said that land was available and she had dreamt that I was guardian of the portal. I said, "I'm sorry, I'm really busy, I'm not looking for land right now, I'm doing my thesis."

'But she had planted that seed in my mind. I paid my assistant who was working with me in the Pantanal to go there. I gave her ten pages of questions to answer. How many springs? What species live there? She sent me a thousand photographs of the place. "These are the rocks that the monkeys use to break coconuts." "These are the cliffs where the araras nest and have their babies in May." I had to go have a look myself. The land was very degraded. I wondered if this was really going to be the promised land. I slept the night on the roof of the abandoned, ruined house, and I connected with the land straight away. The lady had known.'

Her hand reaches down to stroke the head of one of her large dogs, the oldest one of whom follows her devotedly.

'I didn't move here straight away, but then the cats started to die, and I decided to sell my flat in London. It gave me the abundance to create another space. I started to build my own house here, using second-hand wood. At the same time, I was planting a lot of seedlings to reforest the land.

'I started to go mad with imagination. I wanted to build a tower I could see very far from, across the land. At the same time, Philipp came to town, wanting to build a treehouse. He asked around, "If I had to speak to one person about building a treehouse, who would it be?" And he was told to come and see me. He arrived here, with a little folder on his computer with lots of pictures of treehouses and said "You've called me unconsciously." He built Kura Kura, the first treehouse, in ten days, using recycled bits and bobs. It felt really amazing. He then built Araras, which is even taller. I'm hoping that he will come back, there is still lots of material that needs to be used.'

Mari listened to the call of the trees and this land to come and make her home here and is now inviting others to come and learn how to listen to and care for the land. She is also dedicated to campaigning to raise awareness among local farmers and in schools about the destructive effect that setting fires to clear forest for cattle has on ecosystems and wildlife.

I have always wanted to sleep in a treehouse, but until now I never have. The Treehotel in Sweden, with its designer treehouses, is on my bucket list. Philipp is from Auroville, India, my second stop on my journey to the trees after Finland. His parents moved there from Germany when he was six years old. When I spoke with him on WhatsApp, he was in Auroville and kept having to move to try and find a better signal. He told me how he had always wanted to come to Brazil because of the trees in the Amazon but, although he has been to the country now three times, he has not made it to the Amazon as yet.

Philipp and a couple of his friends built Kura Kura from materials left over from other construction projects. The only things they bought were some screws and bolts and the roofing material.

Seed Six: In tune with the rhythms of the earth

'We built it as cheaply as possible,' Philipp said. He returned in 2015, and built Araras, the second treehouse at the lodge, which is a little more elaborate and connected to the ground with a rope bridge decorated with prayer flags that jingle as you walk across. Kura Kura has the cosiness of being surrounded by the trees; Araras has the openness of the view, with a deck on two sides that looks out across the top of the trees and towards the mountains and the setting sun.

Philipp has a mission to build 500 treehouses by 2027. This mission is based on the premise that treehouses are not only the stuff of our childhood fairytale dreams. They are also a way to provide us with a physical connection to nature.

I wander through the grounds of the lodge. Many of the trees have a label, with their species name. I am reminded of a nature connection exercise that I practised when I was in New York. The invitation was to go to a place and to name the trees there. This practice invited looking at and listening to the trees and creating a personal relationship. A practice of really slowing down and connecting. I remember looking up at the branches of one tree and it seemed to me like they were spinning around. I called it The Roundabout Tree. When I went back the next day, I found myself spinning around underneath it and videoing the spinning of the branches with my phone. Now, here in Brazil, I practise slowing down and looking at the trees around me.

Angico

The Angico has a rough bark at the base, smooth trunk higher up. I'm struck by the feathery nature of the leaves, which shimmer in the wind, refracting the morning sun, and the toughness of the base of the trunk. The trunk has red undertones, with grey peaks, ants hurrying up and down the crevasses. I think of the tree as someone who portrays themselves as having a tough exterior but in fact is approachable and wants to add to the beauty of the world. I call it the feather tree. Its medicine is to lighten the soul. Now I see it, I see it all across the property.

Mamoeiro

The mamoeiro tree is by the entrance to the property. It has a smooth light brown straight trunk, with leaves radiating from the top. The bulbous fruit hang, full, ripening in the sun. I am struck by the markings on the trunk of the tree. There are scars all the way up from the branches that have been shed as it has grown. Shadows of butterflies imprinted. Scars that mark growth, transformation. And the shape of lips, calling us to speak out to make that transformation happen. The butterfly calling tree.

Inga

It's a young tree, less than a metre tall, by the yoga shala. Its branches are leggy, and its leaves have holes in them. My initial reaction is to want to ignore it, move past it. I stop. I think of it as the 'finding your way' tree. It looks like it is establishing itself in the world. It's splitting off in different directions, doesn't have one strong trunk. The bark is papery and peeling. And then I look at the underside of the leaf. I see the beauty of the veins, of the sunlight illuminating the leaf. And it is not just the plant that is finding its way. I need to find my way with each plant, to see the beauty of it, to see past initial appearances.

Yet, exploring these trees at the lodge, I still hadn't found my tree. Ultimately, it was the taste of the baru nut that caught my attention. I'm a sucker for nuts in all their forms – peanut-butter sandwiches and handfuls of salted peanuts, pecan pie, the sweetness of marzipan, walnuts cracked from their shells at Christmas, purply-green pistachios rewarding the effort to prise them from their hiding place, crescents of creamy cashews. The only nut I do not love is the Brazil nut, with a fattiness I find cloying. The baruzeiro tree and its nut hooked me via my taste buds, in an unlikely place – an unprepossessing roadside diner on the way back from a visit to the waterfalls that the area is famous for.

I am with a small group, just a mother and her red-haired daughter, and our guide Fabrizio, possessed by the easy confidence of someone who spends their life outdoors. The daughter is in her early twenties and an aspiring influencer, adept with the self-timer on her Nikon camera to capture shots of herself with plunge pools and waterfalls as backdrops.

We drive out of town and are immediately surrounded by the grasslands of the Cerrado. The trees are short, shrub-like, twisting. Isolated hills rise from the flatlands. Maybe it is the presence of the green aliens in town, but I think of the moon. I think that the aliens would feel at home landing here. As we go further, the hills become mountain ridges, with steep ravines, and plateaus. There are groves of palm trees dotted here and there on the lower ground. The morning grey burns away to the bright familiar blue.

We stop in São Jorge, the village nearest to the park. A dust road runs through it, and the houses are painted dust yellow, dust pink, dust lavender, and with exuberant murals of birds and women's faces. The waterfalls we are going to are on a private reserve, so we pay our 25 reais entrance fee and continue on our way. Now we are driving up among the ridges, then we turn off the main road and bump down another dust road, fording a clear-watered river a couple of times. The road is thickly forested on either side with slender trees. The crisp curling leaves are dust-covered.

I set an intention for the walk, 'Show me what I need to know.' It's a simple intention, but one that I know can open me up to connect with the land. We park up at the end of the track, in the shade of some trees. They are medium-sized trees – scrubby, not shapely. I see they have beige-coloured nut cases hanging from them.

'What are these trees?' I ask Fabrizio.

'They are the baruzeiro tree. They grow the baru nut which we can eat.'

I remember seeing the young baruzeiro trees at Terra Booma, establishing themselves as part of the forest garden. But I still don't make the connection that this is the tree for me to focus on – there are just so many different species of tree here. We set out on our walk. The path takes us along and across a river, and we criss-cross the water numerous times on stepping stones. Fabrizio points out some of the trees and I ask him about others. The sheer diversity of the trees and the variety of their uses is astonishing. The pequi tree has a trunk covered in spikes, and its fruit is green outside and yellow inside. The fruit of the wild guava is less sweet than the cultivated tree. Fabrizio rubs the trunk of the almecega tree until some white powder comes off in his hands, which he gives to us to smell. I inhale the sweet, pine-like scent. Fabrizio tells us that the resin, known as White Breu, is used in healing rituals to ward off dark spirits and invite good energy. I wonder if inhaling it will bring good energy for my journey.

We stop to look for alligators. These waters flow into a river which in turn flows into the Amazon, 4,000 kilometres away. Sometimes, in the rainy season, an alligator has been known to swim up the other way and make its home here.

Fabrizio explains why this is the Secret River and the Secret Waterfall. The miners used to take their findings into town, and

Seed Six: In tune with the rhythms of the earth

they were asked where they had found the crystals. 'It's a secret,' they used to say. Maybe the energy of the crystals will point me in the direction of my tree.

We stop at a swimming spot, cooling off in the clear blue-green water, and continue on to the waterfall. The landscape opens up to a wide valley, with views across to the mountain ridges, and the land dotted with trees with short palm-like trunks and long thin narrow drooping leaves. I am slow in my crossing, as I stop to take pictures. As we get closer to the river again, the plants become denser and more lush, with a dotting of palm trees, and welcome shade. In one place, entire bushes are covered with the web of the funnel spider. Then, around the corner, is the object of our walk. 'Our majesty,' Fabrizio says, as water pours down a 112-metre drop into a deep dark pool below.

'Are you going in?' Fabrizio asks. 'It's colder than the other one.'
'Of course,' I say.

I still have my swimming costume on, and take off my clothes and socks and shoes, and then carefully pick my way over the rocks. He's right, the water is cold. But I take the plunge. I want to be immersed in the energy of this water, falling from that height. The water feels alive on my skin, or perhaps it is my skin that feels alive. I dunk my head under water a couple of times to get the full immersion. I invite in the energy of the water and swim until I am too cold.

On the way back, I am still stopping to take pictures, while the other three are now in going back mode. I want to stop again in the valley, and soak in the openness and the sunshine and the view and the particular energy of this place. It makes me think about how perhaps 75 per cent of the purpose of the walk has been to reach the waterfall. We did stop to look at a few of the trees but it feels like a lot of the time the landscape is just something we are passing through, and we occasionally stop to say, 'How beautiful'. Nature is a backdrop for selfies, to show how we are so connected with nature, while the very focus of the activity distances us from it.

We stop for a late lunch at a roadside restaurant which serves two meals – a meat and a non-meat version, which has beans, rice, sliced tomato and manioc fries. The fries are light and crispy. The waiter brings us a plate of *dulce de leche* for us to share for dessert. We tuck in, and even though I am already full, I find space for this creamy sweetness. The restaurant makes its own *cachaça* as well, the Brazilian spirit made from fermented sugar-cane juice, best known as the base of Caipirinha cocktails. Bottles of different flavours are open for us to taste in little plastic shot glasses. I try the tree-based varieties. The passion-fruit flavour is the distilled essence of the fruit. The *jatoba* version has pieces of the tree bark in it; the taste is strong and catches the back of my throat. And then there is the *baru cachaça*, creamy in colour and texture and taste, almost like a strong Baileys. I wish I had enough cash on me to buy a bottle.

This third encounter with the baru is the one that finally captures my attention. Sometimes it is the taste that you need to listen to. I want to learn more about this nut and tree that is particular to this area.

Seth is the founder of a company he set up to import baru products into the United States. He was introduced to the baru nut by his business partner, a self-professed superfood hunter, who came across the baru nut when he was travelling in Brazil. He brought it back for Seth to try. Seth loved the flavour – they tasted like almonds – but it was the nutritional chart that sold him on the baru nut's potential.

'Protein, minerals, potassium, high in fibre and lower in fat, which meant they had fewer calories than other nuts.'

Seed Six: In tune with the rhythms of the earth

Seth had previously been involved in a number of businesses helping people to lose weight. He knew that dieticians often recommended people eat more nuts because of the minerals and fibre they provide. But the downside is the amount of fat they have.

'It exploded in my brain – this was a low-calorie almond.'

Seth was hooked on the opportunity and went to the Cerrado to find out more. He met with some of the farmers and asked why they didn't collect more of the fruit. The biggest problem was that the local co-operative purchaser couldn't guarantee to buy them.

As Seth saw it, 'I was just trying to solve a problem. I've spent my life as a business executive. The solution was pretty straightforward.' He offered to buy all the baru nuts the farmers could collect.

The next challenge was how to get the fruit open to access the nuts. Seth explains that the local people stopped seeing the trees as useful because it was hard to extract the nut. When they discovered peanuts, they saw they were much easier to open. Seth realised that if they were going to create a new future for the baru nut and tree, having an efficient way to get to the nuts was vital.

'For a while, there I was, running around the world to nut equipment manufacturers. I assumed that one of them would have a machine that could open the nuts or be adapted to do so. But no one could get them open, they all quit trying.'

For the moment they are continuing to crack the nuts using the hand tools, while they work on developing automated equipment.

It's not only the nut that is valuable, but also the fruit that surrounds the nut. There is 18 times as much fruit pulp as there is nut, so it makes financial sense to recover this, and it also avoids waste. The fruit is high in antioxidants, fibre, vitamins and minerals.

The baru tree has been identified by the Slow Food Foundation for Biodiversity as one of the trees which can help to save the Cerrado.[7] Baru nuts are included in the 'Ark of Taste', an initiative which identifies small-scale quality products from around the world that are in danger of disappearing. The Manifesto of the Slow Food Foundation called on people 'to defend themselves against the universal madness of "the fast life"… escape the tediousness of "fast-food" [and] rediscover the rich varieties and aromas of local cuisines.'

In *Eating to Extinction*, Dan Saladino writes about how the Slow Food Foundation identified that 'When a food, a local product or crop became endangered, so too did a way of life, knowledge and skill, a local economy and an ecosystem.' I am struck by the contrast between the baruzeiro, the slow food tree, and the fast-food industry which is changing the face of the Cerrado. Many of the crops that are produced here go towards feeding its insatiable demands, whether cattle for burgers or soy to feed the chickens which are served up fried or as nuggets.

Seth has seen first hand the deforestation of the trees that has taken place. A chain is thrown around the tree, and then a tractor is used to yank the tree up and light it on fire. The initial tree clearing is often done for cattle ranching. 'But what the farmers don't understand is that the tearing up of the trees has messed up the water ecology of the ranches themselves and it hurts the ability to raise cattle.'

Seth is working with cattle farmers to try and persuade them to plant baruzeiro and other types of trees on their ranches. The trees help to restore the water ecology and provide shade. He estimates that farmers could reforest up to 25 per cent of their land, and that this would create better outcomes for the cattle.

The first part of Seth's plan is to get more people collecting more of the fruit from existing trees. The second part of the plan

Seed Six: In tune with the rhythms of the earth

is to plant more trees. Planting baruzeiro trees on cattle ranches is an ideal solution. The trees need to be part of a diverse ecosystem. If they are planted in a monoculture, they don't thrive. The baruzeiro tree is ideal for reforestation projects because of its fast growth rate, resistance to dry climates and high-quality wood. The tree has a very long taproot so it can seek out water. It is a typical Cerrado tree in that its root network below ground is twice as big as the branch structure which you can see above ground.

The greenish-white flowers appear on the trees in December when it rains. The yellow fruits form in March. Each baruzeiro tree typically bears around 4,000 fruits. The fruits slowly dry on the tree during the dry period and the seed forms just before it drops. I am here in July, just as the seed is forming. The fruits fall to the ground between August and September. By this point, they have formed a hard shell to protect themselves. The sugars in the fruit provide sustenance for some animals. The fruits have to be collected in an eight-to-twelve-week window before they start to germinate at the time of the first torrential downpour. The rule for those collecting the fruits is to leave a third on the ground so that the trees can regenerate.

I buy a packet of the nuts and of the dried fruit from the store in town. The glossy mahogany-coloured nuts are, as Seth described them, like a cross between an almond and a peanut, and about the size of an almond. I would be happy to pop them into my mouth as a snack or add them to my breakfast muesli every day. And there's no need to stop there. There's now 'barutella', a chocolate spread made with baru nuts, and baru pesto. The dried fruit is like orange leather, tough and sweet. The challenge is getting these products into the retail supply chain and the hands of the customers, which will help to guarantee a long-term future for the baruzeiro trees and surrounding communities.

One thousand nine hundred gallons of water are needed to produce one pound of almonds and 80 per cent of almonds are grown in California where drought is becoming a more and more frequent occurrence. The almond trees are sprayed with insecticide and herbicide, and there is a high mortality rate among the bees who are trucked in to pollinate the trees. Baru nuts could be a low-impact alternative, as well as bringing positive benefits to the Cerrado and its communities.

I wonder why amid all the targets about tree planting, the role of food trees, such as the baruzeiro, is infrequently mentioned. Planting such trees would fulfil multiple objectives: carbon sequestration, biodiversity and food for humans.

It seems that one answer is money. It is cheaper to plant monocultures of conifers or eucalyptus than it is to plant fruit trees. And, in the UK, at least, it seems as if knowledge is a barrier. The Woodland Trust says that historically farming and forestry have been seen as two separate disciplines with little transfer of skills or knowledge between the two. There is the same split at policy level and support has not been provided by the government for agroforestry in the same way as it has been for farming.

On my second to last night, I am woken about 1 o'clock in the morning by an unfamiliar sound. It is high-pitched but there is also a long, haunting quality to it. I can't place where it might be coming from. It is a calling. It doesn't sound like a bird or animal that I know. The only thing that I can think of is that it is from a festival that is taking place in town, maybe music of the shamans. But that would be a long way for the sound to travel. It lasts maybe an hour or so.

As I lie awake, I think back over what I have learnt. This call to slow down and live in tune with the rhythm of the earth.

Seed Six: In tune with the rhythms of the earth

In the morning, I mention it to Karin, Mari's friend who has come to help run the lodge for a few weeks.

'I heard it too. It must be the tapir,' she says. 'I haven't heard it before, but when I heard the sound, that was the answer that came to me.'

I look up the symbolic meaning of tapir. It is a custodian of the forest. The tapirs are threatened in South America because of the destruction of the forests, and it is one of the 60 endangered species in the Cerrado.

I read up on the symbolism of the tapir. 'Tapir can share with us the secrets of the complex energies of the forest, and teach us how to also look after complex, rare and ancient eco-systems. Tapir is often quite generous with this kind of knowledge, and as a guide can help us share the burden of custodianship.'[8]

The tapir wants its cry, and the cry of all the other endangered animals, birds, trees and plant species to be heard. I will take the spirit of the tapir with me as I continue on my way.

As I do so, I will try to continue to slow down to the rhythm of the earth. This is what we need to do to live in harmony with the land.

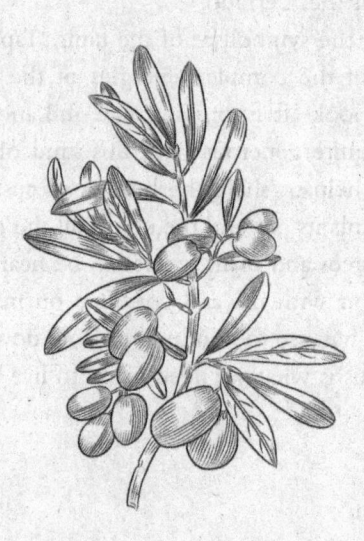

Seed Seven: Joy calls me home

Olive tree, France

> 'Because in trying to articulate what, perhaps, joy is, it has occurred to me that among other things – the trees and the mushrooms have shown me this – joy is the mostly invisible, the underground union between us, you and me...'
>
> Ross Gay[1]

I am staying for a month in an apartment in an old, white stone building in Nice. It is up two flights of stairs and has a small kitchen and living area, a bedroom and a bathroom. It has a floor-to-ceiling windowed balcony door that opens out on to the courtyard, which fills the white-painted kitchen with bright Mediterranean light. And, in the courtyard, there is a tall olive tree, maybe 15 metres high. It is unmistakably an olive tree from the colour and shape of its leaves, but I am surprised by its height.

It turns out that the height of the tree is characteristic of the olive trees of Nice and the surrounding area. I have much to learn.

During university, I lived for a year in France, working as a teaching assistant in Rennes in Brittany. I hadn't spent any time in the south of the country, and never quite understood why the English seemed to be so obsessed with it. Yet, when I saw the opportunity to sublet an apartment in Nice for four weeks across July and August, I was immediately hooked on the idea. I needed a place to stay for a month after Brazil where I could take stock of my journey so far and write. A month in the sunshine next to the sea sounded perfect.

It was only after the arrangements were in place that I realised that Nice was famous for its olive trees. What would *salade niçoise* be without its sprinkling of pungent black olives? The olive oil and olives from Nice proudly carry the prestigious French AOP certification, short for Appellation d'Origine Protégée. And the olive tree is, after all, my namesake tree. In my garden in London was a somewhat spindly olive tree in a pot, given to me by my ex-boyfriend's mother when we moved in. It seemed that the olive tree (*Olea europaea*) knew it had to be part of my journey, even if I had not figured that out myself.

The day after I arrive, I visit the Musée Marc Chagall. Chagall, a modernist artist, lived in the nearby village of St Paul de Vence for 20 years, until his death in 1985. The museum, a contemporary glass building, is set in a garden of olive trees. Chagall worked with the architect on designing the museum and gardens. He had planted olive trees around his house, where he used to walk every day; maybe this was the inspiration for the garden here. Yet it is one of the paintings in the museum that highlights the long-standing relationship between humans and olive trees.

Noah is in the middle of the painting. He is the calm at the centre of the storm. To his right are a huddled mass of women and children, their arms wrapped around each other. To his left are the animals, including mythological-looking creatures and a peacock with a long tail dragging on the ground. The people and animals alike are submerged in shades of aquamarine. The water is dominant, even inside the ark.

Seed Seven: Joy calls me home

But Noah's face and white beard are illuminated. His long, flowing, wavy hair merges into his cloak. He is looking down with kindly eyes. His left hand is resting on the head of a white cow with stubby curved horns, who is looking up at him. His right arm is outstretched and in his hand is a dove. The dove is about to take flight, to take off through the square window, into the blue. We can't tell from looking at the painting if this is the dove's first flight, or its second or its third. But we know how the story will end. We know that the dove will return with an olive branch in its mouth. We have that certainty. We have that sign of hope, given to us by the olive tree, that even after the flood, there is the possibility to begin again. The olive is the tree that has survived the catastrophic floods.

'Noah's Ark' is one of the 17 biblical paintings that are on display in the museum. The accompanying label explains that, while there have been many representations of the building of the ark, or the ark in the context of the flood, this painting, from 1966, is the first one that shows the inside. There has been a shying away by artists, not wanting to consider what it might have been like. Imagine the smell from hundreds of animals and humans after 301 days. It is more hopeful to show the act of building the boat, or the boat bobbing bravely on the flood waters, than to imagine what the reality of the story might have been. The ark is usually held before us as at a distance, as a symbol. Chagall chose to take us inside it, to show the tumult of humans and animals.

In his other paintings in the series, he also confronts the reality of human suffering. Across the room hangs a picture of Adam and Eve, who are being expelled from Paradise by a wrathful angel, having dared to taste the fruit from the tree of knowledge. In Christianity, taking from the trees can get us into trouble.

The museum is closing for the day. I step outside into the

sunshine and into the garden. The air is bright with the scent of lavender. The olive trees bear small green fruit. They have some way to go until they are ripe in November, although maybe they will ripen early this year, given how hot it has been. We think these ancient olive trees will survive anything, even the flood. But will they survive this change in climate? And what can we learn from them to help us survive?

Visiting an olive tree which is the oldest tree in France seems like a good place to start. She is called the 1,000-year-old olive tree. But this is a misnomer. Biologists have dated her to be 1,800–2,200 years old, leading to her claim. It's thought that the Romans introduced olive trees to Marseilles around 600 BC, from where they spread in France. So, at the older end of her suspected age range, she was planted 400 years after olive trees arrived in France.

Perhaps she is a *grande dame* who doesn't want to share her true age. She's certainly not been burdened with the names of a general or a president like the giant sequoias in California – General Sherman, General Grant, the Lincoln tree. If she was in America, she would probably have been named after the man who saved her from being cut down: Gabriel Hanotaux. In 1931, the former government minister and historian bought the land where the tree stands, to spare her the axe.

I ask the lady in the tourist office at Roquebrune-Cap-Martin where the tree is.

'It's a 40-minute walk up the hill. Take the bus.' Her tone is discouraging. 'And in this heat, at midday. It is 800 stairs.' She offers alternatives. 'You could go to Menton, and then get a bus from there.'

But I'm determined to give it a go. I start to climb the broad stairs. I begin to count them and get to eight. One hundredth

Seed Seven: Joy calls me home

of the way there. I stop counting. The stairs wind round the back of houses, with numbers on gates, sometimes names – Olivule, Le Repos. Trees shade the path in places. I don't pass anyone. I arrive in the village with its yellow and pink stone buildings, turquoise shutters. I am covered in sweat. Walking through the square, I glance somewhat enviously at the people at the outside tables, having lunch with a glass of wine under the shade of sun umbrellas.

I keep going. I am on a mission. I spot the signs to the 1,000-year-old olive tree and follow them out of the village. There she is, up on a terrace, at the side of the road, her roots spilling down six feet or so. She is so much bigger than I expected. She does not look like one tree, as she has four trunks. But she is all one.

I climb up on the terrace. The two trunks in the centre are noticeably more pockmarked and twisted than the outside two. I clamber around the back of the tree and sit down. An orchestra of cicadas is playing, filling the air with their sound of summer. I try to sketch the tree, to listen to it in this way, paying attention by drawing. It is a poor sketch and I wish my artist friends were here to do it justice. I tell myself it is not so much the finished article that is important, but the act of drawing. As I trace my pencil on the page, I am looking more closely, I am seeing where a limb has been cut, where there are pockmarks, the differences in the bark, the twists of each trunk.

A group of boys walk past on the road below. They are chatting to each other. They don't see me, they don't look at the tree. I think of the 12-year-old boy in Italo Calvino's book *The Baron in the Tree,* who decides he is going to live in a tree, and from his vantage point looks down on the passers-by. Here is a middle-aged woman looking down on the boys.

Four English-speaking people park their car in the space

opposite the tree. They are carrying baguettes for their lunch, or maybe their dinner. They don't look up either.

I put pencil and paper aside. I sit still. I feel heat start to rise in my left hand, followed by tingling in both hands, and then in my feet. It feels like there is a complete circuit of connection between me and the ground. The energy is running around my body, through my heart.

I don't need the olive tree to tell me anything. At the beginning of my journey, I was wanting to hear messages from the trees, thinking that I had failed somehow if I couldn't hear a message coming through loud and clear. But this act of connection is listening. This act of paying attention, to myself, to the tree, just this feeling of energy, the act of being present with the tree is enough, in a world where the default mode is to be a passer-by. And who knows what the unseen message is that is being planted in my unconscious, that might resurface later.

I make my way back down to the road. A tour group comes past. The guide says that the tree is 23 metres in circumference. The youngest member of the group, a girl maybe ten years old, wearing a back-to-front cap that says 'Nice', seems most interested by the tree. She runs her hand along the roots and takes pictures. Then she moves away to take a selfie doing a backbend.

I look up and see small green fruit hanging from the branches. This tree intends to keep on going, whether we care or not.

'The car is easy to spot. It's a green Kangoo.' I'm in the town of Grasse, an hour's train ride from Nice, 400 metres above the sea. I'm on the phone to Jean-Marie, the owner of an olive grove where I am going to stay for the night.

A few minutes later, I see the distinctive van shape of the Kangoo come down the hill, go past, turn around at the next roundabout, and pull up. It's what could be described as olive-green. Jean-Marie's wife, Marianne, gets out. She's blonde, with fancy-framed sunglasses and wearing a simple black dress. She's taking the advantage of the ride into town to run some errands.

'Welcome,' says Jean-Marie. It's a ten-minute drive to the farm and we start to chat. Jean-Marie had said in an email that he was new to the area. I ask him how long he has been here.

'Two and a half months,' he says.

'Wow, really new.'

Jean-Marie has been living in Sweden for the past 12 years, which is where he met Marianne, who is Swedish. Before that he had lived in Brussels and in London. He's been away from France for a long time. But now he is returning to his roots. He tells me he grew up in Fontainebleau, outside Paris. 'It's a forest of pine trees, and I was always in the forest.'

I ask him why olives. 'I've always loved olive trees. I told a friend 30 years ago that I was going to buy an olive grove.'

'How did you find this place?' I ask.

'It was random. I was looking in another area, in the Var, and looking for a bigger place. I then heard about this one, and it just was right.'

He opens the gate with a remote and we pull up the drive. There are terraces of olive trees on either side. The yellow house faces out over the valley and towards the sea. The spot is nestled in a cradle of mountains curving up on three sides.

He shows me to my room, on the top floor of the house. The window faces out over a red-tiled roof, framing the view to the sparkling turquoise sea, with an armchair and footstool conveniently positioned for sea-gazing.

'We can meet downstairs in five minutes and we can start to talk?' asks Jean-Marie.

I find him in the terracotta-tiled kitchen, making coffee in a cafetière.

'This kitchen used to be the chapel for the monks,' he tells me. 'There were only five of them here, so it didn't need to be very big.' The kitchen of an olive farm once being a place of worship seems highly appropriate.

The monks were here 500 years ago. They were from the Abbaye de Lérins, on the island of Saint Honorat, off the coast of Cannes. They didn't have room on the island for olive trees, so they needed an outpost where they could grow the fruit needed for olive oil. And this must have seemed like the ideal spot, in its protected position. A few of the trees here are 800–1,000 years old, so it was already a well-established olive grove when they arrived. I imagine a Renaissance estate agent showing the monks the land and the trees, and assuring them it would fulfil all their needs, with room for expansion.

The property is 1.5 hectares and has about 220 olive trees, spread out on the terraces. All the trees are of the Cailletier variety, typical to the region. They are vigorous trees and grow tall. They need to be cut every two to three years to keep them in optimum shape.

As we sit talking in the orangery next to the kitchen, it starts to rain big, fat drops. Jean-Marie looks out of the window with concern. 'I've just sprayed the trees against the olive fly, which took 12 hours. If it rains too much, it will wash the spray away, and I will need to do it again. I checked the weather forecast, it didn't show rain today, but you never know here. And we do really need the rain.'

'The life of a farmer,' I say.

He nods in agreement.

The spray is aluminium silicate, white clay. It makes the leaves and the olives white, acting as a disguise. The olive fruit flies are the biggest threat to the trees here. The females lay their eggs in the fruit as it is ripening and, when the larvae hatch, they feed on the pulp. This damages the fruit, and for olives destined to be made into oil, it reduces oil production and lowers quality by increasing acidity.

The spraying of white clay is allowed under the regulations for organic production. But irrigation is not. The lack of irrigation means that the olives are more concentrated.

I'm surprised at the ban. I've been reading about how irrigation will be needed more in the future, because of reductions in rainfall.

'Maybe that means the organic trees will actually be more resistant to climate change and falling levels of rainfall because they are used to being self-sufficient in water and not relying on irrigation. Perhaps they have stronger developed root systems.' I'm thinking out loud.

'It could be, let's hope so,' says Jean-Marie. 'But you know that they have their own in-built tank system in the roots.'

I had noticed the tenting of the roots in the olive trees that I had visited the other day, and how this created a space under the tree. It made sense now.

'This system allows the tree to collect water when it rains, so it can make the most of the rainfall. But then the biggest danger to the tree is in January, when it is full of water from all the rain. If there is a frost, the water inside the tree can freeze, and the tree becomes damaged and can die.'

We go outside so Jean-Marie can show me around. As we walk through the groves, he points out trees who have suffered such damage. But they are still growing, resilient. They might just twist another way, away from the injured part. The trunks of the trees tell stories about what they have experienced and survived.

They are not the small, spreading trees whose image springs

to mind when I think of olive trees, as you might find in Greece. I wonder out loud why they grow so tall.

'Maybe because of the mountains, and because water is more abundant here,' ventures Jean-Marie. 'And also, because space is limited on the mountainsides, they need to grow tall, to make the most of the space.'

'The skyscraper principle,' I say.

There are more than 1,000 varieties of olive tree, each with their own taste profile, of which the Cailletier is one. Some olive varieties have become better known, for example Kalamata olives, which are principally grown in Greece. The most planted cultivar or variety of olive tree is the Picual, which is the predominant variety in Spain. About a third of the world's olive oil production comes from these olives. All olives begin as green and they become black when they are fully ripe.

I ask Jean-Marie how he thinks the trees will cope with climate change. 'I think they will adapt,' he says. 'For example, in strong heat, the leaves turn in, to reduce exposure to the sun, and to stop them burning. I think they will continue to adapt, they should be able to survive hot weather. But I could be wrong. Ask me in a couple of years' time.'

'Of course, yield could be affected,' he adds. 'Last year, the harvest was 2.5 tonnes. In 2011, it was 7.5 tonnes. But there are so many factors that can affect the harvest. The trees are wind-pollinated. So the harvest depends on the way that the wind is blowing, to ensure good pollination of the trees. So far this year, though, it looks like we will have a good crop. Touch wood.' He puts a hand to his head. I do the same.

He explains that there is an early and late harvest, which affects the taste and the level of polyphenols in the oil – the early harvest has more polyphenols. The polyphenols are the antioxidants which provide many of the health benefits of extra-virgin olive oil, and also the peppery burn at the back of your throat when you taste it.

This peppery taste comes from a polyphenol known as oleocanthal, one of over 30 polyphenols in extra-virgin olive oil, and which shares anti-inflammatory characteristics with ibuprofen. Fifty grams or four tablespoons of extra-virgin olive oil is equivalent to approximately 10 per cent of the recommended adult dose of ibuprofen for pain relief. Along with anti-inflammatory benefits, the polyphenols in olive oil have been shown to reduce the risk of heart disease, strokes and diabetes, as well as neurodegenerative diseases such as Alzheimer's. One 24-year study of 93,000 people showed that consuming just half a tablespoon of olive oil daily could lower the risk of contracting heart disease by 14 per cent.[2] It is also beneficial for the gut, helping to stimulate the growth of beneficial bacteria. It has even been shown to help protect from the development of depression[3]. It's little wonder that taking a tablespoon of good-quality extra-virgin olive oil in the morning has become a wellness trend.

Some olive oils are now being specifically marketed for the high level of polyphenols they contain. The polyphenols are present in extra-virgin olive oil and, to a lesser extent, virgin olive oil. Extra-virgin olive oil is made with the first pressing of the fruit, and no heat is used in the extraction of the oil, which preserves the polyphenols. The amount of polyphenols also depends on when the olives were harvested, the variety of olives and how old the oil is – the polyphenols in the oil degrade with age.

'Would you like to taste the oil?' Jean-Marie asks.

'Of course.'

There are two oils for tasting, the early and the late harvest. He starts with the late one, pouring some of the golden liquid into a small cup. I inhale. The smell is pungent, but I lack the vocabulary to describe the individual notes. Or perhaps the memories to make the associations to trigger the words.

'If we have families come for a tasting, and the teenagers don't want to try, I always encourage them to. At least it plants the seed of an association and, if in ten years' time they taste it again, there is a memory for them to draw on. Make sure you coat your mouth with the oil,' he advises. 'Different parts of our mouth have different taste sensors, so they will pick up different nuances of the taste.'

As I swish the oil around my mouth, the predominant taste that I am getting is one of creaminess and butteriness. I swallow and I am hit with a sharp, peppery, almost burning sensation. This was the oleocanthal kicking in.

'Wow, it really does get you in the back of the throat,' I say.

'Yes! And what else can you taste?'

'Well, it is creamy, almost buttery in the mouth.'

'Yes, that's one of the tasting notes, patisserie,' says Jean-Marie. He shows me the list of flavours they use for the tasting sessions. 'Did you taste fresh almonds?'

'No, I didn't get that.'

'It takes practice,' he reassures me. 'When I first started tasting, I wasn't picking up on any of the flavours. But I soon started to distinguish between them. It just takes time to train the brain. Try the early one now.'

I take a sip of the oil and cough. The oleocanthals have hit the back of my throat again. My cough is a good sign. One of the ways experts rate olive oil is as one, two or three coughs – with three coughs being the best, because this indicates the highest concentration of polyphenols. Artichoke is one of the tasting notes associated with this oil. I don't pick this up. But I've seen the gangly artichoke plants, with their thistle-like purple flowers, growing by the olive trees. And a few drops of the olive oil capture the flavour of the artichoke. I wonder about the synergies between flavours.

Learning to distinguish the tastes is another way of listening to the plant. What is it communicating through its flavours? Perhaps it's not a coincidence that the different flavours are called notes.

I look down the list of flavours that might be tasted in these or other oils – apple, banana, grass, mint, vanilla. The early-harvest olives where the fruit is less ripe will be at the greener, grassier end of the flavour spectrum, whereas the late-harvest will be more reminiscent of ripe fruits, such as banana or almond.

In San Marino, the country which has the highest olive oil per capita consumption in the world, at 24 litres a year, pupils are taught how to taste extra-virgin olive oil and go to olive mills for tasting lessons. Of course, San Marino is a country where olive trees are grown. But still, why couldn't there be tasting of olive oil in schools in the UK or in the US, helping pupils to appreciate the subtleties of taste and the joy that can come from discerning them?

That evening, I go to sit under the olive trees. To be in their peace. I sit at the foot of a tree and think of the root system that is working underneath.

'The trees support each other,' Jean-Marie had said, as we made the tour earlier in the day. 'And the older growth trees can better support the other trees, they've had more time for their root structures to grow and be interlinked.' This is what the research shows too, why old growth forests are so important. They will be more resistant to climate change than the newly planted forests because they have this well-established support structure.

I didn't learn to like the taste of olives until I was in France for my year abroad for my English and French degree, working as a teaching *assistante* in three schools. In between practising English conversation with my pupils, I had plenty of time to sit conversing with friends, sometimes in English, sometimes in French. In the evenings, we sat outside cafés at small tables in the cobbled streets of the old town of Rennes, with an aperitif in hand, a kir cassis perhaps, white wine in a flute-shaped glass with a dash of the eponymous blackcurrant syrup. The waiter would come round and place little terracotta dishes on the tables, sometimes filled with salted peanuts and sometimes with olives. At first, I would ignore the olives, black and briny, sure I didn't like them, remembering my mother's attempts to feed them to me. Then, they fell into the same category as quiche and aubergine and beetroot: food to avoid. Now, I'd learnt to appreciate quiche and aubergine, although beetroot in all its forms, pickled, roasted or raw, remained and continues to remain off limits.

With olives in front of me, I tentatively started to nibble and found that, in this setting, their meaty sharpness and sourness was perfectly acceptable, and even desirable. It was sitting at these same tables that I learnt to like espresso coffee. My only experience of coffee before then had been instant coffee, which I had found to be unpalatable and undrinkable. But I figured that I could not sit at a café in France and not order 'un café', so I started to order the little cups with a rich, dark, fragrant brew, popped in a sugar cube, and found that I liked it. I was in France to teach English to school pupils, but France was educating me in matters of taste, and of how to live with an appreciation of good food and ingredients. On Saturday mornings, I would go to the market square with my French flatmate. We would wander around the stalls, picking up armfuls of fresh vegetables, queuing at the cheese merchant's van to sample slivers and buy wedges of cheese, or learning from the fishmonger about monkfish and how to cook it, as a slice was wrapped up in paper. In these interactions, I felt a connection to where my food came from that I had not experienced in England, except for the vegetables that my mother grew in her garden. This was years before farmers' markets started to spring up in towns in England. When our baskets were full, we would stop at one of the cafés for 'un café'.

Madame L. is the president of the AOP Association de Nice. She and her husband own an olive grove on the outskirts of Nice, with 1,200 trees. The farm has been in her husband's family for three generations.

'There are only two things which can kill olive trees,' she says. 'The hand of man and the freeze.' In February 1956, there was a big freeze, which killed two-thirds of the olive trees in Provence. She said that landowners then used this as an excuse to clear more trees so they could sell the land for development. The two forces went hand-in-hand with each other.

'There used to be four seasons,' she says. 'It was easy then. Now, we have to adapt. It's become harder the last five years. The quantity of rain that falls is the same, maybe more. But it rains a lot in October and May. And not in between. And the temperature goes up and down, which is not ideal for the blossom. The temperature was low, but then became too high, and the pollen roasted. The stems to the flowers were weak, and the fruits fell. It's not going to be a good season. Two years ago, we were a long time without rain. We started to worry that we would lose everything. In September, the outside of the olives started to turn black. This normally happens in November. But it was only the outside, not the inside. The olive oil was bitter, the table olives became too ripe.'

Madame L. tells me how her husband walks around the olive grove every morning, looking at the trees, observing how they are.

'He sees himself as the custodian of the trees,' she says. 'All we can do is observe, talk to them, touch them. The harvest is not just the result of one year's work.'

Some of these trees are 800 years old, many of them are 400 years old, planted in the olive boom when the *moulin génois* was invented. This mill crushes and kneads the olives between two stones and enabled more oil to be extracted. The mills these days are more high-tech, although some of the old stone ones are still in use.

'What can we do to help?' I ask.

'Buy olive oil from independent and preferably organic farmers,' she advises.

I walk away from the farm, carrying a pot of tapenade, a spread of black olives, capers and anchovies, that Madame L. has gifted me. Her words ring in my ears. 'We have to be at peace with nature.'

I think of the contrast between the care and the attention that Madame L. and her husband give to these trees, and the olive trees that grow in industrial monocultures. There the trees are sprayed with pesticide by plane and are cut down when they reach 20 years old.

There is a Provencal saying: '*à 100 ans, un olivier est un jeune homme*', at 100 years, the olive tree is a young man. I am struck again by the different conceptions of time, and the difference between resource and relationship. Madame L. and her husband have a relationship with their trees. In the industrial farming system, trees are just seen as a resource.

Does this matter? It matters not only for the olive trees, but for the wider implications to the ecosystem that we are part of. The Spanish olive harvest reportedly killed 2.6 million birds in 2019, as agricultural workers vacuumed up both olives and roosting birds at night.[4]

★

Seed Seven: Joy calls me home

The bus reaches the end of the line. I get off and walk to the olive mill that I am visiting. It dates back 150 years. The kindly woman in the shop puts on the English version of the video about the mill for me, which takes me though the process of making olive oil. Picking the olives, then sorting, pressing, straining, bottling. She closes up the shop and takes me to the old stone mill next door. She explains how nothing goes to waste here. The dried-out skins of the olives, all that is left after the second press, are scattered under the olive trees to stop the grass growing, which competes with the trees for water. The wild boars like to eat the skins as well, and as they snuffle around under the trees for this food, they break up the soil, which helps the water get to the roots when it rains. The seeds of the olives are kept to burn for heat in the winter.

I take a few days to visit a friend in Milan, a four-hour train ride away, along the coast, and then cutting inland at Genoa. There's an exhibition called 'Broken Nature' at the Triennale Museum. One quote captures my attention. It is part of a work called *Birdsong* by the Sigil Collective.

> *'What is a bird?'*
> *'What is a tree?'*
> *Asks a 5-year-old boy in a Syrian prison.*

A little boy is being told a story. But he has no frame of reference for what a bird is and what a tree is from inside the prison walls.

In another book on display, 'Excavating the sky' by Khaled Malas of the Sigil Collective, there is a double-page spread with four photographs taken in Syria in 2012. Top left: rows of olive trees. Top right: close-up of olives ripening in the trees. Bottom left and bottom right: red earth, hole in the red earth, people looking at the hole, bare grey tree branches. All that is left of the olive trees, symbol of peace.

I had not thought before of trees as victims of war. Yet here, the olive trees, many of which were likely to be hundreds of years old, were destroyed. As well as the lives of the people who tended them.

One day, I decide I am going to take the morning off from writing. I am going to go out and make the most of the sunshine. I take a walk around a peninsula jutting out into the glittering blue sea. I come across a small beach and decide to go for a swim and cool off. I am floating, held by the water, held by the sun. The thought comes to me, loud and clear:

> *Joy calls me home.*
>
> She sings to me.
> She cradles me in her waves.
> She says, 'You are home.'
> *Joy calls me home.*

In this moment, I am home. I feel the truth of these words. To be at home, I just need to follow the joy. I revel in the joy of this truth, the joy of being in this water, in this sun, under this sky.

On the way home, on the bus and on the tram, I keep turning these words over in my mind, 'Joy calls me home.' As I get off the tram at my stop, another interpretation of the words comes to me. It is not just about me following joy to find my home. I am the place that joy calls home. Joy is at home in me. I feel this like a revelation. Intellectually, I have known this before, that I need to look inside myself rather than outside myself to find joy. But this experience I have had now is a felt experience, an embodied experience, of joy being at home in me.

I look back at my notes from the 1,000-year-old olive tree. I had felt a connection to the earth and tree then and had written about a message being planted in my unconscious that might surface at a later date. 'Joy calls me home.' I feel this message has been sent through the olive tree.

Yet what does it mean to be a home for joy in this age of eco-anxiety? Is that just happy-go-lucky escapism from the harsh reality that we are living in, in this time of extreme weather, floods, drought, soaring temperatures and loss of plant and animal species? When our notions of home are being upended by these changes, and people are having to flee their homes. Joy calls me home. Really?

We need this joy to keep going in this world. If we let despair overtake us, then we will become stuck, unable to take action. Joy can give us the energy to take action. I can be a home for joy by recognising these moments of beauty, these moments of ease when life is flowing through me, when I am open to the pulsing energy of the world. I can then transform this energy into action, action which is fuelled by a love for this world. This is not a joy that can be achieved by searching for something outside of ourselves. It is a joy that comes from the opening of ourselves to the world.

I think back to the beginnings of my journey. How I was living with numbed emotions. How the grief for the baobab trees broke me open. I felt again and felt called into action. I could feel joy now because of this. Joy and grief are both ways of feeling the world. The two co-exist.

My brother shares pictures of Fiona on WhatsApp. She is now six months old. She smiles at the camera, open-mouthed with joy. She has bold, bright eyes and fine wisps of hair on her head. In the crook of her arm is the Mr Fox stuffed toy I had given her before she was born. In another picture, she is held in the crook of the arm of her mother, both of them laughing at my brother behind the camera. I feel their joy, and joy for them as a family, and the grief of not being part of such a family unit. After I leave France, I am going to visit Finland and meet Fiona Grace for the first time.

Sara Maitland has written about the connection between landscape and the human imagination. She writes of the connection between religions and the landscapes they have been born in. The Abrahamic faiths – Islam, Judaism, Christianity – have their roots in the desert, where you 'need a big god to fill the vast spaces and speak into the huge silence.' Tibetan Buddhism emerged from the high peaks, 'where the everlasting silence of the snows invites a kind of concentration, a loss of ego in the enormity of the mountains.' And, what strikes me now, in this context, is the 'joyful, humanistic polytheism of the Classical Mediterranean', with its interplay between gods and humans, which was born 'in a terrain where there was infinite variety, where you can move in a matter of hours from mountain to sea shore..., where one place is very precisely not like another.'[5] Here, it is less than a matter of hours from mountain to sea shore. This place, with its olive trees as part of the landscape, bred joy.

The olive tree is the tree of the gods. According to legend, the city of Athens was named after Athena, following her victory in a competition with Poseidon. The two gods were asked to bestow the most useful gift on the city. Poseidon struck the ground with his trident and released a spring of salt water. Athena knelt down and planted an olive tree. She was declared the winner because of the olive's usefulness. An olive tree still grows at the Acropolis, said to be descended from the original. The olive is also the tree of the humans. Perhaps of all the trees that I have visited so far, it is the one that needs human care. It has been domesticated. If it is left untended, it grows straggly and unproductive.

The olive tree makes me want to ask, 'What does it mean to be human?' It points to the role that we can have in being a steward for nature, rather than exploiting nature's resources – and the benefits that come back to us as a result, from emotional benefits such as joy and protection from depression, to boosts to our health such as reduced risk of heart disease.

Olives intrigue our taste buds and its oil nourishes our bodies, inside and out. Its shade is a place to sit and contemplate or share a picnic. The olive tree is a steady bringer and convenor of joy, made manifest at harvest time as communities gather to celebrate the fruits of another year's co-operation with nature. The branch that the dove brought to Noah is hopeful and joyful. It says life will go on.

As I continue on my journey, I will carry this olive branch with me.

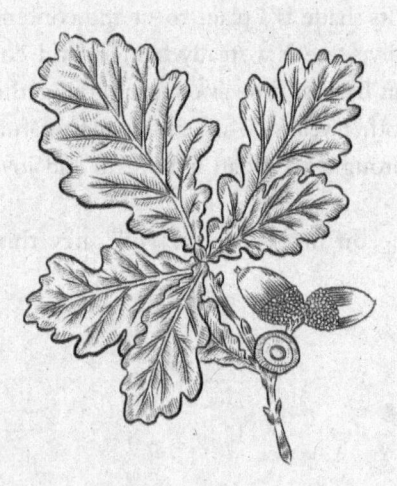

Seed Eight: Be a tree protector

Oak, UK

> 'When the oak is felled, the whole forest echoes with its fall, but a hundred acorns are sown in silence by an unnoticed breeze.'
>
> Thomas Carlyle

I am sitting in a window seat on the train, relaxing my eyes on the green of the English countryside, pastures fringed with hedgerows, dotted with the occasional tree. I spot a few oaks, growing tall from the prickly protection of hedgerows or holding court in the centre of fields, providing shade for sheep and cows, and a home to birds and insects, lichens and mosses.

I am travelling from Sheffield to London. As I look out of the window, I am idly turning an acorn between my fingers like a worry bead. It is smooth, apart from the little knobble protruding at the top, but it also has faint ridges, like those on my fingernails. Nut-brown, it is a length and a half of my thumbnail, and about as wide. It has curved sides and a flat base, so I can stand it up on the train table. The acorn has become separated from the cap it grew in. I turn the cap upside down, so it looks like the hat of an elf, with its bobble on top and woven texture, as if designed to keep the acorn warm as it grew.

If I shake it, it makes no sound. It is solid. There are no loose parts. I tap it with my fingernail, and it makes a sound that reminds me of tapping the top of a loaf of freshly baked bread. Maybe it is the richness of the brown colour, or its doming shape as it now lies on its side, creating this association. Acorn flour can be used to make bread in times when conventional grains are lacking.

I can detect no smell, but if I was a dog, with my nose to the ground, rootling through leaves and earth, then maybe I would be able to sniff it out – and if I was pig or a wild boar, most certainly I would. An image comes to mind of a black and white etching in a picture book, of a pig foraging under an oak tree, searching out acorns. The goddess Circe turned Odysseus's men into pigs and fed them with acorns. Pigs can happily munch away on them, but they are potentially poisonous to horses and cows if they eat too many.

This acorn comes from a tree that was planted about 150 years ago, in a field in the village of Dore in Derbyshire. I say that it was planted, assuming it was a human hand that placed the original acorn in the soil. But maybe it was a jay that laid the acorn under a pile of leaves, as it built up its winter store, one of the 5,000 acorns it hid that year.

Let me plant the seed of an idea since we are here digging in this soil. We tend to think of rewilding and planting trees as something that is exclusively within the gift of humans, as we set tree planting targets to counter the damage we have done. But what if we enabled the other members of our community, such as the birds and squirrels, to contribute? They would likely do a more efficient job than we would and, in the language that tree experts like to use, ensure that 'the right tree is planted in the right place.'

Back to this acorn's story. Derbyshire is in the Midlands,

Seed Eight: Be a tree protector

literally in the middle of England. The village of Dore takes its name from the old English meaning 'door', marking the gateway or passing between two kingdoms, the Anglo-Saxon kingdoms of Deira and Mercia. Around 828, King Egbert of Mercia became the king of the whole of Anglo-Saxon Britain, after defeating King Eanred of Northumbria in a battle here. So there's a long history of clashes and then unification on this land.

If a jay or a human hand planted a small acorn from which this big oak tree grew about 150 years ago, this takes us back to approximately 1860. Queen Victoria had already been on the throne for 23 years. Oak trees do not start to produce acorns until they are approximately 40 years old, so the first would have fallen from the tree around the turn of the century. It was about this time too that the land the tree stood on began to be repurposed. Chatsworth Road, which runs at a right angle to the oak tree, was laid around the turn of the century, lined with tall grey stone houses with peaked roofs. Dore became part of Sheffield in 1934, and it was in the 1930s that Vernon Road was built and became the address of the oak tree. The tree that once grew in a field in Derbyshire became part of a street in a suburb of Sheffield.

And I would not be on this train or holding this acorn in my hand if Sheffield City Council had not decided that they wanted to cut down this tree, along with over 17,000 others – and if a good number of the residents had not decided that they were going to put a stop to this.

The oak tree is the iconic English tree. It has been part of the English landscape for 9,000 years, and it is part of the cultural landscape too. Druids take their name from oaks: the Irish word for oak *dar* was joined with the Indo-European root *did* to mean 'the one who knows the oak'. Oak groves were home to many of the Druids' religious ceremonies. And those cultural resonances of oaks are evident in our language and symbolism. We talk about someone having a 'heart of oak'. The National Trust, which looks after the historic places and countryside of England, has oak leaves and acorns as its emblem. It's not just the British who have a special relationship with oak trees. The ancient Greeks dedicated oak trees to Zeus, king of the gods, and he was known as the oak god.

I wanted to know what lessons this national tree of the country where I was born had to share. With so many ancient oak trees to choose from, the difficulty was making a decision about which to visit. I considered making a pilgrimage to the sacred oak trees, Gog and Magog, in Glastonbury, Somerset. I could have visited the Major Oak tree in Sherwood Forest, Nottingham, where Robin Hood's men were reputed to have hidden. Or there is Bowthorpe Oak in Lincolnshire, which is Britain's widest oak, with a girth of 12.44 metres. It has a hollow trunk, which 39 people once squeezed inside and, in the mid-eighteenth century, 12 people enjoyed afternoon tea in this oak room.

Yet the oak tree that I chose is not ancient; it is only 150 years old. It is not deemed to be sacred in the eyes of those who make such designations; it is just another ordinary oak tree. It is not in a woodland; it grows on a cul-de-sac in a suburb of Sheffield.

But it became a symbol of resistance, embodying the oak tree values of strength and courage. My journey up till now had involved learning to listen to trees in different ways. Now, I was to learn about how a tree was teaching people the importance of community, to listen to their hearts about what mattered most, and giving them the strength and courage to be a tree protector.

Seed Eight: Be a tree protector

I take the bus from Sheffield centre to Dore, on a late August Saturday morning. It's the edge of the Peak District here, and there are a few hikers on the bus, probably heading to Chatsworth House, one of the grand English stately homes, or to the town of Bakewell, on the edge of the Peak District. I had visited both places numerous times when I was growing up in Derbyshire and feel a pull to continue on the bus to revisit them. But I have an appointment with an oak tree.

It's a short walk from the bus stop on the main road to the tree. I walk along Chatsworth Road and then turn into Vernon Road. Vernon Road is populated with newer houses, built in the 1930s and the 1950s. The road slopes slightly upwards. This is Sheffield, after all, and a hill is never far away. The oak tree stands sentinel at the foot of the road, on the left-hand side, outside number one. It is the only street tree on the road. It still wears the yellow ribbon tied around it by campaigners.

There is also a sign fixed to its trunk, proclaiming its CAVAT value: £52,000. I learn later that CAVAT stands for Capital Asset Value for Amenity Trees, and that it is a system for measuring the value of trees. I wonder at the phrasing: 'Amenity Trees'. It sums up a particular world view of trees, where trees are an amenity, their worth counted in how they can be beneficial to us. I read that the methodology was developed to provide a basis for managing trees in the UK as public assets rather than liabilities. I almost laugh out loud at this point. That the starting point that we are trying to row back from is that trees are liabilities rather than gifts is so absurd. If the CAVAT system helps to talk to the authorities in a language that they understand, and helps to stop trees from being cut down, then that is a good thing. But how did we get to this place where these kinds of calculations are necessary?

★

I am half an hour early for my meeting with Margaret and Sue, two of the campaigners who fought to save the tree. I walk around the oak and take pictures from different angles. It is sturdy, with the oak's characteristic bark with deep ridges, and a broad crown, and handsome, as oaks tend to be. I spot acorns on the pavement and pick one up to put in my pocket. Autumn is coming. Five or ten minutes later, a woman comes walking up the street towards me. She stretches out her hand.

'Are you Olivia?'

'Yes! Are you Margaret?'

'No, I'm Sue.'

She has short grey hair and brown eyes.

'I saw you from my kitchen window. I've been making jam. Did I get the time wrong? I thought we were meeting at 9.30?'

'No, I'm early. It was just how the buses ran.'

She says she will go and WhatsApp Margaret and let her know that I am here. I assure her that I am happy hanging out with the tree.

I wonder what the reasons are for the Vernon Oak having been marked for felling. I could see that the kerb was broken in one place by the root of the tree, but the root does not stick out into the road. I ask Sue when she returns.

'It's because of the kerb,' she confirms. 'They said it was a hazard to cars. And then they said that it was a hazard to cyclists. They said that there had to be a build-out to protect cyclists from the hazard, and that build-out would have taken up half the street and made it a one-way street. So we came out and rode our cycles down the street to demonstrate that it wasn't a hazard.' The root barely stuck out beyond the line of the kerb.

This was only the first reason used to try to justify the felling. There were 6 Ds that could be used as reasons: Dangerous, Dead, Diseased, Damaging, Dying, Discriminatory. The root was said to be 'Damaging' the surface of the pavement and the kerb. Then 'Discriminatory' was introduced as a reason. The regulation to prevent discrimination against disabled people specifies between one metre's and one-and-a-half metres' clear space on the pavement for a wheelchair to pass. Sue measured the space from the tree to the far edge of the pavement. It was 1.04 metres, and therefore within the guidelines.

Margaret joins us at the tree, and we walk back up the slope towards her house. We go through the living room and out into Margaret's sunny, flower-filled garden. We sit in a corner of the patio and I breathe in the scent of lavender. Margaret has wispy dark grey hair and I can see a fierceness, a don't-mess-with-me attitude in her eyes. She starts to tell the story.

'This is about an ordinary tree on an ordinary street with ordinary people which became an extraordinary story.'

It was November 2015, a 'gloomy time of year', as Margaret describes it. The residents of Vernon Road received a letter in a plain brown envelope addressed 'To the occupier', tucked in among supermarket discount flyers and bills.

'And we all know what happens to those anonymous brown envelopes,' Margaret says. They are frequently put in the recycling without a glance. But in this envelope was the consultation letter from the Council on the fate of the oak tree that stood on this road. Sue did not receive such a letter because she lived on a neighbouring street, even though the tree had been part of her life for 24 years. Only the people on the street where the tree was located were allowed to have a say.

In February 2016, Margaret read an article about the proposed felling that her neighbour, Tim, had written in the local newsletter. He was the first to christen the tree 'the Vernon Oak'. Margaret realised that it was one of those moments when she could just say 'What a pity' or she could do something. She contacted Tim, and they put leaflets through every door on their street and a few on Sue's street. They asked people to put the leaflet in their window if they agreed that something had to be done to save the Vernon Oak. About half the street showed their support. Sue saw the leaflet in her neighbour's window and got in touch with Margaret. They joined forces and the campaign started.

'We immediately became very creative,' says Margaret. She had never tweeted before, she was not on Facebook, she didn't even own a smartphone. But she realised that the tree needed to have a voice on social media to have a hope of saving it. She created the Vernon Oak Twitter handle and began tweeting in Easter 2016. The very first tweet was 'I was a boundary tree in a field, then houses and roads got built around but I still remind people of that field...'

People have long advocated for trees to be recognised as an important part of the urban public domain. Samuel Hartlib, writing in the 1640s–50s, was an advocate of utopian ideas. He suggested that people should pay a levy for highway maintenance, which would include the planting of trees. He also recommended that fruit trees should be planted, from which people could make cider, reducing reliance on the continent for wine. Having gone scrumping around the street apple trees of Walthamstow, London, with a community group to make apple juice, although not cider, I would fully concur that this is a good idea.

In 1664, the first publication of the Royal Society was *Sylva, or a discourse of forest trees* by John Evelyn. Evelyn also published *Fumifugium or The Inconvenience of the Aer and Smoak of London dissipated*, which proposed the planting of trees around the edge of the city, linked to the ideas of magnificence and public benefit. The eighteenth century saw the rise in importance of the Picturesque movement in Britain and the City Beautiful, and in the nineteenth century trees were seen as a way of addressing concerns about air quality, health and wellbeing. It was at this time that many of the now grand street trees in Sheffield were planted.

Now, the mature street trees in Sheffield formed an important part of the defence against the effects of climate change, for example in helping to protect the city from flooding. Sheffield is located across a bowl of seven hills, and having mature street trees on higher ground offers some protection against the bowl filling up with water. Mature street trees also provide important shade to lower temperatures in cities.

But these considerations were apparently put aside in the decision to 'replace' 17,500 trees, half of Sheffield's street trees.[1] The Council contracted out highway maintenance, including street trees, to Amey, a public company. According to the report of the Sheffield Street Trees Inquiry, an independent public inquiry, Amey proposed to the council to keep the 17,500 figure which had previously been put forward. The report states that 'Their rationale was that this would reduce tree damage to the highways, reduce maintenance costs and produce a tree population that was "more ideal" in terms of "adaptability... to the road infrastructure."[2] The benefits provided by the trees – health, wellbeing, aesthetic, environmental, biodiversity – were seemingly not taken into account. Amey set out a breakdown of when and where they expected to remove and replace trees, with a third of the total to be replaced in the first five years of their contract.

Margaret, Sue and a local writer and poet, Sally, bound themselves together with yellow ribbon to become Vernon Oak and went to Sheffield Town Hall to present their case, but to no avail. Sue emailed the CEO of the Council, with a letter from her heart about the importance of the trees. She didn't receive any reply.

The protest began in order to save the Vernon Oak and the other trees threatened with felling, but it quickly became about much more. It became about listening — or how, in this case, the people of the city were not being listened to by the Council which was supposed to represent them.

'They disrespected and ignored people. Our attitudes quickly hardened. It became a protest about local democracy,' says Margaret.

'Can you imagine,' says Sue, 'at the beginning, we thought that we would write a letter and give it to the individual arbs (arborists), appeal to their better nature.' She laughs. She shows me a copy of the letter, handwritten on the shape of an oak leaf. She speaks of how the protests evolved on numerous roads.

'And then soon we were up against six-foot-tall bouncers, squashing us against walls with the barrier fences.'

'And 30 policemen turning out for the felling of one tree.'

On Chatsworth Road, there was a parade of mature lime trees, with seven out of the 12 marked for felling. Sue and her fellow campaigners sought to save these trees. They managed to save one, but six were felled.

Sue was out walking her mother's dog one morning, early in 2017. Her phone rang. The caller identified himself as being from the CID. Sue said that she would return home and talk to him there.

A male and a female officer arrived shortly after Sue got back. She offered them a cup of tea. They refused.

'Do you remember what happened on 23 October?'

'No,' she said. This was over three months ago.

Seed Eight: Be a tree protector

'Do you remember making some drinks for the tree crews?'

'I might have done,' she said. 'I was always making them drinks.'

'Do you remember making two cups of tea and a glass of orange?'

'I remember,' said her husband, who was sitting in on the interview. 'I thought it was strange that someone wanted a glass of orange, as it was cold out. I thought it was perhaps for a child.'

The upshot of this conversation was that the crew had alleged that laxatives were put in their drinks.

'Well, you can look in my cupboards,' said Sue. 'We're vegetarians, we don't have any laxatives in the house.'

The investigation didn't go anywhere from there. But the press had been tipped off, and they turned up at Sue's house to question her as well. She remembered that before this, she had heard rumours of the 'poisoning incident' and dismissed it. Until it turned out that she was the alleged poisoner.

Art is one of the ways that people connected with the trees during the campaign. I meet with Annette, one of the co-founders of Street Tree Art Sheffield (STARTS) in the Art House Café, an appropriate venue. She has wiry grey hair, pulled back tight, and greets me with a big smile. She apologises if there is still clay on her hands, she has been in the pottery workshop. As she tells her story, it turns out that the tree campaign re-ignited her creativity.

'I was feeling very weepy and emotional because of what was happening to the trees. The feeling of helplessness was intense. It's not only knowing that something is wrong, and you are being prevented by force from doing anything about it. But it's the uncertainty of knowing what's happening. And usually, if you are involved in a campaign, you can go back to your house and it is your safe space but when it is happening outside your house, then you don't even have that. I decided to take my paints to the biggest chestnut that was under threat. You can lose yourself in creative things. I spent six hours there under the tree. The tree had an absolutely glorious canopy, and I thought I am going to lie down and look up at the trees. Then Sarah came along and asked me what I was doing.'

Sarah became Annette's co-founder of STARTS. The following Sunday, seven or eight people painted under the chestnut tree. They supported a project to paint all the memorial trees on Western Road which were under threat, and to do this on Armistice Day, 2017. Approximately 100 people came out to paint the trees. Each person was painting a memorial to these trees that had been planted in memoriam.

Trees are keepers of memories. Trees make memories. Trees are planted as memorials to those who have fallen in wars, from the eucalyptus trees that I had seen in King's Park in Perth, Australia, to this avenue of memorial trees in Sheffield. The trees on Western Road were planted in 1919 in the memory of pupils from the local school who were killed in World War I, with money gathered by public subscription. That these trees which were a living memorial would be cut down caused outrage. The campaigners for these trees were successful. In 2018, the council announced that 32 of the 35 memorial trees that had been earmarked for replacement, including trees on neighbouring roads, would be retained.

After meeting Annette, I visit the Millennium Galleries, where there is an exhibition celebrating Ruskin, the writer and art critic, on the 200th anniversary of his birth. Ruskin was a firm believer in drawing as a means of learning to look, and therefore learning to love nature. He wrote, 'I would rather teach drawing that my pupils may learn to love nature than teach the looking at nature that they may learn to draw.'[3] He described how careful looking at an aspen tree in Fontainebleau changed his perception of it, as well as his own mood:

'I began to draw it, and as I drew, the languor passed away: the beautiful lines insisted on being traced – without weariness. More and more beautiful they became, as each rose out of the rest, and took its place in the air. With wonder increasing every instant, I saw that they "composed" themselves, by finer laws than any known of men. At last, the tree was there, and everything that I had thought before about trees, nowhere.'

STARTS also organised drawing sessions under the Vernon Oak as another way of connecting people with the tree and simply encouraging children and adults to spend time there. I look back at the drawings that Sue shared with me of the Vernon Oak. I saw the time that people had taken to really look at the tree. I think of Annette's description of how spending time with the trees helped to ground her emotions and connect with the tree. And groups such as STARTS provided the link between people noticing the trees and people taking the time to really see them.

Amey, as an external 'service provider', didn't have the same level of accountability to the community as council officers used to have. The tree officers that used to be employed by the council were often local and had a familiarity with both the trees and the community. Amey contractors did not have these relationships.

There was seemingly a lack of transparency around costs as well, with the campaigners feeling that the estimated cost of work to the trees was inflated compared with costs they had obtained from experts. For example, the cost of work to one tree marked for felling, the Nether Edge Elm, a rare 150-year-old elm tree and home to an endangered butterfly, had been estimated at up to £100,000 as reported in a news article. Yet, according to the campaigners, an experienced highways engineer had estimated the cost at £3,500 – not including road closures, utilities and other factors.[4]

Sue saw a contractor come to fix a notice to the Vernon Oak. After he'd left, she came out to read what it said. She phoned Margaret. 'We've got two weeks,' she said. The execution notice had been served.

Sue came to sit under the leaves of the tree every day to meditate. People tied love notes around the trunk. Sally led singing around the tree, and there were readings of poems too.

At a vigil around the tree in the evening before the felling day, the campaigners sang, repeating the chorus of the song, 'You cut us down, down, down.' But they also let their voices raise songs of hope into the air.

The morning of the felling day, in October 2017, Sue, Margaret, Sally and other campaigners came out in the blackness before dawn. They knew that the cutters often arrived in the darkness. A young man pulled himself into the branches of the tree. He sat in the tree all day, talking to the people on the ground, talking to the tree. The campaigners spoke with the TV crews and journalists who had come. Vernon Oak had become a celebrity. As the day went on, spirits began to lift. Perhaps the men with chainsaws were not going to turn up after all.

And they never came. Who knows why the Vernon Oak was spared. Its offending root, breaching the kerb, is still as it was. It must have been decided that the urgent work required was not so urgent after all.

Seed Eight: Be a tree protector

So the Vernon Oak still stands. He is there to provide a home for bluetits. The blackbirds can use his branches as a perch to sing from. Insects have a home – beetles, ladybirds, caterpillars. As do fungi, mosses and lichen. Squirrels have a tree to collect acorns from. Sap continues to rise in the heartwood of the tree.

Robert Macfarlane, the nature writer, wrote the song 'Heartwood' as a charm against harm for Sheffield and trees everywhere threatened with felling. The words of 'Heartwood' were stamped on wooden plaques and hung from trees that were marked for cutting. Sally, together with her friend Val, set the poem to music. I listen now to the recording that Sally gave me of the song, the voices rising pure, like the sap rising in a tree, singing as the tree might sing if we had ears and heart to listen. I imagine the group of residents standing together, sharing their voices under the auspices of the tree, for possibly the last time. Vernon Oak's last stand:

> 'I am a world, cutter,
> I am a maker of life –
> Drinker of rain, breaker of rocks,
> Caster of shade, eater of sun.'

The last lines hang poignantly in the air:

> 'Have you heartwood, cutter?
> Have those who sent you?'

'There was so much singing in the campaign,' Sally said. I meet her at her allotment, down a tree-lined track, through a five-bar gate, tucked away among the other allotments with their garden gates. The last of the summer raspberries hang temptingly from their canes, planted alongside rows of floppy-topped onions. 'We sang songs at the vigil for Vernon Oak. We were singing as the surveillance crews walked up and down. Another time on Chatsworth Road, when we were faced with a large group of police officers, we started singing "The Policeman's Song" from Gilbert and Sullivan. Before Christmas, on Aldam Road, it was freezing cold. I started singing a Sheffield traditional carol on my own under a plane tree, and I was anxious about being challenged by the security personnel. But other campaigners came to join me, and we sang lots of different carols. We adapted the words to fit the occasion: A goldfinch in a plane tree; 12 Amey men, 10 plastic barriers. At the end, the tree crews said that they had enjoyed it. It was part joyous and part angry.

'Singing helps. Campaigns can be grim. It helps to lift people, it helps them to express how they feel. And it disconcerts the authorities, it is not what they are expecting. I think it is also quite a female form of expression.'

I picture the women weaving their voices together into a protective spell for the trees, against the men, and they were predominantly men, wielding chainsaws.

Singing and music is a refrain that is drifting through my journey.

The council made the argument that they would replace the felled trees with new street trees. But the simple fact is that replacing a 100–150-year-old tree with a two-year-old tree is not equivalent. A beech tree which is about 100 years old, 25 metres tall, with a crown diameter of 12–15 metres, has a leaf area of about 1,600 square metres. On a sunny day, this means it can absorb 18 kilograms of carbon dioxide, and it also produces 13 kilograms of oxygen, the daily requirement for ten people. It helps to clean the air, filtering out dust and other harmful substances. It helps to cool the air too, as in the shade of the tree, the air is up to 5°C cooler. To replace the services of this

Seed Eight: Be a tree protector

100-year-old beech with young trees, you would need to plant 2,500 trees.[5] One for one does not 'cut it'. And you cannot replace the sheer joy that can come from being in the presence of a mature tree.

When the felling of the trees came to a halt in March 2018, over 5,000 trees had been cut down. It was a victory of sorts for campaigners as it meant that over 12,000 trees had been saved. But still, there were streets which had lost their mature trees for ever, permanently changing their character and nature. And 5,000 homes for birds and insects and other plant life had been lost, along with the human relationships with these trees and creatures. No wonder the residents felt a profound sense of loss. People tell me they were surprised at the depth of emotion they had felt and how they were moved to take action. For many people, protecting the trees had become the focus of their lives for two years.

'People couldn't even walk down the streets where the trees had been cut down,' said Joanna. 'It tapped something primitive deep inside us.'

Joanna was another one of the campaigners. She spoke of solastalgia and the sense of loss that was experienced through the tree felling. 'Solastalgia' is a term coined by Glenn Albrecht, a philosopher at the University of Newcastle in Australia, in the early 2000s. His definition of 'solastalgia' is:

'The pain experienced when there is recognition that the place where one resides and that one loves is under immediate assault (physical desolation). It is manifest in an attack on one's sense of place, in the erosion of the sense of belonging (identity) to a particular place and a feeling of distress (psychological desolation) about its transformation...

In short, solastalgia is a form of homesickness one gets when one is still at "home."'[6]

It seems to me that solastalgia is a word and, more importantly, a feeling that is going to become more familiar to all of us – whether because of attacks on the environment around us by fellow humans, as was the case in Sheffield, or because of changes due to climate change, such as flooding, storms and wildfires, that cause destruction in the places we call home.

Joanna also helped to bring the book *Lost Words* by Robert Macfarlane and Jackie Morris to all the primary schools in Sheffield. Vernon Oak tweeted to launch the crowdfunding campaign, and Joanna, Margaret and Sue, along with Sarah, the co-founder of STARTS, were the humans on the ground. The book captures the nature-related words that were lost from the *Oxford Junior Dictionary*, including 'acorn' and other commonplace words such as 'dandelion' and 'bramble' and which were replaced with words like 'spreadsheet' and 'block-graph'. If we lose the words to be able to describe and connect to the natural world around us, then we are more likely to lose those beings in the real world as well.

'Do you know what happened to the felled trees?' I asked Joanna.

'There was some suggestion that they were used as biomass, to create energy. It was never made clear.'

The felling stopped, thanks to the voices and actions of all the tree protectors. The tree protectors always preface it with 'for now' because they can never really be sure. Yet it seems that proper tree care and maintenance has also stopped.

'We want all the trees to be cared for,' says Margaret, 'and it seems as if they have now decided not to do anything. Amey have decided to cut their losses. And the trees do need to be cared for and maintained. It's not a long-term solution to do nothing. We need proper tree officers, who take pride in the local area, and who can pass on knowledge.'

Sue is now tweeting about the failing street trees. 'There are thirty-to-forty-year-old trees, which are suffering from lack of care. And where new trees are being planted, they are being planted poorly, there is no preparation. They dig a hole, plonk a tree down. The trees are not going to survive.'

This sentiment is echoed when I speak to Joe Coles, who at the time worked for the Woodland Trust.

'It's not always about planting numbers, it's an issue of maintaining them. Are all of the trees going to thrive into the future? We need to invest in the infrastructure to look after them. The watering that is required for the first two to three years is often overlooked in the planting of the tree.'

The street trees provide a connection to trees and to nature for people who don't have the opportunity to get out into woodlands. There is also the importance of the other benefits that street trees bring. The concept of tree equity is now gaining ground. Based on work first carried out in the USA, the tree equity score measures how well the benefits of trees are reaching those on low incomes and others disproportionately impacted by extreme heat and pollution. Looking at the report for Sheffield as a whole, 34 out of 338 areas are below a tree equity score of 75 out of 100. To get all areas to a score of 75, one square kilometre of tree canopy cover would need to be added, equivalent to 18,000 medium trees. Increasing the cover by this amount would prevent stormwater runoff equal to 319 standard swimming pools.[7]

A Friends of the Earth research study found that 43 per cent of English neighbourhoods have less than 10 per cent tree cover, with lower-income areas having far fewer trees than wealthier ones.[8] The UK Government has acknowledged the physical and mental health benefits of trees, including lowering blood pressure and pulse rate and reducing stress levels. There could be a £2.1 billion saving for the NHS every year if everyone had access to good-quality green spaces.[9] The benefits of trees may also extend to improving educational outcomes. A US study found that tree canopy cover within 250 metres predicted better performance in both reading and maths, even after taking into account factors such as student characteristics, school resources, size and location.[10]

'We need a new strategy for the street trees,' says Sue. 'We need to get the streets involved, to have tree champions on each street. For people to be educated about the trees.'

'And the government needs to say they are valuable,' says Margaret. 'It needs to put them first. And not just the street trees, but the trees in gardens. Forty per cent of the trees in Sheffield are in private gardens.'

I listen to Sue and Margaret and I wonder about who 'owns' the street trees. Ultimately, it is the council who has responsibility for them but there is a problem if they think that they own them, rather than seeing themselves as guardians or caretakers. The language that the council uses is around 'their trees' and 'their decisions'. If residents see the council as owning them, they are less likely to take care of them, even though they might have a natural inclination to. Some of the residents mention that the council planted new trees on their street and stuck on little signs saying, 'Please water me.' But the residents felt hostile towards the council because of the felling of the established street trees and the council had made little attempt to engage the residents or to provide them with tools to water the young trees. As David Elliott, then CEO of Trees for Cities tells me, getting children involved in watering is a wonderful opportunity for them to feel more connected with the trees, to watch and help the trees to grow, as the children themselves grow. There is even greater engagement if the residents do the planting themselves.

There's also the question about what types of trees to plant. Native trees are typically seen as being 'better' than 'non-native' trees and will support more biodiversity. But Joe Coles points out that there are approximately 40 species native to the UK, and only three or four which are suitable for planting as street trees. Jan Woudstra of Sheffield University has suggested that we need to look at the mix of trees that we are planting, not having avenues of one species, as with the great lime avenues in Sheffield, but with a mix of trees that are going to be more resilient to climate change. And we have to look to the future. If there is going to be an average 3°C rise in temperature in London by 2050, with an 18 per cent decline in rainfall, as predictions suggest, what trees are going to be able to survive in that climate? There also needs to be consideration of what trees will help to maintain bird and butterfly populations.

David Elliott says, 'An elm tree in Sheffield which is home to an endangered butterfly was almost cut down because of cost. And how many trees would you need to plant to replace a 300-year-old oak tree? You could make some crude calculations, but it is virtually irreplaceable. You are not going to get any of the same kind of value.'

A couple of weeks later, I head back to the city for the Sheffield Street Trees and Politics conference. Street Trees and Politics seem like an unlikely combination. But the range of speakers from around the world, including the USA and South Korea, demonstrates that it is not just in Sheffield that street trees have become politicised. Professor Wybe Kuipert makes the point that councils should plant more cherry trees because of their blossom. In this Instagram generation, the trees can become a draw. He cites the examples of Washington DC and Berlin, which draw crowds of people in the spring to take selfies with the cherry blossom. His argument is that anything that helps to draw attention to the trees is a good thing. I agree but, at the same time, I wonder how many people are considering the trees for their value beyond being a source of likes on an Instagram feed, a picturesque backdrop for smiling faces. If the cherry blossom is an entry point for connecting with trees and nature, how can we help people to go beyond this, to appreciate the trees for all that they bring, and as living beings?

The campaigners felt deeply for the trees, of that I have no doubt. I also believe there was an extra dimension to their fight because they felt the cutting down of their trees was an attack on their values. It was felt more deeply as an act of betrayal because it was a Labour Council in a traditional Labour stronghold that was behind this act – Labour, who were meant to be on the side of the people, instead of setting all-too-visible police officers and surreptitious evidence gatherers against citizens.

The trees became a symbol of resistance. One of the outcomes of the tree campaign in Sheffield has been the 'It's our city' campaign, seeking to bring back more control of the city to the people. The campaign was successful in collecting enough signatures so that the city had to hold a referendum on governance changes, to make the decision-making process of the council more democratic. In 2021, residents voted for a change to the way that the council works.

The campaign also helped to raise the profile of street trees on a national scale. Michael Gove, at the time the environment

Seed Eight: Be a tree protector

minister in the Conservative government, came to visit the Vernon Oak. However, nearly 50,000 trees were cut down in London boroughs in the five years leading up to the beginning of 2017.[11]

Yet some cities are recognising the importance of street trees. Melbourne, Australia has an Urban Forest strategy, which aims to double canopy cover to 40 per cent by 2040, with the trees helping to maintaining the health and liveability of the city in the face of a changing climate. The council has introduced an email address for each of the city's 77,000 trees, to encourage residents to care for them by reporting if they spot any cause for concern. But people have also taken to emailing love letters to the trees. A golden elm tree is one of the most popular. One email read, 'I used to think you were the Magic Faraway Tree when I was a child. Now that I'm an adult, I still look forward to seeing you as I come around the bend after a tedious crawl down Hoddle Street. A loyal friend always there waiting to say hello.'[12]

I think of the Vernon Oak tweeting to save itself from being cut down. How would things be different if each of Sheffield's trees had an email address? Or, if the Vernon Oak and other trees were hooked up to sensors and were able to live-tweet data such as daily water use, sap flow, stem shrinkage and trunk growth? A 100-year-old red oak tree at Harvard Forest tweets such data under the handle @awitnesstree and has over 10,000 followers. Such innovations help both scientists and the general public learn how the tree interacts with its environment and how it is being affected by climate change.

It's my last day in Sheffield and I am heading back to London. I am standing at the bus stop, on a leafy tree-lined road, under a lime tree, opposite a nursery called TreeTops. The words that keep emerging in relationship to the story of the Vernon Oak and the protests are connection and community. 'We've made so many friends through this.' 'We've met so many wonderful people that we wouldn't otherwise have met.' I think of the root network of the trees, and how the trees naturally support each other. How in our communities we have lost this network, but how it can quickly be re-established, when there is a common cause, in this case the trees.

And it is also about noticing. 'It's about attentiveness. We've learnt to pay attention to what's around us.'

Standing under the trees, I wonder how the two are interlinked. A quote from the artist Georgia O'Keeffe runs through my mind. 'It takes time to see a flower – really – like to have a friend takes time.'

The time to see and listen to the voice of a tree, which then connects you with your voice, your people, your community, your city, your world.

Growing up in Derbyshire, I assumed that my life would follow the conventional path – marriage, two children. Two of my great-aunts had never married and I was sure that I didn't want to be like them, although they were both women who I knew had lived rich lives through the stories they told and the stories the family told about them. Yet it was important to me to have a career too. I remember saying at school, perhaps only half-jokingly, that I wanted to have twins because then I would only need to take one career break. My mother was a twin, after all.

My life had taken a different path. On this trip to Sheffield, I had taken the opportunity to catch up with an old school friend. She didn't have children either. Of my four closest friends at school, only one had had children. There were more and more women like us finding different ways to live in the world.

Seed Eight: Be a tree protector

As I look out of the train window at the green fields that we are passing through, I am aware that I am nearing the end of my journey. I only have two more trees left to visit – the giant sequoia in California and then the baobab. I have found community, as I travel, with people who have shared their love of trees with me. I can only hope that when I finish travelling, I will find such community.

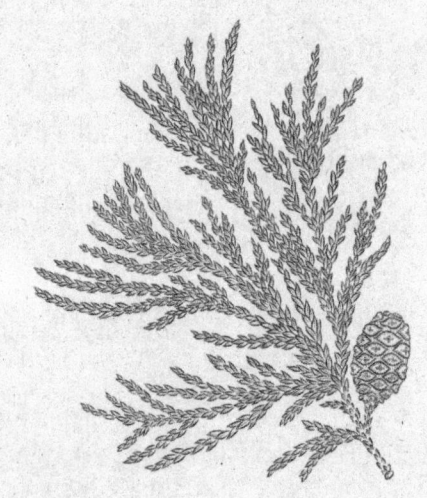

Seed Nine: The forest of the imagination

Giant sequoia, USA

*'The only war that matters is the one against the imagination
All other battles are subsumed in it.'*

Diane di Prima, 'Rant'

Imagine you are walking among trees whose tops reach into the clouds. Imagine you lean your face against the red-brown, grooved, hard yet sponge-like bark of the tree, stretch your arms wide around the tree and they don't even begin to cover the width of the trunk. Imagine you continue on your walk and there is a tree trunk lying on the ground, hollowed out by fire. You climb inside the trunk and crouch-crawl towards the light at the other end through the blackened interior. You emerge into the daylight, into another world. What do you see?

The redwoods take us into another world. A world where some of these trees were this big a 1,000 years before Christ was born in a land far away. A world in which we are truly insignificant in terms of the time we have been on this earth.

The giant sequoias surpass all superlatives. Our language pales into insignificance next to them. Perhaps the only place to adequately meet them is in our imagination.

For they are of this world, and yet they are not of this world.

Who dreamt up these trees that can live to 3,000 years old, and reach 85 metres tall and eight metres in diameter?

Despite their majesty, we are threatening the survival of these giants. Imagine a world in which these trees have all disappeared.

I'm standing at the doorway in the forest. I imagine the voices of the peoples who lived here long ago, calling out praise, voices tumbling in the wind like water over rock. Voices which animated the trees, celebrated their being-ness, sung in relationship with them. And then voices silenced as peoples were forcibly removed, died of disease, died of heartbreak at the denial of being part of this land. The voices of the trees silenced as the voices of these people were silenced. There is a roll call of peoples who were severed from the giant sequoias in what are now Sequoia and Kings Canyon National Parks, with countless stories of loss, and of lives, lineages, languages and knowledge destroyed. These parks are the homelands of the: Mono (Monache), Yokuts, Tübatulabal, Paiute and Western Shoshone.[1] In 1860, the Native American population of California was 20 per cent of what it had been ten years earlier.[2]

The Yokuts-speaking tribes comprised about 50 dialect groups in the territory around the Tulare Lake. Their descendants of the Tule River Tribe manage an 84-square-mile reservation in the Sierra Foothills, with giant sequoia growing there, and bordering on Sequoia National Forest. Many of their historical cultural sites are located within the National Monument. And they are still excluded from decision-making. Harold Santos, a tribal council member has noted, 'There's no buy-in to our culture [from federal and state agencies]... When we say cultural resources, we aren't just talking about archaeological sites. We're talking about all the places and beings that we, Indigenous people, have relationships with and work to protect: from the smallest bug in the ground to the stars in the sky.'³

From the early days of when the settlers arrived, the giant sequoia has been taken out of this web of relationships and objectified. In 1854, in order to prove their existence to the public, the bark was stripped from a giant sequoia in Calaveras Grove, shipped to New York, reassembled in the shape of a tree and put on display there, before being transported to London to be shown in Hyde Park and then put on permanent display in Crystal Palace. The bark exhibit was destroyed by fire in 1866. All of the leaves were gone from the actual tree, known as Mother of the Forest, within five years of it being stripped of its bark, and most of what was left of the tree was destroyed by fire in 1908.

It was a giant sequoia growing in the UK that captured my imagination in childhood, its planting no doubt inspired by this bark shell in Crystal Palace, when it Victorian times it became the fashionable tree to plant. The house in Derbyshire where I lived from the ages of four to eight years old was a timber-framed Tudor house, and in the garden grew this outsized exotic tree.

The Wellingtonia tree was of a different size and scale to the other trees in the garden. It dwarfed the small, twisting 300-year-old mulberry tree with its squishy purple fruits and the lime-tree saplings my mother planted. Wellingtonia is the name that John Lindley from the Royal Horticultural Society gave the species in 1853, in memory of the Duke of Wellington, who had passed away a year earlier. 1853 was also the year that the plant collector William Lobb brought the seeds, shoots and saplings of the giant sequoia he had gathered in California to the UK. I knew that my father came from California and that I had lived there from when I was a baby to when we moved here when I was four years old. At a young age, I remember marvelling that this tree was of the same family as the ones in California, in this garden that belonged to a man who was from California, who had an American accent, and who drove an outsized American car, a green Buick convertible, twice the length of English cars. This tree was as different from the English trees as his car was from English cars. I remember pressing my hand against the fibrous bark of the tree so unlike the bark of the English trees. And looking straight up into its heights, with its one tall singular trunk, different from the English trees with their multiple divisions. The tree connected me with faraway lands. In my imagination, I roamed through forests of these giant trees.

Later, I went to visit my father after he had moved back to San Francisco. We visited the coastal redwood forests where I experienced first hand their collective size and scale and magnificence. He loved those trees as well. I wish I could ask him about his memories of the trees, but he is no longer here to ask.

Maybe the redwood is part of our family tree. In my thirties, when I was imagining where my ideal home would be, I wrote about living on the coast of northern California, in the hills, with coastal redwood trees nearby, with my husband and my daughter and a dog, making a living from my writing. Life has turned out differently.

A law was passed in 1937 to name the redwood as California's state tree. In 1953, this was clarified when the original law was amended to name both the coastal redwood and giant sequoia as the official state trees. The coastal redwoods, *Sequoia sempervirens,* are closely related to the giant sequoias, *Sequoia gigantea,* but differ in a number of respects. One clue is in the name. The coastal redwoods grow on a narrow strip near the Pacific Ocean in northern California. The thick fog that comes in from the sea provides the conditions that the redwoods need. They can absorb

Seed Nine: The forest of the imagination

moisture from the fog through their needles, in a process called foliar uptake. Given that it can take months for a drop of water to pass from the roots to the top of the tree, the fog provides a significant source of water.

The two species also differ in their size and shape. The coastal redwoods are slimmer than their relatives, and taper towards the top. They can grow taller too, up to 100 metres, but the giant sequoias have much more volume, as they have thicker trunks. In the land of superlatives, one coastal redwood claims the title of world's tallest tree, measuring 115.55 metres, its precise location in the Redwood National Park kept a secret. A giant sequoia, the General Sherman tree, is the world's biggest tree, with a volume of 1,486.6 metres. This is the equivalent of more than half the volume of an Olympic swimming pool, thanks to its diameter of 8.23 metres, even though it is a comparatively short 83.8 metres.

The giant sequoia cones are up to 7.5 centimetres long, with seeds the size of an oat flake. The cones of the coastal redwood are smaller, about 2.5 centimetres long and the seeds the size of a tomato seed. It is amazing to imagine how huge trees can grow from such tiny beginnings.

Nine months after I started my journey, I'm excited to be going camping among the giant sequoias with my cousin Greg and his wife Gloria. But first we want to pay a visit to the coastal redwoods in Muir Woods National Monument, near San Francisco.

In 1945, the Secretary of the Interior Ickes proposed in a letter to President Franklin Roosevelt that a meeting of United Nations representatives be held among the redwoods of Muir Woods to focus on sustaining world peace. He wrote about the meeting: 'Not only would this focus attention upon this nation's interest in preserving these mighty trees for posterity, but here in such a "temple of peace" the delegates would gain a perspective and sense of time that could be obtained nowhere in America better than in a forest. Muir Woods is a cathedral, the pillars of which have stood through much of recorded human history. Many of these trees were standing when the Magna Carta was written.'[4]

Franklin Roosevelt died before the meeting took place and so the gathering of 500 United Nations delegates in Muir Woods on 19 May 1945 became a remembrance of his life. But three concepts from the letter stand out. Firstly, the idea of the forest as a 'temple of peace', that there was an intrinsic peacefulness which could influence the thoughts and actions of those who gathered there. Secondly, there is a recognition of the perspective and sense of time that can be gained from being in a forest. Maybe the longevity of the trees would influence participants to act for the long term rather than just in the service of short-term interests. And, thirdly, the idea of Muir Woods as a cathedral.

The depiction of woods as a cathedral is not a new idea. But let's pause to imagine how things would be different both for the woods and ourselves if we did embrace the concept of woods as cathedral. Theodore Roosevelt, another US President and a distant cousin of Franklin Roosevelt, wrote that 'A grove of giant redwood or sequoias should be kept just as we keep a great and beautiful cathedral.'[5]

In Muir Woods, Cathedral Grove, as the board at its entrance explains, is 'set aside as a quiet refuge to protect its natural soundscape in an increasingly noisy world.' People are encouraged not to talk so they can experience the natural sounds of the forest, and so the birds and animals can enjoy the space free from the interference of human voices.

The simple act of intentionally walking in silence through a space engenders reverence. Here in these woods, Greg, Gloria and I walk on the paths through the trees, close to these giants, with their green skirts of frilled ferns. We cross a stream wending its way through the valley floor, water bubbling bright. We take one of the paths that winds up into the hills, and the guardrails disappear, so we can touch these trees. These are younger than the ones on the valley floor. Gloria can almost wrap her arms all the way around one.

It was the ancestors of these trees that the settlers cut down and used to build much of California, including its houses and railroads. In *Trees of California*, first published in 1909, Willis Linn Jepson writes, 'The writer of these lines is a Californian. He was rocked by a pioneer mother in a cradle made of Redwood. The house in which he lived was largely made of Redwood. His clothing, the books of his juvenile library, the saddle for his riding pony were brought in railway cars chiefly made of Redwood... He went to a school in a Redwood schoolhouse, sat at a desk made of Redwood.'[6] He continues to describe all the ways the redwood provided much of the fabric of his life. So it would have been for my ancestors, who first arrived in California at the time of the Gold Rush. Jepson writes, 'California might have done without her gold mines but not without the resources of the Redwood belt.'[7] For the first four years of my life, I lived in a Victorian house in San Francisco, made of redwood, before moving to Derbyshire, where the giant sequoia grew in the garden.

Walking through these trees, whose groves are now preserved only in pockets, it is sobering to think about Jepson's view of these trees as 'standing timber' and his calculation of this amount as 'vast' – a description that is hard to reconcile with his role as a conservationist. In 1892, at the age 25, he was one of the founders, along with John Muir and Warren Olney, of the Sierra Club, which aimed, in Muir's words, 'to do something for wildness and make the mountains glad.'[8] In *Trees of California*, Jepson also recognised the significance of trees beyond the merely practical and useful, and rails against the 'so-called practical man' who has 'locked his door against the ideals and imaginations of humanity.'[9]

Given Jepson's mix of views, I wonder what he would have made of Ronald Reagan saying, when he was running for governor in 1966, 'I think, too, that we've got to recognise that where the preservation of a natural resource like the redwoods is concerned, that there is a common-sense limit. I mean, if you've looked at 100,00 acres or so of trees – you know, a tree is a tree, how many more do you need to look at?'[10]

According to Reagan, a tree is a tree. There is no sense of their individuality. Or what they offer, individually or collectively. A tree is just an object to look at. Or to cut down. The choice is binary. Centred on the human perspective. No recognition of the being-ness of the tree in its own right. Or the tree as part of an ecosystem, supporting diverse forms of life. It is a failure of imagination.

William Blake wrote in a letter in 1799, over 150 years before Reagan spoke his words, 'I know that this world is a world of imagination and vision... The tree which moves some to tears of joy is in the eyes of others only a green thing which stands in the way. Some see nature all ridicule and deformity, and by these I shall not regulate my proportions; and some scarce see nature at all. But to the eyes of the man of imagination, nature is imagination itself. As a man is, so he sees.'

This view of nature as imagination itself is one that was lost on many of the settlers – including, no doubt, my own ancestors. Greg Sarris of the Pomo and Coast Miwok people, who once lived in what is now called Marin County, where the coastal redwoods grow, has written of the settlers as the Forgetters:

Seed Nine: The forest of the imagination

'[T]he Forgetters... killed all of the bears and the elk and the pronghorn. They cut down trees. You see, they forgot the stories. They forgot we are all one People, and the animals, indeed the entire Mountain, began to suffer. Now, we must all try to learn to live together. We must remember the stories again.'[11]

Have we lost our imagination because we forgot the stories of who we are in in relation to nature – and to our own imagination? Do we need to remember and relearn the stories to recover our imagination? And what does that mean for those of us who are not indigenous to one place? My ancestors were settlers and Forgetters in California, as well as native to the woods of Finland. What stories can I remember as I live in a country that is neither of these places?

I am beginning to think that imagination is being connected to the world in all its richness, and to its many layers, the visible and invisible. It is being open to the stories that the trees whisper and the land sings, the stories that speak in the language of dreams and in the rushing of a river. It is being a channel for what the world wants to express through you, in words, in movement, in song. And our responsibility to the imagination is to be open to that which wants to be expressed.

Part of being open is to honour the land we live on, and the stories that have been spoken there for thousands of years, whether by people, by rocks or by trees. And we can honour those stories by remembering them, listening to them, and then passing on those that are ours to tell, in a way that only we can – and that would be lost if we didn't.

The car is packed for the drive to the giant sequoias, loaded with our tents, sleeping bags, food, water, camping stove. We are heading to King's Canyon National Park in the Sierra Nevada mountains. Like the coastal redwoods, the giant sequoias only grow in a narrow range. The range of the giant sequoias is between 1,520 metres elevation and 2,290 metres elevation in California – too low and it is too dry, too high and it is too cold.

From the too dry, dusty lowlands, we wend our way up through the foothills to giant sequoia habitat, as the landscape becomes greener and the trees grow bigger. When we arrive at the campsite, it feels like such a privilege to be able to pitch a tent in the vicinity of the giant sequoias, among their neighbours the sugar pines, incense cedar and fir trees. The sugar pines are giants themselves, being the world's largest pine trees, and growing up to 60 metres tall, with cones up to 50 centimetres long. There is grandness, but also a softness, with the light filtered through the green branches and sounds hushed by the carpet of pine needles.

We are keen to get out and explore before it becomes dark. On our walk from the campground, we come across the General Grant tree, the third largest tree by volume in the world, and the widest known sequoia at 12 metres across. The signage lays out some of the comparisons – the trunk could hold 159,000 basketballs or more than 37 million ping-pong balls. If Greg, Gloria and I wanted to hold hands around the base of the tree, then we would need another 17 people to complete the circle.

But the facts and figures don't really make sense of the trees. The English language – or at least mine – struggles to capture them. I wonder if languages that grew out of the area, out of the landscape of the trees, would do better. I try that night in my journal by torchlight in my tent in wobbly handwriting, and I get as far as 'The trees – words fail. Awe. Can't believe how big they are. To be able to walk inside those which are fallen and hollowed out. To camp under these stars whilst the trees stretch to the heavens, connecting them together. Truly, magnificently.'

Seed Nine: *The forest of the imagination*

Awe is the emotion that I keep coming back to over the next few days.

The interpretation board for the General Grant tree names it as a 'Living Shrine', to honour the men and women who have given their lives in service to the nation. It continues: 'Strong. Uplifting. Inspirational. Enduring. Sequoias and other "trees of life" inspire profound emotion reminding us of ideas above and beyond ourselves.'

Another way to describe this emotion would be 'awe'. The Greater Good Science Center at Berkeley defines 'awe' as 'the feeling of being in the presence of something incredible that challenges our understanding of the world,'[12] and suggests that awe is most likely to occur where there is physical vastness and novelty. The forests of giant sequoia certainly have both of those characteristics for me. I wonder about the novelty aspect – if I lived close to redwoods, would I lose my awe for them? I hope not. But maybe it is easier to access awe when we are somewhere new because we are more open to the world around us, rather than passing through somewhere that feels familiar.

Experiencing awe has been proved to have health benefits, sharpen our thinking and make us more generous.[13] Awe makes us feel part of something bigger, reducing our sense of an individual self and increasing our sense of the collective. One study looked at the difference in behaviour between a group of American college students who stood in a grove of tall eucalyptus trees and looked up for one minute, compared to a group in the same location who faced the other way and stared at a building. Afterwards, a person working with the researchers 'accidentally' dropped some pens on the ground. The students who had been looking at the trees were more likely to help by picking up the pens. The researchers reported that the tree group were also less inclined to act in unethical ways and felt less strongly that they were entitled to preferential treatment.[14]

The study shows that spending time simply looking up into trees can make us better human beings. Another practice is taking an 'awe walk' in nature, setting out with the intention to experience awe, using your senses to feel, see, touch, hear and even taste what is around you. A research study of a group of older adults taking daily 15-minute awe walks found that as well as experiencing greater awe during their walks than a control group also taking daily walks, they also reported greater joy and pro-social positive emotions during their walks and afterwards. In photographs they took of themselves, they showed an increasingly 'small self', filling a smaller part of the photo than at the beginning, and showing increasing smile intensity over the period.[15]

The next day, we visit the General Sherman tree in Sequoia National Park, the biggest tree by volume in the world. We line up to take a group selfie with the tree, but it is impossible to capture its scale. We hike through the forest, soon escaping the crowds who have come only to see the main attraction. We cross open meadows, criss-crossed with shadows and light, and we jump streams of mountain water that is the trees' vital life source. That evening, I can still summon up only a few words. 'Grateful.' 'Peace.' 'Amazing trees.'

In Sequoia National Park, one of the interpretation boards states that the original mission of the National Park Service was 'to conserve the scenery and the natural and historic objects and the wild life therein and to provide for the enjoyment of the same in such manner and by such means as will leave them unimpaired for enjoyment by future generations.'[16]

This anthropocentric statement is concerned only with preservation of the 'natural objects' in terms of how it benefits humans. The language does not recognise the trees as living beings. They are objects to be managed for our benefit. The latest incarnation of the mission reads 'The National Park Service preserves unimpaired the natural and cultural resources and values of the National Park System for the enjoyment, education, and inspiration of this and future generations.' The language has changed only slightly from 'objects' to 'resources', and the focus is still on the benefits nature can bring to humans, with added doses of education and inspiration as well as enjoyment.

In her book, *In Search of the Canary Tree*, Dr Lauren Oakes travels to Alaska to study the yellow cypress and how it is being affected by climate change. She speaks to Teri Rofklat, a weaver from the Tlingit peoples, who makes a powerful case for moving away from the language of resources, saying, 'One of my goals… is to eliminate the term "natural resource". I think it's just – it's an atrocity – you know, it is the resourcing of everything. There's no relationship. If you replace the words "natural resource" with "relationship", you're good to go.'

How about if the National Park Service spoke about fostering relationship with the natural world, rather than preserving natural resources? It would be a step on the journey to break down the barriers between us and the natural world. The word 'environment' is another example of making a separation between humans and the natural world. It comes from the French *environ* and means 'that which surrounds'. It is not something that we humans are part of.

The language of the current National Parks land management strategy acknowledges that preservation in a static state is not possible because of climate change. The strategy is based on the principles of Resist – Accept – Direct.[17] The choices are to resist the change that is happening, working to restore or maintain conditions; to accept the change, allowing the ecosystem to change without interfering; or to direct change, actively shaping the ecosystem towards desired new conditions. With changes happening so fast, it seems to me that resistance will soon be futile — if it is not already.

It is on our last day among the sequoias that I have the deepest experience of them. Maybe it was because it was the day when we went to the part of the forest without designated 'world's largest trees' and therefore there were fewer people. Maybe it was because it takes a few days to relax into being with the trees. Maybe it was a combination of both.

As we walk into Redwood Canyon the energy immediately feels even more peaceful. Here is just the quiet of the forest. I set an intention to connect with the magic and the roots of the world. As I say this, I have an awareness that magic is the root of the world.

The magic is shimmering in the forest as we walk, illuminating yellow autumn leaves on branches and the gold that has made its way to the forest floor. A little way into the walk, I spot a movement on a fallen tree trunk by the side of the path. I stop and look. A low-slung, long-tailed brown creature with little triangular ears pops back into view on the top of the trunk and returns my gaze, holding still. Quietly as possible, I try to capture Greg and Gloria's attention, and they stop as well. 'I think it's a pine marten,' Greg whispers. The animal looks at us for a while and then whisks himself out of sight. We collectively exhale.

'Wow, that was special,' says Gloria.

It is only later, when we ask at the visitor centre, that we learn how rare such a sighting is as pine martens are usually nocturnal. I read on a website, 'The Marten Spirit Animal has close ties with Tree Wisdom and Magic. Like the Marten, trees have a language all their own. So consider pondering the meaning and

Seed Nine: The forest of the imagination

symbols of trees and their energetic signatures.'[18] Seeing the pine marten feels like magic at work.

We carry on, walking beside a creek, and reach a grove of giant sequoias. I lie down on the ground in the middle of the trees, looking up at their vast height, being drawn ever upwards towards the infinite sky. I feel a strong connection with the earth from my root chakra, as if I am pulled down into the earth. I experience such a sense of bliss and want to stay lying here. But we need to keep moving – we have a climb ahead of us. It is a steady climb out of the canyon of 1,200 feet, through yellow-leaved oaks and rocks covered with lichens.

We reach the top of the ridge and there a surprise awaits us. A grove of giant sequoias. I hadn't read any descriptions of the trail beforehand, so I wasn't expecting to find more redwoods here. This is Sugar Bowl Grove. The red bark of the trees is aglow in the sunset light. It is an unusual redwood grove as there are only the sequoias growing here; they are not mixed through with pine and firs. It is pure sequoia magnificence. On one side of the ridge the full moon is rising over the mountains and the sun is setting on the other side. I feel like the luckiest person alive to be able to experience this moment in this place.

Darkness falls as we are still wending our way down through the forest, through the moon shadows. There is a moment when we think we have lost the path, but then it reappears. Over black bean tacos for dinner around the campfire, I share that this has been one of my best hikes ever, and that I am so grateful for the beauty, wonder and magic. I ponder aloud if I experienced more magic because I had set out the intention to do so.

'Maybe you were more open to the noticing of it,' Greg says.

In 2021, two years after our hike, Redwood Canyon was one of the areas burnt in the KNP Complex Fire. Lightning strikes ignited two major fires, which then combined. It took firefighters three months to contain the fire. It is estimated that between 1,330–2,380 large giant sequoias were killed or would die in the next three to five years,[19] and that in total in 2020–21, nearly 20 per cent of the world's giant sequoias were lost in wildfires.[20] I see the pictures of the devastation wrought by the fires and the blackened, charred remains – and remember the time we spent there and where we felt such peace. I wonder if the pine marten survived.

Fire has always been part of the story of the giant sequoias. Fire releases the seeds from the cones on the forest floor, having prepared the ground to provide the best possible conditions for growth. Ash returns nutrients to the soil and there is increased sunlight for young saplings as fire kills some of the surrounding trees. The native peoples of California managed the forests through prescribed burns, like the native peoples of Australia did. They knew that fire was needed to keep the ecosystem in balance. Without fire the growth in the understorey would build up, meaning that when lightning inevitably struck, the fire would burn more fiercely and for longer. However, when the settlers arrived, they attempted to control the landscape by suppressing fire, as well as moving native peoples from the areas where they had lived and which they had managed.

Although giant sequoia are highly fire-adapted, they are not adapted to extensive high severity fire, which is becoming more frequent. In several places that burnt in the KNP Complex Fire, it appears that previous prescribed fire work reduced fire severity.[21] This points to the crucial importance of forest treatments to reduce the risk of high severity fires.

When I speak to Dr Kristen Shive, it is in her role at the time as Director of Science at Save the Redwoods League. Here, a large part of Dr Kristen Shive's job was related to changing the story about the fire. It is because of fire she made the switch from anthropology to science. She tells me, 'I didn't know as a girl whether I could do science. So I studied anthropology. The summer after I graduated, I went to work as an intern in the visitor centre of Bandelier National Monument in New Mexico.'

Bandelier is an ancient site, with a human presence going back 11,000 years. I had visited and walked the narrow paths leading to the cave dwellings in the cliffs and seen the petroglyphs on the rock walls. I could understand why it would have been of interest to an anthropology graduate.

'I arrived a month after they had lost control of a prescribed burn in the forest. Because of the damage caused, the burn was controversial.'

The Cerro Grande Fire in 2000 burnt across 47,000 acres. In total, over 400 families lost their homes, including some members of the park staff with whom Kristen was working. The Los Alamos National Laboratory also suffered damage. Reports relate that a combination of the drought conditions and high winds led to the fire getting out of control. But if they hadn't proceeded with the burn, there was the risk that a lightning strike or human carelessness would have started a random fire, and the results could have been even more devastating.

In learning about the fire, Kristen became interested in how we can use our understanding of the forest to manage it better. She started to work on prescribed burn crews and firefighting crews, becoming immersed in the science of forest and fire. She went on to study for a master's degree in forestry, and then a PhD in Environmental Sciences at the University of Berkeley, specialising in fire ecology.

At Save the Redwoods League, a key part of her role was outreach and education. 'In California, there is no "no fire solution". The idea is not to prevent fires. We want to make the forests more resilient for when fires do happen.'

Kristen mentions a research project that is studying the effects of the interaction between fire injury, drought and beetles on the giant sequoia. It is the combination of all three that is proving fatal for the trees. The intensity of the fires is now severely damaging the trees, if not killing them. Many of them have already been weakened by drought. And this means that they are now vulnerable to the beetles, which bury inside the sequoias' bark.

Kristen tells me, 'The beetles were previously a nuisance; now we think that they may contribute to the death of these trees.' A few months later, the preliminary research report is published, showing the interconnection of these threats, and the danger they pose for the trees.

Dr Christy Brigham, chief of resource management and science for Sequoia and Kings Canyon National Parks says, 'It's unheard of. It's never happened before. You think giant sequoias don't die in fire, you think giant sequoias can't be killed by insects. That's not true any more.'[22]

John Muir wrote of the sequoias, 'Most of the Sierra trees die of disease, insects, fungi, etc, but nothing hurts the big tree. I never saw one that was sick or showed the slightest sign of decay. Barring accidents, it seems to be immortal.'[23]

The once unimaginable is becoming reality.

It occurs to me that there is a strong tendency for us to want to eradicate anything that may be potentially troubling in our lives, to suppress it, as with the approach that has been taken to managing fire. But when we do so, it comes back with the force of fire to strike us down. Seemingly healthy young people have heart attacks or are in a pre-heart-attack state because of the pressure of their jobs. Often we shy away from confronting aspects

Seed Nine: The forest of the imagination

of our lives because we are afraid of what we may find if we confront the wildness of our existence. But the body finds a way to make us listen if we refuse.

On our visit to the sequoias, we had queued to take our picture in front of General Sherman. Two years later, the pictures of General Sherman feature not tourists in the foreground, but firefighters, protecting the giant tree with a foil-resistant blanket to ward off the fire, flames filling the background of the picture.

I read a poem by Ellen Bass, 'Wrapping the Sequoias', written in response. The poem ends with the lines:

> 'I try to imagine
> one tree saved, alone, roots reaching out to touch
> nothing, a monarch without a realm, survivor
> who escapes a burning house
> while the bones of his family smoulder, embers
> flickering, alive through the winter.' [24]

This image of the lone survivor lodges in my mind, 'roots reaching out to touch/nothing'. These trees with their vast interconnected root systems, these root systems which have held them upright and together for so many years, can no longer resist the changes that are happening.

It is this image, more than the science, which stays with me. It appeals to the imagination. It calls to me to identify with this tree, to relate to it, in a way that science cannot. This is why we need poetry, metaphor, the imagination, as much as science as we seek to respond to climate change. Science provides the 'what', the description of what is happening. Poetry can unlock the 'why' of our response. It is the agent of action where science is the instrument.

★

What is the future? The future is the result of the actions of the present. What is the present? The present is the result of the actions of the past. So what matters is what we do now, in this present. This will determine the future.

After I return from the giant sequoias, I dream about two children dying. I feel the grief of this loss. It is not clear in the dream if they are my children, but they are related to me. And then the children turn into animals, a racoon and another similar creature. They have been let out and they come running towards me, ignoring the other people that are with me. I stroke and pet them for a while and then they run off into the city.

Perhaps the other animal along with the racoon was the pine marten I saw among the redwoods. That feels right to me. The dream is clearly saying to me that although I feel grief for not having had children, I can have a connection with animals. And the fact that the animals run into the city shows me that nature can exist there too, if only I look.

I first came across the work of the Animas Valley Institute through Bill Plotkin's book *Soulcraft*. In a follow-up book, he describes the concept of 'deep imagination' as 'the images, symbols, dreams, visions and revelations that we do not command or control but that arise unbidden and possess the immediate ring of truth... Our deep imagination not only shows us what might be but also illuminates what already is.' [25]

On the first 'Deep Imagination' course I had taken, in the Joshua Tree desert in southern California in 2018, I had an experience which showed me the interconnectedness of life, and I declared that I wanted to live in a way that honoured the land. But I was still left with the question of what this looked like in practice. When I saw that there was a follow-up facilitation training course for

Seed Nine: The forest of the imagination

'Deep Imagination', scheduled to coincide with when I was going to be in California to visit the redwoods, I knew I had to go.

It's a dramatic change in scenery from the grandeur of the giant sequoia forests to the sandy, rocky desert of this section of Joshua Tree National Park. There are none of the eponymous Joshua trees here – they are in the northern part of the park. Leafy cottonwood trees provide welcome shade in the dry creeks where they grow. I am taking part in an exercise where one of the other participants in the course, bell selkie, is guiding me on a journey into my imagination, as I lie on the sand of the desert floor. In my journey, I start with the image of a dragonfly. The dragonfly leads me to a pond, and then to a river. And then the river becomes the stream that ran through the Redwood Canyon. I describe out loud the quality of the light on the water and the beauty of the place. I am completely transported into that place and overwhelmed by emotion. I feel a deep joy at the beauty of the place and then an overwhelming sense of needing to hold that space and protect it from threatening forces. My arms reach straight up into the air as if I am trying to hold back invading forces from overwhelming this space, as if I am forming the walls of a protective canyon. My body starts to physically convulse and tremble with the effort of holding back these forces. The pine marten appears and this intensifies the grief at the threat that the trees face. I have the sense of the pine marten looking at me and asking me to take action. In the midst of the grief, I deeply feel that the beauty of the place gives me the strength to hold back those that would seek to destroy it.

During my imagined journey, I hear wings beating fast beside my head and I wonder what is there. Bell selkie tells me that a hummingbird came and hovered right next to me. Afterwards, I hear the knocking of a woodpecker. The appearance of these two birds who have been with me on my journey, from the woodpecker's knocking in Menla to the hummingbird in Brazil, seems like a blessing for which I am deeply grateful.

Again, I wonder, what is the role that I have to play in protecting the redwoods from destructive forces. It is not humans and their saws they need defending against. It is the effects of man-made climate change which puts them at risk of destruction from fire, drought and now beetles.

It was my imagination that took me on a powerful journey to connect again with the redwoods, after I had had the privilege of seeing them in real life. I can share the beauty of the redwoods through my writing, but now I feel that perhaps I have another role to play as well – to help people reconnect with their imaginations so they can imagine what they can do in their own lives, families, workplaces, communities and societies.

I have seen how children look with wonder at the trees, focus on the intricate swirl of petals of a flower and conjure imaginary worlds that are as real as the world they see around them. I imagine drawing maps of fairy kingdoms with Fiona Grace, when she is older. Children have an innate connection to the world around them, and to those worlds we cannot see. When do we lose this connection? Perhaps our awe and curiosity are shut down by adults. Instead, adults should respond to the child's excitement about what they are seeing with the same level of vibration. To validate what the child is seeing and feeling, and encourage this response to grow, rather than squash it.

I think of the message I would want to pass to on to Fiona Grace. It would be:

Don't look at the trees through my eyes. Look at the trees through your own eyes and respond to them with your own imagination.

Seed Nine: The forest of the imagination

And maybe it won't be trees that spark your imagination, maybe it will be birds or ants or lizards or lilies or coral reefs or crickets or dolphins or grasses. But perhaps that is my greatest wish for you — that you will continue to look at the world with wonder and love and amazement as you grow older, even in the face of grief for what has been lost and what is continuing to be destroyed. And then act from this place of your heart.

The only war that matters is the one for the imagination.

Seed Ten: The art of being in place

Beech, UK

> 'Strength comes, healing comes, from aligning yourself with the grain of your place and answering to its needs.'
>
> Scott Russell Sanders[1]

> 'If we can learn to listen to the land, we can learn to listen to each other. This is the beginning of ceremony.'
>
> Terry Tempest Williams

The baobab, the inspiration for my journey, was going to be my last tree. But none of us had planned for the pandemic and lockdowns.

I was sitting in my friend's light-filled kitchen in London.

'I feel like I need to stop somewhere. Rest. Recuperate. Write. But where to do that?' I had visited nine trees and needed somewhere to base myself while I organised my trip to the baobabs.

I was back to the question of 'Where?'

But then what?

From a practical point of view, it was easier for me to stay in England, rather than go back to the United States. I had more contacts so I could pick up work and replenish my bank account. But it was expensive to find a short-term let in London and I had a sense that this was the perfect opportunity to try living somewhere outside London. But where?

The town of Lewes popped into my head. I had been walking there a few times. It is a small market town in the south-east of England, just over an hour from London on the train, seven miles from the coast and right on the edge of the South Downs National Park. There is easy access to nature, and it is known for its artists and writers, so perhaps I would find a community. I also knew that there were active sustainability groups – they had even created their own currency, the Lewes Pound, to encourage people to spend money with local retailers. I looked on a property website for six-month furnished lets. I spotted one that was the right size and looked like somewhere I could live.

I took the train there to look at the house. It was a two-up, two-down terraced cottage, with wooden floors and agricultural implements – part of a plough, a wooden rake, a pitchfork – hanging from the walls. From the main bedroom window, you could see one of the towers of Lewes Castle, still standing strong from when it was completed in 1070, just a few years after the arrival of William the Conqueror from Normandy. There was a true cottage garden, with a climbing rose, sprawling lavender, spiky rosemary and a small wildlife pond.

I said yes to it. It was one of those decisions that I did not have to make, like the one to set out on my journey to the trees. The decision had already been made for me, and I just had to give my consent.

I moved into my new house, with my rucksack and a suitcase. 'It's just for a few months,' I told myself. I would write, I would visit the baobab tree. And I would see what would happen.

I enjoyed learning the ways and rhythms of a new place but over the winter I started to struggle. I suspected I was starting to become depressed. I wondered why I was here and not in New York or San Francisco or a warmer country. The familiar pattern was re-emerging – my desire to be somewhere else rather than the place where I was. And yet, in the words of Thoreau, as he wrote in his journal, 'The man who is often thinking that it is better to be somewhere else than where he is excommunicates himself.'[2] I was cutting myself off from place through my thinking.

I travelled to Finland for Christmas, spending it at my mother's house, along with my brother, his wife and Fiona Grace. She was crawling now, exploring all the time, spreading her smiles, wearing a red Christmas hat headband. I wondered about moving to Finland, to be part of this family life. I could get residency through my mother's citizenship. But on my return, I don't move forward with the process. Somehow, I think there is less chance of meeting a partner in Finland. Plus, there are the long dark winters. I make a choice not to be with family.

'Relax.' Gordon Hempton's advice on listening from my time in Ecuador came to mind as I was walking home one February Saturday afternoon. I was at the top of a hill, the road sloping away in front of me, rising up again on the other side. The far side was lined with terraced houses and punctuated with old-fashioned lampposts, the lanterns coming from Victorian central casting.

In order to listen to a place, you have to relax, including those tiny muscles in your ears. Following this logic, it is not possible to connect with a place unless you are relaxed. I hadn't thought about it like this before. Relaxing allows you to be open, otherwise the tension in your mind and body will act as a barrier. It strikes me that this is why I had felt so deeply the insight in France that 'Joy calls me home.' Floating in the warm sea, I was deeply and utterly relaxed.

Five years ago, I had opened up a new document on my computer, with the title 'The Art of Being in Place'. I'd written a few lines and then abandoned it. Now I was wondering, is the secret simply to relax? If I am open to the place, I am more likely to be connected to it. If I am relaxed, I am more likely to be present. If I am not lost in my thoughts, I am actually here and more likely to appreciate what is in front of me, and therefore want to be here.

The news began to talk of little else except the coronavirus. Despite the government not telling us to stay at home yet, I was already adjusting my behaviour, avoiding crowded places. It was slowly dawning on me that I was going to be staying here longer than six months. Perhaps this was the universe teaching me, teaching us all, 'The Art of Being in Place'.

Two days before the first lockdown began, I went for a run. My route took me through a wood. I stopped in a clearing by a majestic, grey-green, smooth-skinned old tree, freckled with lichen. Some impulse made me take a picture of my shadow, its length falling away in front of me, over the edges of the roots of the tree. When I arrived back home and looked at the picture, I noticed there were two shadows arcing around me. It looked as if I was about to step through a portal or across a threshold. I wondered at how I had thought to take this picture, when I hadn't consciously registered the portal qualities in it. But some part of me – or maybe something outside – had guided me to do so.

The next day, I went back to the tree again. An older gentleman, who was walking his dog and who I had passed at the gate entering the woodland, caught up with me.

'It's a beautiful tree, isn't it?' he said.

'It really is,' I agreed.

'When it rains, water gathers in the bowls of the roots, and the dogs stop here to drink.'

Seed Ten: The art of being in place

'A natural drinking fountain,' I said. 'Do you know what type of tree it is?'

'A beech tree, I think.'

'Oh, of course, the beech nuts.' Looking down now, I could see them on the ground, their spiky shapes merging with the brown of the earth.

The first day of lockdown, it was the morning of the new moon. The dark moon. I went for my morning run, making the most of my allowance of one form of exercise a day. I stopped by the beech tree. I put my hand on her trunk. I felt her strength. *'You are strong,'* I heard the tree whisper to me. I rested my cheek on the coolness of the bark. I needed this touch. I looked down at the roots, thick and strong, mossy in places, reaching into this earth, connecting with the other trees.

I had found my tree. This tree had called me to venture along this path when I needed it.

Back at home, I received an email to say that the work project that I had been counting on to sustain me for the next month had been pulled. I felt fear rise in my heart. I went to sit in the sunshine in the garden, to watch the bees, take in the bright blueness of the forget-me-nots.

I thought back to the beech tree. *You are strong.* I looked up the symbolism of the beech tree. The first reference I found said, 'Beech can signify the end or death of something, but also stand for the changes that arise through realisation... Beech suggests you should cross the threshold that is challenging you, gain experience from the unknown, seek revelation and increase your knowledge.'[3]

I had come across the beech tree, which stood for crossing thresholds, just at the time when we were crossing into the unknown of the deepening of the pandemic and the aloneness of lockdown. What you need will come to you when you most need it.

I let out a prayer of thanks to the trees. 'Thank you, trees, for looking out for me and being here for me always. May I be here for you too.'

I wanted to know more. I googled books about beech trees. The one that stood out was called *Casting Deep Shade* by C D Wright. I nearly fell off my chair. I had bought this book, after having seen it recommended in a bookshop by Richard Powers, the author of *The Overstory*. It was in a stack of books beside my bed, waiting to be read. I picked it up and opened it at random. The first sentence I saw was 'The beech is a witness tree.'

I had been thinking the day before that maybe I would have to let the baobabs go. Who knew when I would be able to travel to Africa? Close one door, and a portal opens.

I visit the beech tree a few times a week, on my walks and on runs. Sometimes I stop and sit on the fallen trunk of a tree, opposite the beech, just to be in her presence, to feel her strength, to listen to what she might have to say. When people pass by, sometimes I feel guilty that I am just sitting here, not exercising, in contravention of government guidelines. But I live alone. The tree is my support. How did I once not know her name? It is a feeling that Helen Thomas, wife of Edward Thomas, the poet, wrote about: 'It seems strange now that there was ever a time when I could not recognise the beech's fine-textured skin like bark, and the set of the trunk and branches like human limbs, and the beautiful curve that the leafy branches make, like a hand opened for giving.'[4]

It would take the arms of three, maybe four, people to hug around you. To wrap around your smooth bark, crinkled in places, with a veneer of mossy green and patches of white lichen.

You are tall enough that your branch tips wave gently in the wind that passes over the top of the woods. Your branches are

Seed Ten: The art of being in place

dream-time bare. Just one brown leaf hangs by a thread, not wanting to let go and make its way back to the earth.

Your roots spill out over the soil, stake your claim to being here. They do not burrow so deep into this land of chalk, but wide. The folds provide drinking bowls for thirsty animals when it has rained, and crevasses for woodland folk to shelter in. Your roots sweep around you like a skirt on the woodland dance floor, keeping a clear space. You are the queen of the forest, after all.

Your trunk splits into two, with a third smaller division. A family, I think. Your body is tuned to the vibrations of birdsong, and picks up the passing of feet, their tempo and weight, their hurriedness or their attention. In this season without leaves, your wind song remains silent. You listen to the evening choir of birds. I wonder how the cry of lambs for the comfort of their mothers reverberates inside you. Do you notice the noise of the cars from the road at the end of the track? Do you hear more quiet now in these days?

I look to the swelling-bellied moon which you hold beyond your branches. You are a participant in this closing ceremony for the day. The dissolving of what has passed, and the rising of what is to come. In three minutes, the sun will set. I look to the west and the yellow-orange sky, the sun already sunk behind the chalk hill. The birds release their final song, crisp in the cooling air. The crows are cawing their way home. I wonder how many sunsets and sunrises you have seen, you the witness tree. Seventy-five thousand perhaps? Is there one particular sunrise imprinted in your rings?

A teenage boy, his sister and his mother pass you by. The boy trips on your root. He utters an *'Ow!'* They carry on. You stand at a crossroads on the crest of a hill, paths branching in four directions. I wonder what you will dream tonight. I feel the cold rising from the land. I imagine you spinning on the dance floor, under the moon. Maybe the stars are your dancing partners. Or the moon herself. As we all spin through this life. Across the twilight, there is final flurry of birds, as fast as bats. Dream well, dance well.

Another day. I sit by the tree again and write.

To do

Look at the topmost tips of the branches.
Pale pink against this spring blue sky.
Observe the buds, candles reaching to the light
while the branches below remain bare.

Crane my head backwards,
see filigree of twigs as finely branched
as lungs. Feel in my body the warmth
of the spotlights of sun upon your trunk.

Absorb through my feet like roots
the call and response of the lambs
and mother sheep. Breathe in the oxygen
you have given back to the air.

Wonder at the new green of the leaves
encircling you, glittering like offerings,
as you bide your time, knowing there is no rush.
There is enough sunlight to feed us all.

And there is grace in waiting.

Now we have the time and seek to fill it.
But what if we sought to empty it?
To empty it as empty it will go.

Seed Ten: The art of being in place

> To leave the branches bare.
> Not rush to fill them up again.
> I ask this of the one tree in the woods
> not yet in spring leaf,
> the queen, the beech.

It is three weeks into lockdown. On my walk to the tree, I am thinking about holding space. The beech holds off on releasing its leaves into the world in the spring, which gives the other trees around it a chance to have light. The beech tree was often a site for ceremonies because it had a clear space around it, its dense shade canopy denying sunlight to the undergrowth. It makes me think this is why the beech tree is associated with thresholds, as ceremonies create a liminal space. I remember Randy saying in the Amazon that indigenous people are practical. It makes sense that the beech tree was a place for holding ceremonies because the clear ground around the tree literally provides a space to do so.

I arrive at the glade. It is the most cathedral-like I have seen it. The light slants through the branches as if through arched windows and the young leaves on surrounding trees glow like stained glass. I am carrying a bottle of water. It is water that has been blessed in an online ceremony I attended before setting out on my walk, blessed so it may bring healing to us and the Earth. Ceremony is taking a different form these days as we live much of our lives online. But still, I can make this connection. I walk around the beech tree and sprinkle the water in a circle, leaving a broken trail of damp earth. I offer the water to the roots of the tree so she may continue to bring us healing. Holy water.

And now, today, suddenly, I see for the first time the buds of leaves on the lower branches. It sparks joy in me, that the beech tree is ready, that it is joining the spring party. Looking up, I see the first small green leaves, right at the tip of one of the lower branches, but probably still at least ten metres above the ground. I count the leaves. Seven. Glowing in the late afternoon light. I am happy that I will see the tree filling with leaves over time. I stand under the budding branches to take a closer look. The leaf buds are maybe two or three centimetres long already, pointed as candles, slanted out and upwards. A bud candelabra.

'We live in one big ceremony.' I am gifted these words by Mac Macartney, the founder of Embercombe, a place of nature connection, one evening, in an online session. I set out on my daily walk. I leave my headphones at home. I think about how upset I was at the lack of ceremony before my overnight solo in the Ecuadorian Amazon. As I walk, I realise why I was wrong to see it as an absence. Because everything is ceremony. Like everything is sacred. Why would you make a distinction?

Back home in the kitchen, prepping my dinner, I remember when I had made a vow in the Joshua Tree desert, that I wanted to live in a way that honoured the land. Only I did not really know how to do this.

But if I live life as a ceremony, then I will be honouring the land through my daily actions. It is as simple and beautiful as that.

Mac had also spoken about how ceremony is belonging. Through ceremony we belong. How I make and eat my dinner can be ceremony and can connect me to the world around me – even as we sit in our separate bubbles.

I sit in the garden and listen to the spring awakening of the birds.

The voice of the blackbird rises and falls, clear-throated, sure. Do birds have chakras, I wonder? If birds represented chakras, then the blackbird would represent the throat chakra.

Seed Ten: The art of being in place

I listen to the seagulls and wonder, if I did not know, would it be obvious that they belonged to the sea. I listen to their voice and hear how it is suited to surf and rise above the roar of the ocean waves, high-pitched enough to carry, but not so high that it is lost.

The wood pigeons. A low, reassuring note, a warm grey, at home in a dappled glade of light and shade. A vibration for trees to grow to, slow and steady. There is no hurry here. Resonating in the root chakra. A hug of a call.

Still the busyness of the sparrows, the crescendos they create rising and falling, a flock of sound.

The starlings whistle, sending their voices shooting up and down the scale. Bird on a wire.

That evening, I walk through the fields. I notice the yellow tubular bells of the cowslips, nodding in the breeze. It seems as if the earth itself is singing, there is a song rising from the grass. Yet it is the song of the skylark, unseen on its wing. Trilling the thrill of the thrill of the world.

Each of the birds has its own unique voice, its song, its place in the world. Their song expresses their belonging to place.

I walk to the woods again and sit among the trees. What can one place teach us?

It can teach us to learn to look at one piece of ground and all the life that is within this one space.

To see:

The root of the beech tree breaching the soil, like the back of a whale.

A piece of chalk. The coccoliths of plankton from millions of years ago, when this land was under a warm sea.

A scrap of blue-green lichen, intricate in its warp and weft, fallen from a tree branch, on to a bed of moss, another micro world.

The tufts of the moss.
Last year's beech nuts becoming food for the soil.
A small grey woodlouse navigating this terrain.
Pieces of twig, slowly, slowly breaking down back into this earth.

The days have rolled into summer. Life seems to be bursting out of every inch of soil. I look with eyes that now see magic all around me.

What makes a place magical? What do we mean by magic?
It is the play of light and shadow.
The birdsong, the trees, the ivy creeping over the ground.
I don't need to go to the Amazon, to take plant medicine.
The plant medicine is here, in the way that the light illuminates the leaf.
And now, a small brown bird lands in front of me.
She has a white feather in her beak. She flies to a tree behind me, and then to the right of me.
Encircling me.
She returns to her starting place. She dances, hopping in place, aware of me.
I wonder why she doesn't take the feather to her nest.
And there make a home.
And then I realise I am asking the question of myself.

It is early autumn. I change up my morning routine. I decide I need to get out of the house before I begin the day's work. I need to connect to the world around me.

It has rained heavily the night before. The air still has some warmth to it. I stop to look at the hawthorn berries, red-polished to gleaming, with spheres of water hanging underneath, not quite ready yet to make the drop to earth. The trunks of the trees are

Seed Ten: The art of being in place

criss-crossed with the glide paths of water. The greens of the lichen are heightened and illuminated. A snail is crawling up the tree, already above my head. I pick a waterlogged blackberry, crunch its sweetness and its seeds.

The world is made anew each morning. I have asked before the question of how I can be of service. These brief moments of connection this morning lead me to think, 'What am I in service to?' I am in service to the perfect redness of the hawthorn berry and its attendant pendant jewel. I am in service to this snail, making its slow, deliberate way. I am in service to these rings of lichen, to this bramble thicket and this blackberry that I pick and eat.

I promised to live in a way that honours the land. To live in a way that honours the land requires being in service to the land.

It changes everything to think about my day from the perspective of how I can serve the hawthorn berry, the snail, the bramble. It is not even a question of how I can use my skills to be in service. It is a question of who I am. I am a being who is in service to the hawthorn, the snail, the lichen, the bramble.

On this rain-washed morning, this is a revelation to me. If I was indigenous to the land, it would not have to be. I would have been brought up knowing that these trees and other beings were my tribe and that I had a responsibility to them.

There are layers and layers to pick through, to unlearn. All I can do is to keep on learning, learn from each of these beings. Each of these are in service to each other. The snail will climb into the tree and become food for the birds. The hawthorn berry will become food for the birds and its seed will be passed on. We are all part of a chain of service. Interconnected interbeings.

I've woken early because of the wind. I am tired now. Not just because of a sleepless night, but by the ongoing buffeting of the pandemic, the politics, the changing restrictions, the uncertainty of when this will ever end. The isolation and loneliness is becoming harder.

In some ways, I was well prepared for the isolation. I was used to living on my own. Now, with what I had learnt from my journey, I had extra resources to draw on. I knew that the trees were part of my bubble. I was physically safe. I could speak to my mother, and my brother's family. I could see Fiona Grace growing into a toddler on video clips my brother shared with me. I see her in my mother's garden, picking redcurrants from the bushes as I had once done, and then running into the arms of her mother, my mother standing there too, delighted. I have a deep pang of longing, for my own child, and also just to be with my family, to experience these everyday joys.

Humans are not meant to live alone. Like trees are not designed to grow alone. The trees thrive through connection. And we are social animals, we need to be part of a wood or a forest. Research has revealed that showing people pictures of social activities after they have been in isolation lights up areas in the mid-brain similar to when people are shown pictures of food after they have fasted.[5] Loneliness is a hunger for connection.

I have cried today and, when the tears are not falling, I feel that they are not far from the surface. The clouds of tears have gathered. A wind is moving them along till they reach a hill and fall. Maybe these tears will be nourishment for growth, all part of the water cycle. My heart is as waterlogged as the earth. The rain from the sky stops in the afternoon. There is blue sky. I head out for a walk. I try not to focus on my tiredness. I ask myself, 'What is right now?' I am walking. The sky is blue. There are acorns on the ground. I go to my beech tree.

★

Seed Ten: The art of being in place

In high winds, we need to have strong foundations. Yet the beech trees have shallow roots. When they are toppled by the wind, they make way for the next generation of trees. And the downed tree becomes nourishment for the soil and the saplings, along with providing a home for insects and fungi. These fallen trees are called 'nurse' trees and are a vital part of the woodland ecosystem.

The beech tree is known as the mother of the woods. Her usual lifespan is 300 years, although she can live to 500. It seems to me that there is a mother's generosity in giving her body back to the woods in this way.

Sitting under the beech tree, I consider I'm lucky to live near her. The beech tree is only considered native to the south-east of England. Yet the Royal Horticultural Society is now advising that planting them in southern and eastern England is 'not a wise choice'[6] because of the increased risk of drought, which beeches find hard to tolerate because of their shallow roots. On the plus side, Scotland and other northern and western regions could become better suited to the trees. Climate change is affecting where we can all live.

To stay in one place requires discipline. In the time of the coronavirus crisis, we are told to exercise discipline and shelter in place. The discipline to stay in place is provided by the authority of the government. We are to be punished if we stray. The etymology of discipline leads back to the Middle English 'penitential chastisement, punishment for the sake of correction'. No wonder we shy away from discipline when there are these authoritarian connotations lurking in the background. But if you dig back deeper, the original root of the word is the Latin *discere*, meaning 'to learn'. *Discere* is the root of 'disciple'. 'Discipline' can also mean a field of study. In thinking about the discipline required to stay in place, maybe it is more helpful to think about it as a place of learning. How can we be a disciple to place?

Writers including Robin Wall Kimmerer and Scott Russell Sanders have written about how the United States of America, as a nation of immigrants, is a restless nation, and how restlessness is a quality that is prized. I think of the stories that are told in my family of our history, and how the focus of these stories is on movement. My great-great-grandmother left Dorset, in the UK, to make her way to America, and other members of the family made the voyage across the Atlantic from Ireland. Once they were there, they continued on across the continent, from east coast to west coast. There are stories of strong women, who set out from New York to travel to California, travelling by boat to Panama, crossing the isthmus on foot, and then taking the boat to San Francisco to join their husbands, and to live in houses made of the giant redwood trees. My father was born in the Philippines, where his father was working, and he lived in countless places, including England, where I was born, and France, where he passed away.

Of course, that is only half the story. My DNA test reveals that I am 50 per cent Finnish. My Finnish forefathers and mothers stayed in place, in the land of trees and lakes. But my mother did have the restless gene.

These are the stories that I have grown up with, of people striking out to make a new life in a new place, often repeatedly. They are not stories of people making a life in one place – and if there are those stories, they are stories mentioned in passing, perhaps because they are seen as lacking in adventure. I certainly saw them as such.

I remember telling my father when I left university that I wanted to go travelling, to live in another country. He offered me the example of George Mackay Brown, a writer, who lived on the same Hebridean island all his life. I puzzled at this, given that my father's life was the polar opposite of this. Still, I decided to stay in England – and then chafed against this decision for the next 20 years or so, while never putting down roots, wanting to be somewhere else.

Reading Ursula K Le Guin's essay, 'The Carrier Bag Theory of Fiction', goes some way to explaining why these stories of adventure, of the lone hero striking out on a quest, are the ones that have dominance in our society, rather than the story of those who stayed by the fire and told stories of the wild oats. Her theory is that in the time when the men went out to hunt mammoths and the women stayed behind, it was the men who returned with stories of derring-do, and it was these stories that were shared around the fire in the evening, rather than the accounts of the women collecting the wild oats. If we translate this to a larger scale, of stories of place, it is the stories of our ancestors who went out to discover new lands that are the ones that we are drawn to, rather than those who stayed in one place.

It is now nearly a year since the first lockdown began. I look back at the words I wrote then. I wonder at how connected I felt. I don't feel that now. I am chafing again, to travel, to move beyond the confines I walk in.

I think back to the invitation of Martin Shaw, the storyteller, to get to know the life within a five-kilometre radius of where you live.

There is so much life here. There are new discoveries to see. The other day, I stood and watched five peregrine falcons flying above the disused quarry where they have made their nest. I knew they nested here but had only seen one or two at a distance. Now, they were flying close, the yellow of their feet clearly visible as they swooped by.

And yet, there is the old familiar tension. I want to pack my bags and go somewhere new. At the same time, I want to put down roots. To buy a house. To tend a garden. To be part of a community.

What have the trees taught me? That my place is in community. The trees are interconnected with their roots, they support each other. Trees are the masters of being in place. It is time for me to take my place in that community of beings. I know that.

I want to share my life with someone else, a partner. But maybe the only way I am going to find a partner is to put down roots.

There is no simple answer. There is no moment of absolute revelation, at least not for me.

During the first lockdown, I wrote a series of letters, addressed to 'Dear Solitude'. I wanted to make friends with solitude. Now I write a letter, 'Dear Community.'

Dear Community

I walk through the town. I see people with each other. I see people laughing together. How do I become part of a community? I think I missed out on these skills somewhere along the way.

I hear community whisper back: you become part of community by giving to it.

What can I give? I can give my praise and my love.

But it has to be more than that. It has to be by the labour of my hands as well as my heart.

I think back to the start of the journey. I wanted to begin by getting my hands dirty. The ending is mirrored in the beginning. How can I get my hands dirty?

I have been walking this land. This is now the calling of spring. To get my hands dirty.

Perhaps the restlessness I feel is actually a call to dig deeper, rather than to move on.

Seed Ten: The art of being in place

Feel the feelings and drop the story. It's a mantra I have written on the whiteboard on my fridge. I am so used to interpreting the story in one way, that restlessness means time to move on. But maybe there is another interpretation of the story, that it means time to drop deeper.

We engage with the world through the asking of questions. In sharing stories of the Pomo and Coast Miwok people of present-day Marin County in California, Greg Sarris tells of the twin sisters, Question Woman and Answer Woman, Coyote's daughters. 'Answer Woman knows all of the answers but she cannot think of them unless she is asked. Question Woman, on the other hand, cannot remember a single answer, not one story, and she must always ask her question in order to hear the answer again.'[7]

I am like Question Woman. I am continually forgetting the answers, and must ask the questions again and again to Answer Woman. I see the land and the trees as Answer Woman. They are waiting to share their answers, if only we will ask the questions and then listen.

I return to the question, 'What is the art of being in place?' Suddenly, after years of holding the question, I see the answer. The answer is in the question. The answer is art. To live as if life itself is art.

I listen to a meditation one morning. The teacher shares a quote from Hafiz: 'I am a hole in a flute that the Christ's breath moves through... listen to this music.' I replace 'Christ' with 'spirit'. This is the invitation. To see ourselves as the hole in a flute that the breath moves through. This is one of the lessons of my journey. To unblock that which is stopping the breath move me, which is stopping the music.

★

I think back to that day beside the pond at Menla. How the flute-player let the music move through him. How he answered the woodpecker's call with his music.

The breath of the world moves through the trees. The trees draw down the carbon dioxide we breathe out, and share oxygen, that we fill our lungs with and make music with. This is the song, the give and take, which is now out of balance.

In the same way that the tree offers its leaves to the sun, and through the alchemy of photosynthesis transforms light and air into matter, this is what we can do: transform light and energy into matter, whether words, music, touch, a carved piece of wood or a smile. These become offerings into the world, the oxygen that helps to sustain us and others.

I set out on my journey with the question, 'What is my place in the world, in this time of crisis and change, when the baobab trees are dying?'

The first place I need to belong to is myself. A place where joy calls me home, where I am rooted in and accepting of myself. Accepting means taking down the walls I have put up. To let go. Then I am open to belong, and to take my place in community. Open to receive the support of the earth, and to contribute consciously as part of an interconnected web.

How we choose to listen to the trees shows us who we are. Whether we are a photographer, musician or farmer. A soul-whisperer or scientist. Yet these are all outward expressions of who we are. Maybe what the trees truly reveal is who we are beyond these external facing roles. Who we are when only the trees are looking, and speaking to us, as we listen to them.

★

Seed Ten: The art of being in place

I read in scientist Suzanne Simard's book, *Finding the Mother Tree*: 'When Mother Trees – the majestic hubs at the centre of forest communication, protection and sentience – die, they pass their wisdom to their kin, generation after generation, sharing the knowledge of what helps and what harms, who is friend or foe, and how to adapt and survive in an ever-changing landscape. It's what all parents do.'

I still feel the loss that I do not have children to whom I can pass on any wisdom that I might have. Yet, perhaps, instead it is through community that I can share my knowledge, as I transition to becoming an elder. I need to live from a place of acceptance. This does not diminish the loss I feel, which will be there, as friends talk about their children and, in time, their grandchildren. Yet the trees had called me on a journey to open up my life in a different direction, and I needed to continue to honour that calling.

I am looking through a stack of old notebooks. They are medium-sized Moleskine notebooks, a mix of black, red and beige, with the date written on white stickers. I pick up one, labelled 'April 2009'. Turning to the first page and what I have written there, I am stunned:

Muse = Tree Goddess

I imagine my muse. I call my muse towards me. I shut my eyes. I have an image of a tree. I draw the tree towards me. It is the tree goddess, the spirit of the tree. Why have I called a tree to be my muse? I stand in the shade of the tree, and I absorb its coolness, its energy which it freely gives to me. I think back to the beginnings of the tree, when it was an acorn perhaps, and it was full of heat, and it was starting off on its own journey. No one could have known looking at that sapling what height it would grow to. In the beginning it needed the protection of others, and needed to escape being trampled or eaten. But it believed in what it could be and continued to grow and grow — until one day it could be a shelter for others, it could be a home for others, and it could generate new trees of its own. That is why the tree goddess is my muse. The tree that stands tall, powerful, but gentle. Each morning, before beginning my writing, I will invite my muse, the tree goddess.

I have no memory of writing these words. Yet, ten years before I began my journey to the trees, I had called the tree goddess into my life. An acorn had been planted then. The tree goddess had been an invisible guiding force towards and throughout my journey. 'It believed in what it could be and continued to grow and grow.' Reading this, it felt as if the tree goddess had believed in me. She had believed I did have the strength to make this journey, to continue to grow and grow.

I return again to the beech tree. I thank the tree goddess. For staying with me, even when I had forgotten her. For calling me on the journey. For being with me. For inviting me to step over the threshold of home and into place, through this beech tree. I now realise that when I stepped through the threshold, I was stepping into a liminal space. The word 'liminal' comes from the Latin for 'threshold', *limen*. The time of lockdown and its accompanying isolation was a space that was out of time. The trees had granted me a moment of transformation in calling me on the journey, inviting me into learning a different way of relating to the world. My journey of travelling to the trees had ended but I would continue to grow and grow, and grow my relationship with the trees.

★

That night, I have a dream that I am being talked through a process of rebirth. I am in a narrow, confined space, and I am moving forward very slowly, inching my way through. Suddenly, I am catapulted, ejected into the light. But there is no ground beneath me, I am hanging over the side of a cliff. Hands reach out to catch me. I try to find footholds for my feet in the side of the cliff. I am full of the energy of this rebirth. I wonder what would happen if I just let go.

I am sitting at my desk. It is the day after the easing of lockdown. It is the day after the full moon. A text comes through on my phone. It is from my ex. 'Hi. I received the last divorce papers. How are you doing in these mad times?' The last message I have from him is from five years ago, when I arrived in the United States. I feel tears come into my eyes. But they do not fall. I cannot say that there is closure. But there is an ending. And in the ending, there is a beginning.

The washing machine is beeping the end of its cycle. I go outside to hang the wet clothes on the line, for the first time this year. It is going to be a warm spring day. The birds are singing. I watch a blackbird fly from one tree to another. I am going today to look at a house to buy. This land is singing to me. And I am now ready to listen.

Epilogue

I visit a birch tree near my house. It's a young birch tree, growing on the edge of a former quarry, in a thicket of trees. There's a view out across to the river valley below.

I sit on the grass, and feel the springy moss under my hands, and a cool bright May breeze on my face. The birch tree is where I began my journey in Finland. She is also the tree of endings.

Dear birch tree teacher, what can you tell me about beginnings and endings?

They are all one. There is no distinction between them, except in language.

Dear birch tree teacher, how I can honour what we call beginnings and endings?

Dear one. Place your hand on your heart. Feel your heartbeat. Feel this present moment.

Dear birch tree teacher, how can I move on from this present moment?

Dear one, move on in this present moment.

Dear birch tree teacher, how can I thank you?

I give freely, so you can do the same.

Practices

These practices are designed to help you explore for yourself the themes of each of the chapters, through writing, connecting, listening, walking and reading. Listening is used here in the broadest sense of connecting to the tree with all our senses. Work through them at your own pace or pick the ones that speak to you most. You could also explore them with a group.

Practice one: Know your roots

Writing

- Write about your roots in the natural world – how did you experience nature when you were growing up? How has your relationship with nature evolved over time?

Connecting

- Speak to older members of your family or your community about their experiences of nature and place. Where did they grow up? Do they have a favourite tree or plant? What changes have they noticed over time? You could also seek out (or reread) a classic epic piece of literature or mythology from your heritage or the place where you live. (In my case, I read the *Kalevala,* a Finnish epic.) How does nature feature?

Listening

- Find a birch tree or another tree that speaks to you of new beginnings. Sit with the tree and ask it for guidance for new beginnings – whether beginning or continuing your exploration of connection to nature, the beginning of a new day or at the time of a new moon. What does it tell you? If you hear nothing, don't worry, it is all a practice. Write down your experience.

Walking

- The purpose of the walk is to reflect on the paths you have chosen to follow in life. Go for a walk which takes in different types of spaces and terrains, for example pavements, open space, woodland etc. As you walk through each type of space, how does it feel to walk that path? Reflect on how the different types of path might relate to the path or paths you have chosen in life, what type of path you might want to choose now and how you want to walk that path.

Practice two: Selfless service

Writing

- Journal on what the concept of service means to you. How can you be of service to the trees and other-than-human beings, as well as to humans?

Connecting

- Get your hands dirty – plant a seed, water, nurture it, learn to listen to what it needs.
- Volunteer for the trees. Find out where you can plant trees and look after them, or take care of a community garden. See how one action leads to another.

Listening

- Find a tree near to you that you can visit on a daily basis for a week. Commit to spending ten minutes a day with the tree and seeing what arises. Jot down any thoughts that come to mind at the end of the practice. At the end of the week, reflect on what you have learnt from spending time with the tree.

Walking
- Go for a walk. Take a moment at the beginning to ask for guidance, 'How can I be of service?' Then let go of this question and see what comes to you. Use all of your senses to tune into the environment – sounds, what you can touch, any plants you can safely taste, what you can see, what you can smell. Note these as they arise, along with any thoughts and feelings. At the end of the walk, take a few minutes to write down your answer to the question, 'How can I be of service?' Don't worry if you don't have an immediate answer. You have planted a seed, and it will grow in good time. If you can't go for a walk, you can do this practice sitting at a window, ideally looking at a tree or a garden and using the senses in the same way.

Practice three: Awakening to co-arising

Writing
- Practise listening to the singing of the birds – go somewhere you can hear the birds, listen to their individual songs and sounds. Try to transcribe the sounds, write down what you are hearing. Then move on to listening to yourself, what song are you singing, what is arising within you?

Connecting
- Try chanting. You may be able to find a local group. Or you can listen to chants online and then join in with the chanting when you feel comfortable.

Listening
- Sit for five minutes outside. Close your eyes and open your hearing.

What is the sound furthest away that you can hear? What is the sound nearest to you? After five minutes, open your eyes to a soft gaze. Look at what you can see around you in detail. Take a few moments to note down your experience of listening and seeing.

Walking

- At the meditation retreat, we engaged in different kinds of meditation. Walking meditation, sitting meditation while savouring a cup of tea, sweeping meditation as we looked after the grounds, weeding meditation. Try walking meditation – walking slowly, paying attention as you put one foot down on the earth, and then the other. Feel the earth beneath your feet, what walking feels like in your body. When you notice your thoughts, come gently back to the sensation of walking.

Practice four: Trees are kin

Writing

- Choose a tree. Write a letter to it as if you were writing to a relative, perhaps a grandparent. You could tell the tree about your life, perhaps ask it for guidance. If you like, write a response back from the tree to yourself.

Connecting

- Dreaming. Put a notebook beside your bed. Write the date at the top of the page. Set an intention to remember your dreams. If you don't remember, then repeat the practice again the next night. If you do remember a dream when you wake, write it down, disturbing your body as little as possible, so you keep hold of the dream. Identify what the feeling of the dream is.

Listening

- Find a plant that you are drawn towards. Ask 'How does it feel?' Speak your response to the plant, enter into conversation with it.

Walking
- Go on a walk to open your heart to the plants. Praise the plants, show you have noticed them, thank them, be in a relationship with them.

Practice five: Feel the unseen

Writing
- Read 'Eagle Poem' by Joy Harjo. (This can be found online.) Read it a couple of times out loud – you may choose to do this outside. Then choose one of the lines in the poem that speaks to you as a springboard for freewriting for ten minutes.

Connecting
- Use a hand lens to look at plants more closely and what lies unseen.

Listening
- In spring when the sap is rising, use a stethoscope to experiment with listening to trees, placing the stethoscope against the bark of the trunk. You can buy stethoscopes which are relatively inexpensive.

Walking
- On a walk, experiment making recordings of the natural world. Most smartphones have an audio recording app built in. You could try recording birdsong, the sound of a stream, the noise of leaves in a wind. Listen back to the recordings – what do you notice? How does it differ from and/or enhance your listening?

Practice six: In tune with the rhythms of the earth

Writing
- Write an alpha poem on the theme of Rhythm. (An alpha poem is one where each line begins with a letter of the word, e.g. the first line begins with R, the second line with H, etc). See what comes up for you on the theme of rhythms of the earth.

Connecting

- Connect with your morning cup of coffee or tea. As you sit with your hot drink, start by giving thanks for being able to enjoy it. Then start to think back through all the people and processes that have brought this drink to you. If you don't know, look up the origin of your tea or coffee. What country has it come from? Can you find out anything about who grew it, how it was grown, what the ecosystem is like?

Listening

- Go to a tree, spend time with it, look carefully at it, from roots to the crown. What features stand out to you? What is the energy of the tree? What qualities does it have? Let a name come to mind for the tree. Be as playful as you like with it.

Walking

- Go for a walk. Observe the different heights of plants and trees. Think about how they are growing in community with each other. What is the role of the different plants in the ecosystem? Do they, for example, provide shelter, food or ground cover? Are there fallen leaves which will decompose and return to nutrients to the soil? Stop at one point with a mix of plants. Working from ground level up, notice the number of different plants present.

Practice seven: Joy calls me home

Writing

- Use the prompt: 'Joy calls me home.' Questions to explore could include how does joy feel, when have you experienced joy in nature, how can you be a home for joy?

Connecting

- Hold an olive oil tasting with friends. Ask each person to bring an olive oil from a different country or buy a range of small bottles of olive oil and see whether you can identify the different characteristics of olive oil. You can find guidance online on how to organise an olive oil tasting and flavour characteristics to look out for, from buttery to grassy.

Listening
- Think about what natural sounds bring you joy. It could be birdsong or the sound of waves. See if you can go somewhere you can listen to these sounds. If you like, write about how listening to these sounds makes you feel.

Walking
- Go on a joy walk. Look for objects that bring you joy – it could be the colours of a leaf, the shape of a flower, the pattern on a stone. Take pictures if you have a camera. If you like, write about the characteristics of those objects that brings you joy.

Practice eight: Be a tree protector

Writing
- The spirit of the oak tree is of the protector and inviting you to take the right action. What in your life do you love and want to protect? Write to the oak tree and ask for guidance. Then write back to yourself from the oak tree – what guidance does the oak tree provide?

Connecting
- Find out about trees which are under threat, either near you or further afield, and if there is an action you can take to help support them, whether signing a petition or visiting the tree in a show of support.

Listening
- One of the activities that the tree protectors in Sheffield did was to draw under the trees. Drawing can be a way to learn to listen to trees through close observation. Take a sketchbook and a soft pencil

or some charcoal. Find an oak tree to sit by, or another tree that catches your eye. Observe the tree from different angles. Draw what you see and feel.

Walking

- In a town you live in or are visiting, take a walk with the intention to pay attention to the street trees. Where are they planted? How old are they? Do they look healthy? What kind of trees are they? What do they contribute to the street? What would be lost if they were felled? If you can't see any street trees, think about where they could be planted and what they would add. Take notes and share pictures if you like on social media.

Practice nine: The forest of the imagination

Writing

- Write a letter to the imagination of your six-year-old self. Start 'Dear six-year-old-me, I'd like your imagination to be a bigger part of my life.' Describe how you are going to invite imagination into your life. Make yourself a home for imagination.

Connecting

- Light a candle or tea light. As you do so, ask the fire what gift it wants to share with you. Watching the flame, or with eyes closed, knowing the flame is there, let this gift come to you. When you have it, sit with it. After a period of time, say five minutes, sit with how you could share this gift with your community.

Listening

- Find a natural object that calls to you, either on a walk or inside, that you can hold in your hand. This could be, for example, a rock, a piece of bark or wood or a shell. Explore it with your fingers with your eyes closed. Feel its texture and qualities, its temperature, how hard it is. Feel where it has come from. Now imagine that it can grant you a wish. What would this be? Write in your journal about what arises for you.

Walking

- Take an awe walk among some trees. At the beginning of the walk, set the intention to experience awe. Take a deep breath in to ground yourself. As you walk, keep coming back to the breath and using your senses. Pay attention to what can you feel, hear and smell, as well as see. Open to awe, whether that is the light on the trees or a tiny flower. At the end of the walk, write down what you noticed.

Practice ten: The art of being in place

Writing

- Read the poem 'When I am Among the Trees' by Mary Oliver. (You can find this on the internet.) Read it out loud a couple of times. Notice which phrase or line stands out for you. Journal on this. Then use the phrase 'When I am among the trees' as a prompt to write, setting a timer for seven minutes. Try to write continuously for seven minutes. Then read what you have written and, if you like, continue to develop it further.

Listening

- Go for a walk or sit outside. Wait for a question to come to mind. Then, as you walk or sit, look around you for clues as to what the answer might be. Listen with your whole being. See what answer comes. Don't worry if an answer doesn't come at first, keep holding the question tenderly (and know that in the holding there might be part of the answer).

Connecting

- Find a tree that speaks to you of endings. Sit or stand under the tree. Ask the tree what guidance it has about endings and next steps. This could relate to a specific situation in your life, or to a season.

Walking
- Go for a walk with the intention of noticing the relationship of other beings to one place. For example, this could be an insect living on a tree, a tree rooted in one place, or a hole in the ground where an animal lives. In one of these places, sit for a while and imagine what it is like to live in that one place, and how the being relates to the place around it. Write some notes or draw a picture on an aspect of that experience. (With thanks to Tariki Trust for the inspiration for this exercise.)

My approach to developing the exercises has been shaped in part by my training in ecotherapy with the Tariki Trust, including poetry therapy training with Mary Reynolds Thompson. I am grateful to my human teachers, as well as my tree teachers.

Acknowledgements

Writing these acknowledgements, there is a strong theme of those who have encouraged me to keep going with writing this book. I knew I owed it to the trees to share their stories, but it truly is thanks to the support and encouragement of so many people that it happened. Thank you to everyone who has touched the book in some way.

Thank you to my agents Michael Alcock and Charlotte Seymour, of Johnson & Alcock, for believing in the book. Thank you to Jamie Hodder-Williams, to Myfanwy Moore for her clear-sighted edits and to the whole team at Bedford Square Publishers, including Polly Halsey, for bringing the book into the world.

Thank you to all those people who I met on my travels, were part of the journey, helped me and shared their stories. My travels took place in 2019 and inevitably circumstances and people's lives may have changed since then. Thank you to: Aviram and Yorit and the community at Sadhana Forest; the teachers and staff at Nilambe Meditation Centre; Rae and Yuri and my fellow artists-in-residence at BigCi, to Chris and to Monica Gagliano. To: Gordon Hempton, Randy Borman, the Cofan community at Zabalo, my fellow listeners in the rainforest and Jake at Explorer X. To Mari and Craw at Mariri Jungle Lodge and Carlos and

Acknowledgements

Henny at Terra Booma; to Jean-Marie; to Margaret, Sue, Sally, Annette and the other tree protectors who shared their stories; to Mary and Nate of Animas Valley Institute and to Kristen Shive. Thank you to everyone who spoke with me, and who facilitated introductions.

Thank you to my teachers, who have been numerous over the years. Thank you to those who have directly helped to shape the book including Kathryn Aalto, as a mentor, Lulah Ellender for her advice and edits and Clare Whistler and Kay Syrad, aka kin'd and kin'd, whose correspondence course on eco-poetry through the medium of letters was such a gift during lockdown. To the teachers whose courses supported the writing of the book, including Jessica J. Lee, William Atkins and Cal Flyn. To Tanya Shadrick for her timely encouragement.

I'm fortunate to be part of several communities who have provided support and encouraged me to get the work done. Thank you to Barbara and Amelia, who I met on an Arvon course – our weekly check-ins and monthly meetings have kept me on track. To Chalk & Stream Writers, my local nature writing group, for providing writerly community and in particular to Ruth, for reading chapters. To London Writers' Salon, for hosting a space to write in. To Selina Barker and the community she has created, for being cheerleaders when I needed it. To 26 Writers and John Simmons - the rich community and inspiring projects have helped me develop as a writer over the years. To the teachers and community of Tariki Trust, for helping to root and continue to grow what I learnt on my travels.

Thank you to my family. To my mother for, as she says, always knowing that I was going to be a writer, and encouraging my writing from a young age, as well as sharing her love of trees and fuelling my imagination with stories. To my brother Robert and sister-in-law Therese, who cheered on the idea from the beginning, and their children Fiona Grace and Robert. To Greg and Gloria for our trip to the redwoods. To Aunt Kay for being a source of inspiration. To Omaid. Thank you for believing in me, for your insights, ideas and enthusiasm, and helping to put things into perspective when needed.

Thank you to the trees for calling to me and setting me on this journey and sharing their wisdom with me. It is a continuing life-long journey of learning.

Further reading

Included here are some of the books that were part of my reading as I researched and wrote this book.

Anna Lewington, *Birch* (Reaktion Books, 2018)
Bill Plotkin, *Soulcraft* (New World Library, 2003)
Bill Plotkin, *The Journey of Soul Initiation* (New World Library, 2001)
Bob Randall, *Songman: The Story of an Aboriginal Elder* (Australian Broadcasting, 2003)
C D Wright, *Casting Deep Shade* (Copper Canyon Press, 2019)
Danu Forest, *Celtic Tree Magic* (Llewellyn Publications, 2014)
Glennie Kindred, *Walking with Trees* (Permanent Publications, 2019)
Greg Sarris, *How a Mountain was Made: Stories* (Heyday, 2017)
James Canton, *The Oak Papers* (Canongate Books, 2020)
Joanna Macy, *World as Lover, World as Self* (Parallax Press, 2007)
John Lewis Stempel, *The Glorious Life of the Oak* (Doubleday, 2018)
Mike Shanahan, *Ladders To Heaven: How fig trees shaped our history, fed our imaginations and can enrich our future* (Unbound, 2016)
Monica Gagliano, *Thus Spoke the Plant* (North Atlantic Books, 2018)

Ross Gay, *Inciting Joy: Essays* (Coronet, 2022)
Scott Russell Sanders, *Staying Put: Making a Home in a Restless World* (Beacon Press, 1994)
Sharon Blackie, *If Women Rose Rooted* (September Publishing, 2016)
Stephen Buhner, *Plant Intelligence and the Imaginal Realm* (Bear and Company, 2014)
Suzanne Simard, *Finding the Mother Tree* (Allen Lane, 2021)
Thich Nhat Hanh, *Zen and the Art of Saving the Planet* (Rider, 2021)
Toko-pa Turner, *Belonging: Remembering Ourselves Home* (Her Own Room Press, 2017)

Notes

Introduction:

1 Hermann Hesse, *Wandering: Notes and Sketches* (Farrar Strauss Giroux, 1972)
1 Agence France-Presse, 'Giant African baobab trees die suddenly after thousands of years', 11 June 2018 https://www.theguardian.com/world/2018/jun/11/giant-african-baobab-trees-die-suddenly-after-thousands-of-years

Seed One

1 University Of Michigan. 'Birch Trees To Edge Out Aspens In Warming World.' ScienceDaily, 7 September 2007. www.sciencedaily.com/releases/2007/09/070905151422.htm
2 Diane Toomey, 'Exploring How and Why Trees "Talk" To Each Other'. Yale Environment 360, 1 September 2016 https://e360.yale.edu/features/exploring_how_and_why_trees_talk_to_each_other
3 Renata Soukand, Nora Papp, Iwa Kolodziejska, Raivo Kalle, 'Use of tree saps in northern and eastern parts of Europe', https://doi.org/10.5586/asbp.2012.036
4 Fact.MR, 'Birch Water Market to Grow More than Double as Application in Cosmetics and Personal Care Sector Rises',

8 November 2022 www.prnewswire.com/news-releases/birch-water-market-to-grow-more-than-double-as-application-in-cosmetics-and-personal-care-sector-rises-301671549.html

5 Seppo Vuokko, *Cultivation and care – forestry and biodiversity.* (Finnish Forest Association, 2019) https://smy.fi/en/materials/cultivation-and-care-forestry-and-biodiversity

6 Hannes Mantyranta, 'Forest Sector in Finland', June 2019 https://forest.fi/article/forest-sector-in-finland

7 Benjamin Laker, 'What Leaders Should Know About Climate Change and Carbon Negativity,' Forbes, 24 February 2024 www.forbes.com/sites/benjaminlaker/2021/02/24/what-leaders-should-know-about-climate-change-and-carbon-negativity

8 Matti Sarmela, *The Finnish Folklore Atlas*, www.sarmela.net/folklore-atlas

9 Horatio Clare, *Kalevala* (Vintage Classics, 2017)

10 Sandy Dunlop, quoted on www.herstory.ie/who-was-brigid?

11 Translated by John Crawford, *The Kalevala*, https://sacred-texts.com/neu/kveng/kvrune44.htm

12 Rupert Sheldrake, Terence McKenna and Ralph Abraham, *Chaos, Creativity and Cosmic Consciousness* (Park Street Press, 2001)

13 https://onbeing.org/programs/katy-payne-in-the-presence-of-elephants-and-whales/#transcript

14 https://soundcloud.com/generation-anthropocene/the-soundtracker

Seed Two

1 Hermann Hesse, *Wandering: Notes and Sketches* (Farrar Straus & Giroux, 1972)

2 Paul Blanchflower, 'Restoration of the Tropical Dry Evergreen Forest of Peninsular India' https://auroville-tdef.info/pdfs/TDEF-Auroville.pdf

3 Joan Benham, *Brilliant green: the surprising history and science of plant intelligence*, Choice Reviews Online www.academia.edu/79916233/Brilliant_green_the_surprising_history_and_science_

Notes

of_plant_intelligence&nav_from=86323adf-f89d-4565-a8a6-8b85b-7902cff&rw_pos=0

4 Mike Shanahan, '10 things you need to know about banyan trees' https://underthebanyan.blog/2016/09/04/10-things-you-need-to-know-about-banyan-trees/

5 https://herbaria.plants.ox.ac.uk/bol/plants400/Profiles/EF/Ficusb

6 *Auroville: Aims and Ideals – selections from the writings and aims of the Mother* (Auroville Publication Group, October 2006)

7 Andrea Vecchione, 'Koyilkatu: Modern Day Sacred Grove Nature Temples of Tamil Nadu: Traditional Ecological Knowledge Integrated in Modern Times' https://www.academia.edu/28635949

8 Ditto

9 Sophia Easthaugh, 'India's 105-year-old mother of trees', CNN https://edition.cnn.com/2016/11/04/asia/saalumarada-thimmakka-trees-india

Seed Three

1 Joanna Macy, excerpt from *Greening of the Self*. Copyright © 2012 by Unified Buddhist church, Inc. with the permission of Parallax Press, Berkeley, California, www.parallax.org.

2 Joanna Macy, *World as Lover, World as Self* (Parallax Press, 2007)

3 Interview with David Jay Brown http://www.davidjaybrown.com/purce-int/

4 Diane Beresford Kroger, *To Speak for the Trees: My Life's Journey from Ancient Celtic Wisdom to a Healing Vision of the Forest* (Random House Canada, 2019)

5 Damanpreet Singh, Bikram Singh, Rajesh Kumar Gael, 'Traditional uses, phytochemistry and pharmacology of *Ficus religiosa*: A review', *Journal of Ethnopharmacology*, Volume 1, Issue 3, 12 April 2011, https://doi.org/10.1016/j.jep.2011.01.046

6 Auroville Herbarium, www.aurovilleherbarium.org/contents/medicinal.php?id=64

7 K P Ariyadasa, 'Fire Situation in Sri Lanka', Food and Agriculture

Organisation, https://www.fao.org/4/AD653E/ad653e52.htm
8 Joanna Macy, *World as Lover, World as Self* (Parallax Press, 2007)
9 Sam Harris, *Waking Up: Searching for Spirituality Without Religion* (Black Swan, 2014)

Seed Four

1 David Abram, *Becoming Animal: An Earthly Cosmology*, (Vintage Books, 2011)
2 Harriet Ampt, 'The Ideal Australian: The role of the gum tree in an Australian collective cultural identity', https://hdl.handle.net/10523/10403
3 Australian Government Department of Agriculture, Australian forest profiles: Eucalypt, https://www.agriculture.gov.au/sites/default/files/abares/forestsaustralia/publishingimages/forest%20profiles%202019/eucalypt/AusForProf_2019_Eucalypt_v.1.0.0.pdf
4 Australian Academy of Science, 'The story of our eucalypts', www.science.org.au/curious/earth-environment/story-our-eucalypts
5 See Monica Gagliano's book *Thus Spoke the Plant* (North Atlantic Books, 2018) and Sci News, 'Mimosa Plants Have Long Term Memory, Can Learn, Say Biologists' https://www.sci.news/biology/science-mimosa-plants-memory-01695.html
6 For more on time see Oliver Burkeman, *Four Thousand Weeks: Time and how to use it*, Bodley Head, 2021, page 24
7 Diane Beresford Kroger, *To Speak for the Trees* (Random House Canada, 2019)
8 John J. Bradley. 'Can my country hear English?: Reflections on the relationship of language to country'. Monash University. Journal contribution. https://doi.org/10.4225/03/5ab86f0221aa1
9 Robin Wall Kimmerer, 'Nature Needs a New Pronoun: To Stop the Age of Extinction, Let's Start by Ditching "It"'. *Yes Magazine* www.yesmagazine.org/issue/together-earth/2015/03/30/alternative-grammar-a-new-language-of-kinship

Notes

10 Bob Randall, *Songman: The Story of an Aboriginal Elder* (Australian Broadcasting, 2003)
11 Toko-pa Turner, *Belonging: Remembering Ourselves Home* (Her Own Room Press, 2017)
12 Associate Professor Lauren Bennett, Dr Sabine Kasel, Dr Tom Fairman, Ruizhu Jiang, University of Melbourne, 'Why Australia's Severe Bushfires May Be Bad News for Tree Regeneration', Pursuit. https://pursuit.unimelb.edu.au/articles/why-australia-s-severe-bushfires-may-be-bad-news-for-tree-regeneration

Seed Five

1 Janeth Lessman et al. 'Large expansion of oil industry in the Ecuadorian Amazon: biodiversity vulnerability and conservation alternatives.' *Ecology and evolution* vol. 6,14 4997 – 5012. 24 Jun. 2016, doi:10.1002/ece3.2099
2 Manuela Andreoni, 'A Collapse of the Amazon Could Be Coming Faster Than We Thought', 14 February 2024, *New York Times* www.nytimes.com/2024/02/14/climate/amazon-rain-forest-tipping-point.html
3 Joseph Campbell, Diane K. Osborn (editor), *Reflections on the Art of Living: A Joseph Campbell Companion* (Harper Perennial, 1995)
4 https://amazonaid.org/resources/about-the-amazon/the-amazon-biome/
5 Victoria Tauli-Corpuz, 'Indigenous people are guardians of global biodiversity but we need protection too', 7 May 2019. https://www.reutersevents.com/sustainability/indigenous-people-are-guardians-global-biodiversity-we-need-protection-too
6 Joanna Macy, 'The Greening of the Self,' *Spiritual Ecology*, edited by Llewellyn Vaughan Lee (Golden Sufi Centre, 2016)
7 Wendell Berry, *The Unsettling of America* (Counterpoint Press, 2015)
8 Carlos Andrés Baquero-Diaz, 'José Gualinga Montalvo: "The jungle

is a living, intelligent and conscious being" https://sumauma.com/en/jose-gualinga-montalvo-a-floresta-e-um-ser-vivo-inteligente-e-consciente/

9 Ditto

Seed Six

1 Agenda Gotsch, 'Life in Syntropy', https://www.youtube.com/watch?v=gSPNRu4ZPvE
2 https://noosaforestretreat.com/whats-the-difference-between-syntropic-farming-and-permaculture
3 Inez de Oliveira, 'Ernst Götsch: The creator of the real green revolution', Believe.earth, https://believe.earth/en/ernst-gotsch-the-creator-of-the-real-green-revolution
4 https://agendagotsch.com/en
5 Inez de Oliveira, 'Ernst Götsch: The creator of the real green revolution', Believe.earth, https://believe.earth/en/ernst-gotsch-the-creator-of-the-real-green-revolution/
6 I wrote about this in more detail in the Creativist Manifesto, published online in 2010.
7 Sharon Guynup, 'Can "Slow Food" save Brazil's fast-vanishing Cerrado savanna?', Mongabay, 25 March 2021 https://news.mongabay.com/2021/03/can-slow-food-save-brazils-fast-vanishing-cerrado-savanna/
8 http://www.wildspeak.com/animalenergies/tapir.html

Seed Seven

1 Ross Gay, *The Book of Delights: Essays* (Algonquin Books, 2022)
2 Daniel Dawson, 'Olive Oil Health Benefits', *Olive Oil Times*, 10 December 2022, www.oliveoiltimes.com/health-news/health-benefits-olive-oil
3 Elena Paravantes, 'Olive Oil May Protect from Depression', 26

January 2011, www.oliveoiltimes.com/health-news/olive-oil-may-protect-from-depression
4. Erik Meijaard, 'Why coconut oil may be worse than palm oil for the environment', 8 July 2020 www.independent.co.uk/news/long_reads/science-and-technology/coconut-oil-worse-palm-oil-deforestation-environment-ecology-a9605761.html
5. Sara Maitland, *Gossip from the Forest* (Granta, 2013)

Seed Eight

1. Sheffield Street Trees Inquiry report, page 7, https://www.sheffield.gov.uk/sites/default/files/2023-03/sheffield_street_trees_inquiry_report.pdf
2. Ditto
3. From exhibition, 'John Ruskin, Art and Wonder' at Millennium Galleries, Sheffield. Quote from John Ruskin, *The Elements of Drawing*
4. The Star, 'Rare elm could be saved for £3,500', 7 July 2016, https://www.thestar.co.uk/news/rare-elm-could-be-saved-for-aps3500-456533
5. www.berlin.de/senuvk/umwelt/stadtgruen/stadtbaeume/de/einzelbaeume/index.shtml
6. Zoe Schlanger, 'A philosopher invented a word for the psychic pain of climate change', *Quartz*, 13 October 2018 https://qz.com/1423202/a-philosopher-invented-a-word-for-the-psychic-pain-of-climate-change/
7. Tree Equity Score UK, Sheffield. https://uk.treeequityscore.org/reports/local-authority/E08000019
8. Friends of the Earth, https://friendsoftheearth.uk/nature/new-data-shows-glaring-disparity-england-tree-cover
9. UK Government, https://www.gov.uk/government/publications/plant-your-future-the-case-for-trees
10. Ming Kuo, Samantha E Klein, Matthew H E M Browning, Jaime Zaplatosch, 'Greening for academic achievement: Prioritizing

what to plant and where', *Landscape and Urban Planning*, Volume 206, 2021, https://doi.org/10.1016/j.landurbplan.2020.103962.

11 https://eandt.theiet.org/content/articles/2017/05/our-canopy-is-vanishing-london-councils-remove-almost-50-000-trees-in-five-years/

12 Simon Leo Brown, 'Punt Road golden elm is Melbourne's most emailed tree', ABC News, 22 July 2015 www.abc.net.au/news/2015-07-22/most-emailed-tree-in-melbourne-is-punt-rd-golden-elm/6639062

Seed Nine

1 https://www.nps.gov/seki/learn/historyculture/native-americans.htm
2 https://tulerivertribe-nsn.gov/history/
3 Jeanine Pfeiffer, 'Wildfire Management and Recovery on Tribal Lands Complicated by Policy Inequities', PBS SoCal, 18 August 2022 www.pbssocal.org/news-community/wildfire-management-and-recovery-on-tribal-lands-complicated-by-policy-inequities
4 https://www.nps.gov/articles/the-united-nations-memorial-service-at-muir-woods.htm
5 https://www.amnh.org/exhibitions/permanent/north-american-forests/giant-sequoia-tree
6 Willis Linn Jepson, *The Trees of California* https://archive.org/stream/treesofcaliforni00jeps_0/treesofcaliforni00jeps_0_djvu.txt
7 Ditto
8 http://vault.sierraclub.org/john_muir_exhibit/about/sierra.aspx
9 Willis Linn Jepson, *The Trees of California* https://archive.org/stream/treesofcaliforni00jeps_0/treesofcaliforni00jeps_0_djvu.txt
10 Robert Hass, 'The Nature of Gary Snyder', *The Paris Review*, 10 September 2020 https://www.theparisreview.org/blog/2020/09/10/the-nature-of-gary-snyder
11 Arwen Spicer, 'Greg Sarris's *How a Mountain was Made: Stories as a Transformative Indigenous Futurism*', SFRA Review, Vol 52, no 1., https://sfrareview.org/2022/01/17/greg-sarriss-how-a-mountain-was-made-stories-as-a-transformative-indigenous-futurism

12 https://ggia.berkeley.edu/practice/awe_walk
13 Summer Allen, 'Eight Reasons Why Awe Makes Your Life Better', *Greater Good Magazine*, 26 September 2018 https://greatergood.berkeley.edu/article/item/eight_reasons_why_awe_makes_your_life_better
14 Piff, Paul K et al. 'Awe, the small self, and prosocial behavior'. *Journal of personality and social psychology* vol. 108,6 (2015): 883–99. doi:10.1037/pspi0000018
15 Sturm, Virginia E et al. 'Big smile, small self: Awe walks promote prosocial positive emotions in older adults.' *Emotion* (Washington, D.C.) vol. 22,5 (2022): 1044 – 58. doi:10.1037/emo0000876
16 https://www.nps.gov/grba/learn/management/organic-act-of-1916.htm
17 Schuurman G W et al. 'Resist-accept-direct (RAD) – a framework for the 21st-century natural resource manager.' Natural Resource Report. NPS/NRSS/CCRP/NRR – 2020/2213. National Park Service. Fort Collins, Colorado. doi:10.36967/nrr-2283597
18 https://whatismyspiritanimal.com/spirit-totem-power-animal-meanings/mammals/marten-symbolism-meaning/
19 https://www.nps.gov/articles/000/2021-fire-season-impacts-to-giant-sequoias.htm
20 www.cnbc.com/2021/11/19/fires-have-killed-nearly-20percent-of-the-worlds-giant-sequoias-in-the-last-two-years.html
21 https://www.nps.gov/articles/000/2021-fire-season-impacts-to-giant-sequoias.htm
22 Patrick Greenfield and Mette Lampcov, 'Beetles and fire kill dozens of "indestructible" giant sequoia trees', *The Guardian*, 18 January 2020 www.theguardian.com/environment/2020/jan/18/beetles-and-fire-kill-dozens-of-california-indestructible-giant-sequoia-trees-aoe
23 John Muir, *The Yosemite*, https://vault.sierraclub.org/john_muir_exhibit/writings/the_yosemite/chapter_7.aspx
24 https://www.sierraclub.org/sierra/2022-1-spring/poem/wrapping-sequoias-ellen-bass
25 *The Journey of Soul Initiation* © Bill Plotkin Copyright 2021. Used by permission of New World Library

Olivia Sprinkel

Seed Ten

1 *Staying Put: Making Home in a Restless World* by Scott Russell Sanders Copyright © 1993 by Scott Russell Sanders Reprinted with permission from Beacon Press, Boston Massachusetts
2 https://www.cliffsnotes.com/literature/t/thoreau-emerson-and-transcendentalism/henry-david-thoreau/introduction-to-thoreaus-writing#:~:text=The%20man%20who%20is%20often,may%20the%20better%20express%20myself
3 John Matthews and Will Worthington, *Green Man Tree Oracle*, quoted on www.thegoddesstree.com
4 Quoted by Robert Macfarlane, *The Old Ways* (Penguin, 2013)
5 Stephen Braren, 'The Evolution of Social Connection as a Basic Human Need', https://www.thesocialcreatures.org/thecreaturetimes/evolution-of-social-connection
6 https://www.rhs.org.uk/plants/types/trees/for-climate-change
7 Greg Sarris, 'A Woman Meets an Owl, a Rattlesnake and a Hummingbird', *Emergence Magazine* https://emergencemagazine.org/fiction/a-woman-meets-an-owl-a-rattlesnake-and-a-hummingbird/

About the Author

Image Credit © Kristen Perers

Olivia Sprinkel is a writer and sustainability consultant. She is half-Finnish, half-American, and grew up in Derbyshire. She now lives in East Sussex, UK.

www.oliviasprinkel.com

@oliviasprinkel

Bedford Square Publishers is an independent publisher of fiction and non-fiction, founded in 2022 in the historic streets of Bedford Square London and the sea mist shrouded green of Bedford Square Brighton.

Our goal is to discover irresistible stories and voices that illuminate our world.

We are passionate about connecting our authors to readers across the globe and our independence allows us to do this in original and nimble ways.

The team at Bedford Square Publishers has years of experience and we aim to use that knowledge and creative insight, alongside evolving technology, to reach the right readers for our books. From the ones who read a lot, to the ones who don't consider themselves readers, we aim to find those who will love our books and talk about them as much as we do.

We are hunting for vital new voices from all backgrounds – with books that take the reader to new places and transform perceptions of the world we live in.

Follow us on social media for the latest Bedford Square Publishers news.

@bedsqpublishers
facebook.com/bedfordsq.publishers/
@bedfordsq.publishers

https://bedfordsquarepublishers.co.uk/